Streets

To
Peggy Elenbaas Ploem,
dear *sobat* of many, many years

Sampeh bertulisan lagi ...

STREETS
Exploring Kowloon

Jason Wordie

Photographs by Anthony J. Hedley and John Lambon

香港大學出版社
HONG KONG UNIVERSITY PRESS

Hong Kong University Press
14/F Hing Wai Centre
7 Tin Wan Praya Road
Aberdeen
Hong Kong

© Hong Kong University Press 2007

ISBN 978-962-209-813-8

All rights reserved. No portion of this publication may be reproduced or transmitted in any form or by any means, electronic or mechanical, including photocopy, recording, or any information storage or retrieval system, without prior permission in writing from the publisher.

Secure On-line Ordering
http://www.hkupress.org

British Library Cataloguing-in-Publication Data
A catalogue record for this book is available from the British Library.

Printed and bound by United League Graphic & Printing Co. Ltd. in Hong Kong, China

Contents

Acknowledgements	vii
User's Guide	ix
Introduction	1
Tsim Sha Tsui	**16**
Salisbury Road	20
Nathan Road	28
Haiphong Road	35
Chatham Road South	41
Observatory Road	46
Austin Road	51
Yau Ma Tei	**56**
Jordan Road	60
Saigon Street	66
Gascoigne Road	70
Kansu Street	75
Reclamation Street	80
Shanghai Street	86
Portland Street	91
Waterloo Road	96
Mong Kok	**100**
Peace Avenue	104
Argyle Street	110
Kadoorie Avenue	116
Prince Edward Road West	122
Boundary Street	129
New Kowloon	**134**
Anchor Street	138
Yu Chau Street	142
Apliu Street	146

Contents

Yen Chow Street	151
Tai Po Road	157
Cheung Sha Wan Road	163
Lai Chi Kok Road	168
Tsuen Wan and Beyond	**172**
Tsuen Wan Market Street	176
Sai Lau Kok Road	183
Route TWISK	190
Shing Mun Road	195
Castle Peak Road	200
Kowloon Tong	**204**
La Salle Road	206
Cumberland Road	211
Waterloo Road	216
Broadcast Drive	221
Kowloon City	**226**
Hung Hom Road	228
Ma Tau Wai Road	233
Sung Wong Toi Road	239
Nga Tsin Wai Road	245
Tak Ku Ling Road	250
Tung Tau Tsuen Road	255
East Kowloon	**260**
Wong Tai Sin Road	262
Clear Water Bay Road	267
Cha Kwo Ling Road	272
Lei Yue Mun Road	278
Bibliography	**285**
Photograph Credits	**291**

Acknowledgements

Streets: Exploring Kowloon, along with the earlier volume *Streets: Exploring Hong Kong Island,* derives in part from an idea by Susan Sams, formerly associate editor (features) of the *South China Morning Post.* The weekly column, from which these books subsequently evolved, first appeared as a series in the newspaper's *Post Magazine* several years ago.

When we embarked in earnest on *Streets: Exploring Kowloon*, shortly after *Streets: Exploring Hong Kong Island* was published in 2002, none of us realized that for various reasons completely unconnected to this book, the project would take some years to finish.

First and most, heartfelt thanks must go to Tony Hedley and John Lambon, whose patience and enthusiasm for the book never diminished; both revisited locations numerous times to get just the right shot. Their desire for photographic perfection has, without doubt, helped to keep at least one camera shop in Hong Kong in business for the last couple of years. Without their skill, enthusiasm and dedication, this would have been a very different book, if indeed it had appeared at all.

Colin Day of Hong Kong University Press participated in this project in numerous behind-the-scenes ways. Jenny Day was also very helpful and accepted numerous weekend commitments with humour and good grace.

Peter Cunich, Sarah Draper-Ali, Vaudine England, Sheilah Hamilton, Julia Kneale, Sarah Kneale, Ko Tim Keung, David and Evangeline Ollerearnshaw and Edward Stokes have all provided a great deal of encouragement and sound advice in their own way at various times, in a few cases without fully realizing it. Ko Tim Keung has kindly granted permission to reproduce the photograph of the Wakabayashi Inscription on p. 199.

Wee Kek Koon hand-drew the maps and icon-like illustrations used throughout the book, and has been very helpful throughout.

Wong Nai Kwan was a great resource on often obscure points of local history and culture. A fund of detailed local history knowledge, he has provided a great deal of practical help in the preparation of this book.

STREETS

Acknowledgements

My own research on various local subjects over the years has been greatly enriched by the friendship and enthusiasm of several long-time residents of Hong Kong, both past and present, who have given me numerous insights into local life and society that I would never have otherwise obtained.

In this connection I would especially like to thank Gloria d'Almada Barretto, Ruy and Karen Barretto, Felix Bieger, Irene Braude, Cecilia Maria Fok, S. J. Chan, John R. Harris and the late Lady May Ride. Irene Smirnoff Garfinkle and Nina Smirnoff Bieger, in particular, provided numerous anecdotes of post-war Kowloon life, and Irene read and usefully commented upon the manuscript at an early stage.

No one who writes on subjects related to local history in Hong Kong can fail to acknowledge the tremendous debt we all owe, whether directly or otherwise, to the pioneering work undertaken by the Reverend Carl T. Smith, for decades the doyen of Hong Kong's archival researchers.

Likewise, the encouragement given by Dr Elizabeth Sinn, formerly deputy director of the Centre of Asian Studies at the University of Hong Kong, has been of great assistance to many people interested in the study of Hong Kong, myself included, over the years.

The *Journal* of the Hong Kong Branch of the Royal Asiatic Society has been a tremendous resource, with many obscure details hidden within its volumes. In addition, fellow council members of the society have provided me with a great source of stimulation over the years.

Numerous participants on the historical walking tours that I have conducted for various local organizations over the last decade — it would be impossible to name them all individually, but they know who they are — have provided many off-hand insights into Hong Kong and Kowloon backstreet life, and a great deal of stimulation along the way. These walks started out as a cool-weather diversion for me and have gradually become a most enjoyable seasonal undertaking.

User's Guide

Streets: Exploring Kowloon is intended to be an impressionistic guide towards more individual explorations and discoveries. None of these urban walks are intended to be exhaustive or prescriptive. Each aims to illuminate and represent specific yet complementary perspectives of Kowloon's history, culture and everyday life, and fit them, where appropriate, within a broader contextual framework.

Some locations contained within these pages will already be well-known to readers familiar with Hong Kong. Others will be more obscure, and many places will probably be unknown to anyone beyond those who live in the immediate vicinity.

Various facets of local life featured within specific location groupings were selected for their ability to help understand and better interpret other, more widespread aspects of Hong Kong culture and society. Their inclusion provides a detailed snapshot of the many similar characteristics can be witnessed or experienced elsewhere in Kowloon, or in other parts of Hong Kong.

Readers may question why some places have even been included at all. For example, it is hardly to be expected that a reader would specifically travel to Kau Wa Keng Village near Mei Foo (p. 170), for example, to see some open drains filled with raw sewage, or to Anchor Street at Tai Kok Tsui (p. 138) to experience first-hand the range of recreational facilities on offer in an inner-Kowloon public park.

The inclusion of these places has been done to call reader's attention to some of the more widely representative, yet under-acknowledged, aspects of local life that these encapsulate. By depicting such places, and many other 'ordinary corners', we have tried to put some facets of Hong Kong life, and through these the many other parts of Hong Kong that are very much like them, into some sort of coherent historical, social or cultural frame of reference.

Other urban explorers will encounter many similar characteristics of everyday Hong Kong life — some will be more familiar than others — as they follow these routes or, as we hope, formulate routes of their own with this one indicated as a broad template. Hopefully some of the points raised will illustrate a fuller understanding of what makes life in Hong Kong and Kowloon the fascinating, bewildering, infuriating yet enjoyable, multifaceted experience that it is.

User's Guide

In *Streets: Exploring Kowloon* we have expanded somewhat upon usually accepted geographical definitions. In this book 'Kowloon' incorporates both that part of the Chinese mainland directly opposite Hong Kong Island, and the older urban area's massive expansion in recent decades. As a result, 'our' Kowloon extends around the mainland shoreline of Victoria Harbour northwards beyond Tsuen Wan and eastwards to Lyemun, and includes most of the land area below the southern ridges of the Kowloon hills.

Getting Around 'Kowloon Streets'

Unlike Hong Kong Island, which can be travelled around in a more-or-less circular direction, a comprehensive exploration of the greater Kowloon area requires some pre-planning, and a measure of detailed co-ordination, to get the most out of a backstreet visit.

Detailed sequential routes for each area have been suggested in each individual chapter introduction. These routes follow, wherever possible, a logical walking sequence for the specific locations both contained within, and grouped around, a particular street.

Individual clusters of locations have then been linked, in as many instances as possible, with other locations in neighbouring streets. These clusters then help to form the nucleus of an integrated extended walk through several neighbouring streets. In some areas, such as Yau Ma Tei, Mong Kok and Sham Shui Po, these walks loosely extend across districts.

It has not always been possible to achieve this broad objective. Some individual locations contained within a specific road, especially in parts of northern and eastern Kowloon, are simply too widely dispersed for a walk to be practical. In these instances points of interest have been described in the text, and then indicated on the map.

Detailed public transport links are given within each individual street subsection. In practically every instance, public transport provides the most time- and cost-efficient means of getting about Kowloon. For this reason we have avoided, wherever possible, the inclusion of access details and parking options for private cars.

User's Guide

Most of the locations that we have detailed within southern Kowloon are readily accessible by the Mass Transit Railway (MTR). When alternative bus or minibus routes exist, but where we considered the MTR option to be the most efficient means of getting to and from a specific location, we have only included details of this mode of transportation.

Except where otherwise stated, bus numbers and routes indicated for each location have as their start point the 'Star' Ferry bus terminus, adjacent to the Cultural Centre in Tsim Sha Tsui.

Minibus routes are common all over Kowloon, but are frequently confusing to those unfamiliar with local landmarks. To avoid unnecessary complication, details of this mode of transport are only given for certain locations, such as the Shing Mun Reservoir, where a minibus is the only means of access other than by taxi or private car.

More outlying parts of the Kowloon conurbation, such as the areas beyond Tsuen Wan, use a major local landmark (in that case the Tsuen Wan MTR Station and adjacent bus terminus) as the radial reference point.

Maps provide a guide to those who intend to walk a particular series of streets. These are not to scale, and the 'icons' contained within specific area locations represent only some of the specific aspects of that area which we have covered in the text. We hope these drawings will supply some incidental amusement as you explore Kowloon for yourself.

Introduction

The Kowloon peninsula — or more specifically the southernmost stretch of Nathan Road, fantastically glittering with neon lights and constantly thronged with people — is probably Hong Kong's most immediately familiar district to visitors. Despite this international profile, Kowloon remains a remarkably unexplored section of Hong Kong, in particular by residents from other parts of the territory.

Not for nothing is the lower stretch of Nathan Road known as the 'Golden Mile', as much for the incredible night-time dazzle as the ability of its astonishing assortment of shops — and their canny proprietors — to extract money the pockets of passers-by. But only a few minutes walk from the 'Golden Mile' itself there are quiet, reflective corners, such as St Andrew's Church or Signal Hill, that are little altered by the passage of time.

Modern Kowloon, that sprawling conurbation below the 'Nine Dragon' hills, which now extends to the north and east of the Kowloon peninsula, offers a plethora of widely conflicting, often complimentary, and always compelling images and impressions.

Like Hong Kong Island, directly across Victoria Harbour, Kowloon's constantly varied range of sights, sounds and smells alternatively confront, assault, enchant and delight both the casual backstreet ambler — whether a local or a visitor — and those who actually live and work there. Some of these are obvious; others less so. All are an inherent section of what the Kowloon experience is all about:

> Quiet green corners marooned among the heart of the tower blocks, shaded by copses of vivid purple Blake's Bauhinea (*Bauhinea Blakeana*), the Hong Kong floral emblem, in glorious, gaudy colour; elderly men clad in white cotton vests walking their caged songbirds, and countless cicadas screaming, invisible in the shimmering mid-year heat.
>
> Steadily dripping air-conditioners, right along Nathan Road and its dozens of side-streets; like so much else in Hong Kong, omnipresent, illegal and mostly unprosecuted, there for all to see.

Introduction

Dank entrances to alleys and courts, with clusters of small shops in their entranceways selling watches, handbags and mounds luggage.

Well-made fakes of all possible prices and varieties, that most perennial of Hong Kong specialties, unsubtly offered from every street corner to almost every passing pedestrian.

Insistent Indian salesmen, and tailor's shop leaflet distributors by the dozen, all trying to sell every European passer-by a new suit, blazer, shirt, pair of slacks — or several of each; even the price suits you, sir.

Expensively elegant shops in up-market hotel arcades offer some of the world's most costly designer-label luxuries.

Multi-storied emporia filled with garment outlets, watch shops, electronics retailers and Chinese-flavoured tourist souvenirs; all types, colours, qualities and prices are available.

Genuinely polyglot, polychrome corner of Asia, Kowloon; *Jellaba*-clad Pakistani men gathered in groups; laughing Filipinos in tight jeans and baseball caps; men and women from Ghana and Nigeria and the Ivory Coast with impressive physiques, flowing robes and immensely colourful, turbaned headdresses; wide-eyed, rotund Americans in Hawaiian shirts and sunglasses; elderly British tourists in socks and sandals, sweaty and red-faced; blond and deeply tanned Dutch or Scandinavian backpackers, in Hong Kong for a few days as another stop in an extended round-the-world trip, their well-worn backpacks covered in the small embroidered flags of a dozen countries. And Chinese — over ninety-six for every four of anyone else.

Odd relics of the former Crown Colony's multi-ethnic past, still marooned out of time and context among the tower blocks, the crowds, the noise and the traffic and Hong Kong's increasingly monocultural, determinedly monolingual post-handover present.

The clock tower of what used to be the Kowloon railway station, the red brick and granite base still bearing scarred

Introduction

witness to invasion and long-gone conflict, its lingering presence a forlorn reminder of past times, strangely and controversially spared when all else around it was heedlessly, and at times mindlessly, destroyed by 'progress'.

Solidly red-brick churches that would not be out of place in the more affluent suburbs of Manchester or Sydney or Auckland are still there, and well attended too, but by completely different communities to those who first built them and made them into the centres of community life that they still remain.

Quiet parks and sitting-out areas right across Kowloon, from Tai Kok Tsui to Tsz Wan Shan, enjoyed by simply dressed old people, who read the newspapers, gossip in the shade, play cards or draughts perhaps, or just sit alone and stare into space, their innermost thoughts almost the only privacy that their own overcrowded corner of the teeming city ever affords them.

Luxurious international cruise-liners and equally sumptuous private pleasure launches, green-and-cream painted cross-harbour ferries and slow-moving rusty barges filled with piles of sand and stones destined for ever-more reclamation work, all jostling for space in the annually more narrow stretch of Victoria Harbour that lies between Kowloon Point and Hong Kong Island's northern coastline.

Hustling for business in all its forms at its most unabashed; touts and pimps, leaflet distributors and salesmen; the overwhelming, somewhat oppressive sense that everything in Hong Kong is for sale, that somewhere around the backstreets everything — *anything* — is available for a price.

These are only a few of the many random images and impressions are on offer to the interested, observant ambler. A continuing joy of Kowloon is that every visit, even for an hour or two, will add a few more descriptions to each individual's own personal inventory of experiences.

* * * * *

STREETS

Introduction

You do not need to go too far off the beaten track in Kowloon to experience, first-hand, its contradictions and disparities. Within two hundred metres or so, it is possible to experience three completely contrasting, equally authentic and enjoyable aspects of Kowloon life. One of the most vivid examples can be found right in the heart of Tsim Sha Tsui.

The venerable Peninsula Hotel, last survivor and gracious reminder of Hong Kong's truly historic hotels, still presides, as it has done since 1928, over the Tsim Sha Tsui waterfront. A sleek fleet of racing-green, monogrammed Rolls Royces is lined up out the front, around the fountain. And just outside the hotel Kowloon's cracked, crowded pavements begin, only a few steps away from the hotel's magnificent foyer. Every afternoon of the year, the Peninsula serves one of Hong Kong's finest afternoon teas, with the theme music from the movie, *Love Is a Many-Splendoured Thing* and other nostalgic tunes played for background effect by the discreet string quartet.

This oasis of splendid international luxury is directly across from the world-famous Chungking Mansions. Forty years ago, a *very* long time ago in Hong Kong terms, this was a high-class apartment block. Now, it enjoys a somewhat raffish renown as one of the world's best-known backpacker destinations. In its own unique manner, Chungking Mansions is every bit as cosmopolitan as the Peninsula Hotel, and as characteristic of Kowloon's charm and interest.

The moment you enter the shop-lined arcade from Nathan Road, Chungking Mansions offers up a series of sights and odours — both pleasant and less so — that would not be out of place in Delhi or Calcutta. This place really is like nowhere else in all of Hong Kong, and worth a visit for that reason alone.

This most complex of complexes teems with rats and roaches, curious, slightly daring tourists and in-the-know locals, as well as a motley, highly coloured assortment of businessmen and chancers, backpackers and adventurers from all over the world. And, Chungking Mansions is probably Hong Kong's best place to enjoy a reasonably priced, deliciously authentic curry.

Walk slowly through Chungking Arcade, past the money-changers, the souvenir shops selling gaudy paintings on black velvet

Introduction

and 'I Survived Hong Kong' T-shirts, the racks of brightly coloured *saree* lengths and glistening *salwar khameez*, Hindi, Urdu, Nepali and Yoruba-language video tapes and DVDs, stalls redolent with crunchy, fragrant samosas and sticky-sweet, milky-rich Indian confections, and out to the *paan* ('betel-nut') be-splattered alley-way behind. Just off Minden Row, another sharply contrasting, little explored and delightful corner of Kowloon awaits.

A low yet steep hill, thick with trees, bright with azaleas and other flowering plants, and almost completely marooned within the tower blocks, is only a few dozen metres away. Directly behind Chungking Mansions, one of Kowloon's most atmospheric if grubby landmarks, in among the trees, a red brick and granite tower stands unnoticed on its hillside. A completely different experience to either the Peninsula Hotel or Chungking Mansions, with birdsong instead of Hollywood film themes or *bhangra* beats, lies just beyond both.

Variously known as Signal Hill or — on older maps — Blackhead Point, this green, pleasant, quiet spot is one of the most unexpected, least explored corners of southern Kowloon. Near the top the old signal tower still stands, built of red Canton bricks and local granite, a relic of the days when the tower, and the hill on which it stands, was one of the city's most prominent landmarks, easily seen from all corners of Victoria Harbour.

For a generation this tower was one of the most important places in Victoria Harbour, and gave warning of high winds, and the coming of typhoons. Before the days of radio, and for a long time afterwards, the time ball on its summit was almost the only means for ships in the harbour to set their chronometers accurately. Signal towers, like the sextants and chronometers they complemented, are now obsolete all over the world. Yet incongruously enough, in a quiet corner of modern-as-tomorrow Kowloon, one of the last examples can still be found.

From here, Kowloon's extended area lies densely clotted below and around one as far beyond as Devil's Peak and the eastern entrance to Victoria Harbour. But on most days and at most times, the visitor can be almost entirely alone in this vantage point; Signal Hill is *so* little known to visitors, and unfrequented by local residents.

Introduction

Tsim Sha Tsui's almost dizzying juxtaposition of the opulent and the ramshackle, the overcrowded and the spacious, cacophony and near-silence found within these few hundred metres could not be more absolute and epitomizes, in microcosm, much of the overall Hong Kong experience. Between here and the Kowloon hills, there are dozens of other corners that offer the same variety of sensual experience, all waiting to be explored.

* * * * *

Move northwards from the international tourist strip in Tsim Sha Tsui, and another Kowloon emerges, one that provides a sharply different, yet equally varied window into visitor's experiences of the city. Kowloon's older districts, around Yau Ma Tei and Mong Kok, and the newer districts that extend towards Tsuen Wan and across to Kowloon's eastern reaches are, at first glance at least, rather unlovely and at times, somewhat uninviting.

This understandable initial impression is nevertheless misleading, and discourages many from exploring what are some of Hong Kong's most fascinating, genuinely authentic localities. In Tsim Sha Tsui, visitors converge from all over the world. But in Yau Ma Tei and Mong Kok, Tsuen Wan and Kowloon City, it is mainland Chinese tourists that predominate.

Because of their worldwide presence in recent years and annually, increasing spending power, mainland Chinese are often described as the 'new Japanese'. The label has some validity. Like the Japanese package tourist of a generation or so ago, mainland Chinese are immediately recognizable in Hong Kong and elsewhere, with readily typecast tastes and habits and *plenty* of money to spend. While they become more sophisticated with every passing year, the stereotyped ill-cut suits, white socks, shiny black slip-on shoes, unfeasibly elaborate hairdos and expensive, glittery watches will still be around for some years to come.

Somewhat grudgingly welcomed to the city for the money they bring, all too often mainland Chinese are dismissively referred to by the Hong Kong Chinese as 'Ah Chan' — uncouth country cousins

Introduction

down to the 'big city' for the first time. And well do the mainland Chinese visitors know that they are looked down upon in Hong Kong.

Initial impressions of northern Kowloon are of almost impossibly thronged streets choked night and day with cars, buses, minibuses, and more people than one could think it possible for the land area to contain. Thousands of individual shops and stalls sell every conceivable good and service, as well as more than a few that perhaps even the more curious and adventurous would not even wish to think about.

> Clustered sampans and fishing boats at the Yau Ma Tei typhoon anchorage, washing hung out over the stern, immaculate white-clad children coming home over the gangplank from school for lunch; last glimpses of a once usual way of life all over Hong Kong, now transformed by economic progress and steadily rising expectations.
>
> Omnipresent, immediately recognizable Kowloon backstreet smells; compounded of stairwell mustiness, sandalwood incense, roasted pork, exhaust fumes and the occasional, unmistakable whiff of something overripe, perhaps; fecund with possibility, like Hong Kong itself.
>
> Completely Chinese backstreet scenes, with sights and smells of interest on every corner; elderly herbalists brewing inky-black, pungent *fu cha* ('bitter tea'); traditional medicine shops that seem to sell everything from lizard skins and dried seahorses to 'cloud-ear' fungus and jars of Tiger Balm.
>
> Young, heavily muscled Chinese *laan jai* ('toughs'), with sharply chiselled features, lanky orange-tinted hair and the tail or claws of a swirling dragon-tattoo just showing below the capped sleeves of an overtight, biceps-defining T-shirt.
>
> Serried ranks of public housing blocks clustered below Lion Rock, starkly functional and yet totally human in scope at one and the same time. All gaily, cleanly decorated with the unmistakable, irrepressible 'Hong Kong flag' — hundreds of plastic-covered bamboo poles protruding from every floor, each building festooned with thousands of

STREETS

Introduction

pieces of laundry flapping dry in the breeze. One of Hong Kong's greatest, and most under-recognized success stories, these blocks are the housing of the Chinese multitudes, all firmly anchored 'Beneath Lion Rock'.

A few Chinese characters incised onto a roughly hewn stone, now marooned among the Kowloon City traffic; the last physical reminder of the flight of a tragic boy-king, hastening southwards, away from the invading Mongol hordes, but towards his own death, and the extinction of his dynasty.

The ever-present sense of the Kowloon hills in the distance, sometimes seen, always felt, towering and rocky looming over the near horizon, adds to the sense of being confined, in somewhere close and densely packed, with something else very different just a short away and over and just behind.

These images, like those of the tourist belt, are a part of elemental Hong Kong, which changes and reinvents itself every other month or year. Yet, in essence, Kowloon life remains much as it has been for decades, and in some corners for far longer than that.

* * * * *

Most of Kowloon, indeed much of what lives beyond Tsim Sha Tsui's 'Golden Mile', remains undiscovered by many Hong Kong residents, unknown, unexplored and also somewhat dismissed by those who live elsewhere in Hong Kong, and even by many who actually live there.

The somewhat more relaxed social atmosphere that prevailed among European residents in early Kowloon provoked what must be one of Hong Kong's oldest and most commonly repeated saws; a Hong Kong-side matron meets a young, newly arrived bachelor for the first time and archly inquires, 'Are you married, or do you live in Kowloon?'

Introduction

The implication was, of course, that married people, or at least *respectable* married people, did not live on the Kowloon side, among the Chinese lower orders and Hong Kong's various indigenous species of 'half-caste' and 'gone-native'.

It was much the same way with many of the Chinese who lived in Kowloon too. For much of its early history, and for a long time into the twentieth century, their presence in Hong Kong was a transitory one, and in some places, such as Yau Ma Tei's sampan anchorage, the literally floating population came and went from local waters with almost every passing tide.

As in other parts of urban Hong Kong, in these years it was the 'local' people — the Eurasians, the local Portuguese, the Parsees and various Indian ethnicities — along with migrants from elsewhere in China who had sent down deeper roots, who formed the backbone of a permanent, domiciled community in Kowloon. The numerous schools, churches and clubs that were either established by prominent members of their communities, or were largely peopled by them, are still around.

And they continue to prosper and thrive in more international times, in the Kowloon of today that has always been, and still remains, their only real home.

* * * * *

The Hong Kong Island matron's oblique question slyly hinted at another aspect of Hong Kong life, one which is perhaps most brazenly found in Kowloon these days. From the beginning social, and by implication sexual, mores on the Kowloon side of the harbour were more — shall we say — accommodating, than those of Hong Kong Island, and so it remains today.

Echoes of past activity, and modern extensions and variations, can be found all over contemporary Kowloon. Sign-boards for thinly disguised 'barber-shop' brothels, hoardings for Category Three films and plenty of streetwalkers, both plainly obvious and the not-so-apparent, can be found all over the peninsula. One does not have to

Introduction

look very hard; this aspect of local life is readily apparent to even the most casual, innocent-intentioned observer.

Yau Ma Tei has long been notorious as a centre for Hong Kong's flesh trade. Even before the typhoon shelter breakwater was built in the early twentieth century, the anchorage was home to an unknown number of floating prostitutes. These women plied their trade in the 'flower boats', or waterborne brothels, which were a well-known feature of life in Canton and Macao for decades before Hong Kong became a British settlement. Kowloon's 'pleasure vessels' continued to operate, in various forms, until the late 1980s.

The postwar years, and in particular during the Vietnam War era, was a boom time for the R&R (Rest and Recreation) industry, also rudely if accurately known as I&I (Intoxication and Intercourse). Bars and nightclubs of all types, massage establishments and other types of 'sly' brothels proliferated, and Kowloon's sex industry, like Wanchai's across the harbour, continued to expand.

Exotic, romantic imagery, rather than the gritty, sad reality of the trade, was greatly romanticized in the 1950s by popular novels and Hollywood films such as *The World of Suzie Wong*. Against all the odds, the compliant Asian goddess metaphor still somehow persists in contemporary Hong Kong. The end of the Vietnam War did not end matters; Hong Kong's ongoing tourist boom — in particular, in those years, annually increasing visitor numbers from Japan — provided new markets for the world's oldest profession.

Many were attracted by the widely stereotyped, 'penny dreadful' images of Hong Kong popularized throughout the world since the nineteenth century. In those years the place was seen, with some justification, as a permissive, rather louché colonial society, where more or less anything went and most desires could be satisfied for the right price. And like most popular Hong Kong stereotypes, at least some factual basis underpinned the generalizations.

It is still much the same today — and one certainly does not need to be a *haam sup lo* ('salty and wet man') — to notice the more carnal aspects of Kowloon life; all these images readily accost the casual ambler's eye without invitation or hesitation.

Hong Kong's legions of sex workers, whether mainland Chinese, Hong Kong locals, Southeast Asians or a plethora of other

Introduction

nationalities, such as Eastern Europeans and South Americans, continue to face a hard, uncompromising life compounded of Triad exploitation, police intimidation and public disdain. Their lives mirrors the prurient hypocrisy so noticeable in the wider Hong Kong Chinese society and its attitudes towards anything at all to so with sex. This is not an attractive side of Kowloon life, but nevertheless, it is almost impossible to ignore.

* * * * *

Somewhere beyond the tourist strip in Tsim Sha Tsui, and the ever-thronged streets of Yau Ma Tei and Mong Kok lies a different Kowloon. This is that omnipresent, yet somehow elusive place known as 'the real Hong Kong', the place that offers an authentic, undiluted, not-put-on-for-tourists experience of local life and culture.

But where exactly *is* the 'real' Kowloon? And *what* exactly sums up this place? Definitions change, of course, and depend largely on who is making them, and why they are being made. To my mind anyway, the 'real' Kowloon (and its most perennially interesting aspect) lies in its everyday, commuter territory. This area extends northwards past Mong Kok and to the east of Kowloon City, around the coast towards Kwun Tong. Along with the New Towns, such as Sha Tin, Tai Po and Tuen Mun, this is where the average Hong Kong person lives, and to experience some sense of the sights, sounds, smells and flavours of how that life takes place, one has to go there and spend a few hours just walking about.

Most areas found within the 'real Kowloon', such as Cheung Sha Wan, Tsz Wan Shan, Ngau Tau Kok, Tsuen Wan and Wong Tai Sin, offer some standard tourist sights, mostly popular temples, monasteries and isolated fragments of pre-urban, village Kowloon. Some places such as the massive religious complex at Wong Tai Sin or the hauntingly lovely Chi Lin Nunnery, are of interest to visitors throughout the year.

But for the most part, these districts are worth visiting simply to experience an authentic slice of *real* local life. They are places to see ordinary people going about their everyday lives and for a few hours,

STREETS

Introduction

they offer the possibility to be a part — however tangential — of life as the average Hong Kong Chinese lives it. Here are some random examples of the sights, sounds and smells somewhere out in the 'housing estate heartland':

> Simply dressed *see lai* (housewives) go about their morning or afternoon marketing, plastic bags filled with fresh fish and vivid green bundles of *choy sum* ('Chinese mustard') and other leafy vegetables;
>
> Loudly chattering students in immaculate school uniforms wait for a minibus, and compare their most recent exam results;
>
> Market hawkers and stallholders display their goods and shout the odds and the prices to passers-by;
>
> Wizened old women purchase joss-sticks, *laap juk* (red candles) paper offerings, and then burn them on the kerbside;
>
> Fit young policemen clad in green summer uniforms steadily patrol in pairs, belts bristling with hi-tech equipment, boots immaculately polished;
>
> Red and green-painted taxis queue, engines idling in the heat;
>
> Bright electric lights with red plastic shades illuminate heaped piles of export-quality fruit, and racks of roast ducks and *char siu* (roast pork) glistening with oil;
>
> Lunchtime crowds gather in a *cha chaan teng* (café) or mill in and out of one of the local fast-food chains, or queue for a shared table at a popular soup-noodle stall.

A few hours spent in the 'real Kowloon' will bring you many more such impressions, and unlike a shopping mall in one of the more 'international' parts of Hong Kong — what you will see or experience here is *never* the same twice.

* * * * *

Introduction

Greenery, quiet corners and a relative abundance of open space is not something generally associated with Kowloon. Yet there is far more nature in evidence than most people recognize. Within sight of the massive housing estates in Kwai Chung and Tsuen Wan, or just above Kwun Tong, on the eastern end of Kowloon Bay, expanses of rocky, rugged, almost wild country beckon.

Abandoned gun batteries, tunnels and emplacements lie overgrown in the hills, contemplative corners that remain mostly unexplored and unregarded. Like many aspects of Hong Kong's built legacy from the past, the crumbling Second World War sites are largely unprotected by existing heritage legislation. Bunkers still scarred by bullets and shrapnel, and inscriptions chipped into the concrete when the fighting abated, are all there still, a prey to any passing vandal. Few local residents know, or care, that these historic ruins even exist.

Magnificent hiking trails start in the lower Kowloon hills, and wind their way past superb scenic vistas of rocky coastlines, outlying islands, tranquil reservoirs and wooded slopes. Some trails are little more than gentle paths behind the tower blocks while others, such as the paths around Lion Rock, provide popular and easily reached morning constitutional routes for residents in the places just below. Other tracks are more remote, and to reach them requires stamina and a desire for solitude.

The MacLehose Trail, named after Sir Murray MacLehose (later Lord MacLehose of Beoch), governor of Hong Kong from 1971 to 1981, winds over the Kowloon hills from beyond Sai Kung's High Island Reservoir, towards Kwai Chung, and over Tai Mo Shan, the highest mountain in Hong Kong. The Trail finally ends near Perowne Barracks, the crumbling former home of the Queen's Gurkha Engineers, along the Castle Peak Road just south of Tuen Mun.

Every year, the Maclehose Trail sees thousands of hikers participate in the annual Operation Trailwalker charity fund-raising event. For much of the rest of the year, especially during the summer months, hikers on these remote paths rarely encounter another human being.

Introduction

One of Hong Kong's most enjoyable long tramps, the Wilson Trail, named after Sir David Wilson (later Lord Wilson of Tillyorn and Fan Ling), the colony's penultimate governor, starts near Stanley on Hong Kong Island and continues above and beyond Devil's Peak, and continues all the way to Sha Tau Kok, near the border with China.

For much of the way, the contrast between Kowloon's dense urban conurbation not far below and beyond, and the waving grasses, sweeping views and near-total silence along the trail, could not be more marked. These expanses of readily accessible open country are all an essential part of the peninsula, too. Kowloon without its surrounding ranges is only a small part of the whole.

Just beyond Choi Hung and Diamond Hill the entire Sai Kung and Clearwater Bay districts open up. These areas are easy to reach by public transport and simple to explore, with well-marked trails and a multitude of places to relax. As a respite from urban Kowloon, a bus ride is all it takes.

A few hours — or better still, an entire day — spent out on the Kowloon hills brings one a world away from the massed housing estates, crowded streets, and thronged shopping areas just within sight, and sometimes sound, of the wild country beyond. To many residents, and increasing numbers of visitors, readily accessible countryside is an aspect of Hong Kong life even more surprising and delightful than the obvious appeals of the city itself.

* * * * *

Streets: Exploring Kowloon aims to complement and enhance, but not replicate or stand apart from its companion volume, *Streets: Exploring Hong Kong Island*. Like the two sides of the city bisected by Victoria Harbour, the divisions and differences between both add further dimensions, colour and balance to the whole.

Kowloon and its extended area is emphatically *not* a poor relative of Hong Kong Island, even though it is sometimes seen that way. Neither is Kowloon simply a sprawling urban adjunct to the mountains, open spaces and New Town conurbations of the

Introduction

mainland New Territories. And most of all, Kowloon is not simply a place to be passed through on the way out to the airport and away from Hong Kong altogether.

Like the earlier work, *Streets: Exploring Kowloon* is a personal and particular view of a very varied place and its equally wide-ranging assortment of residents and visitors. It will not fit around everyone's notions of what the extended Kowloon area is, and it does not intend to do so.

If *Streets: Exploring Kowloon* encourages more people, *especially* those who live in Hong Kong, to venture into parts of Kowloon that are unfamiliar to them, to more fully explore the peninsula and its extended areas, and hopefully see this enduringly fascinating place with a different eye, then it will have more than achieved its aim.

Tsim Sha Tsui

Modern Tsim Sha Tsui summons up a rich and heady juxtaposition of initial images and impressions. Many of them are both overwhelming and contradictory: closely packed tower blocks, unremitting traffic and construction noise, neon-lit streets, legions of persistent touts promoting everything from near-authentic quality copy watches to backstairs Indian tailor shops, slightly bewildered, camera-slung tourists, and teeming masses of people on the move and on the make.

Overwhelmingly, perceptions are of a densely compacted part of one of the most highly urbanized places in the world. But Tsim Sha Tsui, like the rest of Kowloon, was not always bustling and crowded. Numerous echoes of a quieter, less frenetic past still remain to be enjoyed, aspects of which can also be found in surprising quantity and variety right across modern urban Hong Kong.

Less than half a century ago Nathan Road, the main north-south thoroughfare through Tsim Sha Tsui, was a pleasant, tree-lined boulevard with relatively light traffic. From its southern end, near the harbour front and the Kowloon-Canton Railway lines, Nathan Road passed through a low-rise, almost suburban townscape and then gradually gave way to barracks, playing fields and open space to the northeast, and the densely packed tenement areas at Yau Ma Tei, Mong Kok and beyond towards Sham Shui Po.

Tsim Sha Tsui means 'sharp, sandy point'. The indented coastline around southern Kowloon bore that shape when the peninsula was ceded to Great Britain in 1860. On a number of early British-era maps, present-day Tsim Sha Tsui is marked in English as Kowloon Point. Gradual phases of reclamation and development over the last century have dramatically altered the shape of Kowloon, as well as greatly enlarged the peninsula's overall land area. No trace of the original Tsim Sha Tsui shoreline still remains.

Before Hong Kong Island was claimed by Great Britain in 1841, Tsim Sha Tsui was a far-flung, sparsely settled place of low hills, sandy beaches and scattered small villages. Tsim Sha Tsui's land-dwelling population were a mixture of Punti (Cantonese) and Hakka, and in this respect the area differed little from villages elsewhere on the Kowloon peninsula and around the mainland coast of Victoria Harbour south of the Kowloon hills.

After the early 1840s, most villagers on the lower Kowloon peninsula lived by quarrying building stone for use in the new City of Victoria, just across the water. Some small-scale market gardening also developed. A similar development pattern occurred at locations elsewhere around Victoria Harbour, after the settlement of Hong Kong Island by the British in 1841, and these activities continued to expand throughout the nineteenth century.

Tsim Sha Tau ('sharp, sandy head') was a very long-established village located around the eastern end of what is now Granville Road; its villagers were resettled further north near Yau Ma Tei after the British took possession of Kowloon in 1860. No trace whatsoever remains of Tsim Sha Tau — not even a road name commemorates this long-vanished hamlet.

STREETS

• Salisbury Road	• Observatory Road
• Nathan Road	• Austin Road
• Haiphong Road	
• Chatham Road South	

By the 1880s the many small-scale granite quarries along the Tsim Sha Tsui coastline had mostly been worked out, and by the end of the following decade all had completely closed down. Other harbour-side quarries operations continued to operate around the eastern shores of Kowloon Bay until the late 1920s.

A large number of British and Indian Army soldiers and service families also lived in Tsim Sha Tsui in these years. Kowloon was home to a substantial army presence from the earliest days of British settlement. In these years Whitfield Barracks dominated the western side of Nathan Road, past Haiphong Road, and Gun Club Hill Barracks commanded the high-ground position between Austin and Jordan Roads.

From the early twentieth century onwards a racially mixed community made their homes in Kowloon. During these years, Tsim Sha Tsui became home to an expanding Eurasian population and by the 1920s, a significant proportion of the colony's well-established local Portuguese community had moved across the harbour as well, and established schools and churches of their own in Kowloon.

Between the wars, Hong Kong had a sizeable European lower-middle class, who worked as foremen and engineers in the utility companies and in the commercial and Royal Naval dockyards, as ship's officers, police constables and sergeants, or as managerial staff in smaller trading firms. Many of these European residents lived in Kowloon, where living costs were lower. Most seemed to mix easily with their Eurasian and local Portuguese neighbours — a contrast to the somewhat more exclusive social atmosphere that prevailed on parts of Hong Kong Island.

In the 1920s a significant White Russian émigré contingent emerged in Tsim Sha Tsui. Large numbers settled elsewhere in China during that period, especially in Manchuria, Shanghai and the Treaty Port cities. Many White Russians worked in the Hong Kong Police, the Hong Kong Jockey Club and as security guards on passenger vessels that operated out of Hong Kong up and down the China coast. Others opened popular restaurants and cafes, such as the long-vanished Cherikoff, which was locally renowned for its high quality cakes and pastries and numerous varieties of savoury *piroshki* ('little pies'). The White Russian community remained a noted feature of Hong Kong life until the late 1950s and was large enough for a small Russian Orthodox Church to operate on Middle Road. This church has long since moved, along with most of its congregation, to Sydney.

Apartment buildings in Tsim Sha Tsui, as elsewhere in Hong Kong, were usually three or four stories high. Before the advent of air-conditioning, these were kept cool with broad verandahs, window shutters and high ceilings. Many flat-dwellers in Kowloon rented flowerpots already in bloom from local nurseries, which were changed with the seasons. The services of a gardener, known as the *fa wong* or 'flower king', was included in the price, and who came every other day to tend them. All these features added to the area's scenic appeal.

STREETS

Tsim Sha Tsui

In addition to numerous low-rise apartment buildings, Tsim Sha Tsui also had several residential hotels. Empress Lodge on Mody Road was one of the most popular. A room with full board cost less than a hundred dollars a month, which made Empress Lodge a popular option for young unmarried men. Renamed the Melbourne Hotel in 1939, the building was later demolished and replaced by the Holiday Inn Golden Mile.

Cinemas were very popular all over Hong Kong and Kowloon and Tsim Sha Tsui had several; the Star Theatre on the corner of Peking and Hankow Roads was probably one of the best patronized. Film programmes changed every week and from time to time, touring Italian opera companies, concert orchestras and other live theatrical performances would perform at the Star Theatre as well.

Kowloon's relaxed pattern of life changed rapidly in the early 1950s. The steady development of international air routes in the 1950s, and the correspondingly rapid development of the local tourist industry, meant that throughout these years prewar apartment blocks gradually gave way to multi-storied hotels and shopping arcades. By the end of the 1960s Tsim Sha Tsui had been completely transformed, and from the 1970s the district looked much as it does today.

Numerous goods and services that catered to the international tourist trade burgeoned exponentially in Kowloon in these years, along with annually increasing number of visitors. At the same time, however, Tsim Sha Tsui's physical

Tsim Sha Tsui

infrastructure remained almost unchanged from half a century earlier. Narrow footpaths originally laid out for quiet suburban streets now saw thousands of pedestrians jammed along them every day. Shady mature trees along the roadsides were felled after shopkeepers complained that branches blocked their advertising hoardings. With every passing year, Tsim Sha Tsui had fewer old buildings or other references to the past.

Modern Tsim Sha Tsui can appear rather overwhelming at first. While this part of Kowloon is certainly very vital, interesting and unexpected in places, for many people the overall Tsim Sha Tsui experience is often less than a pleasant one. Impossibly crowded streets are choked with traffic and pedestrians and often blocked by construction work. Touts accost passers-by every twenty metres or so. Air-conditioner ducts and broken pipes drip on one's head and ambient noise levels — even by Hong Kong standards — can be excruciating, especially when compounded by the heat, humidity and almost constant rain in the summer months.

Largely because of these issues, quite a few local residents avoid a visit to Tsim Sha Tsui unless they have a specific reason to go there. By way of contrast, overseas tourists' impressions of Hong Kong are largely informed by the streets of Tsim Sha Tsui. Tsim Sha Tsui has numerous corners of considerable interest right next to obvious aesthetic or planning shortcomings, and its streets have a densely clotted, cheerfully hucksterish get-up-and-go flavour combined with a highly visible diverse, genuinely international presence, which is largely absent in many other parts of contemporary Hong Kong.

STREETS

Salisbury Road
梳士巴利道

When the British took possession of the Kowloon peninsula in 1860, most of where this unendingly busy stretch of road now runs was located some distance beyond the original Tsim Sha Tsui coastline in Victoria Harbour. Over the following fifty years, piecemeal reclamation provided land for wharves, warehouses, railway lines and Salisbury Road. Salisbury Road was named after Robert Cecil (later Lord Salisbury), British foreign secretary during the 1870s and subsequently prime minister in the 1880s.

Passengers from all over the world once disembarked onto wharves located on the site of the present-day Ocean Terminal and the Harbour City shopping complex, at the junction of Salisbury and Canton Roads. Back in the days when sea travel was almost the only way to go, international and coastal passenger liners all berthed here. Almost every major shipping line in the world — from the stately, class-conscious P&O liners and the Canadian Pacific's famous white 'Empresses', to sleek, black hulled Japanese Nippon Yusen Kaisha (NYK) boats and the French Messageries Maritimes liners, internationally renowned for their excellent food and wine — all called regularly at Hong Kong and tied up at these piers.

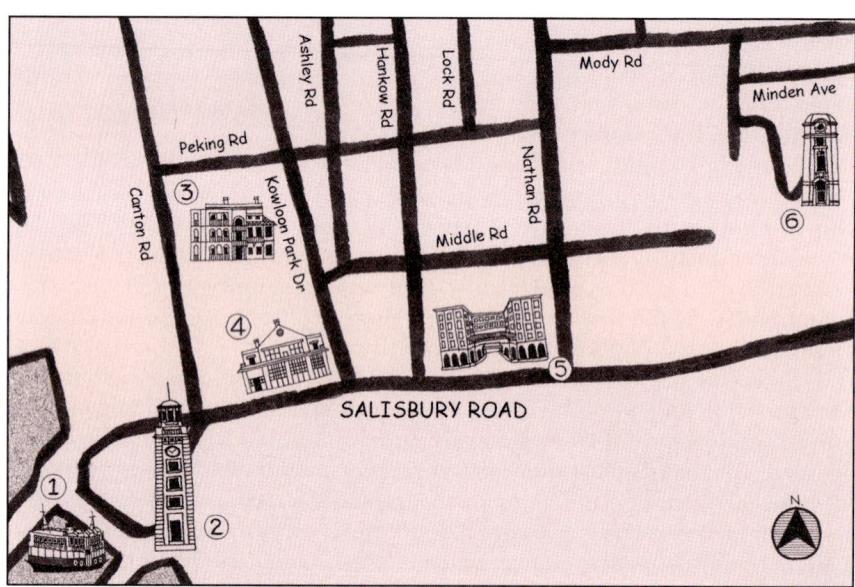

❶ 'Star' Ferry
❷ Former Kowloon-Canton Railway clock tower
❸ Old Marine Police Headquarters
❹ Former Tsim Sha Tsui Fire Station
❺ Peninsula Hotel
❻ Signal Hill

Salisbury Road

One notable exception was the Liverpool-based Blue Funnel Line, which tied up at its own landing stage, known as Holt's Wharf, further up past the railway station just below Signal Hill. With ships named after Homeric figures such as Agamemnon and Achilles, Blue Funnel Line was a popular alternative to other shipping lines: all one-class, fares were cheaper and many passengers regarded 'the Blue Funnel' as far less stuffy than the line's competitors.

Improved international air services throughout the 1950s and 1960s gradually rendered scheduled passenger liners uneconomical, and the last scheduled P&O passenger vessel to call at Hong Kong, the *Chitral*, sailed for England in 1969. Massive cruise ships, however, such as the *Queen Elizabeth II*, still regularly berth alongside the Ocean Terminal. The dominance of air travel now means that there are few chances to enter and leave Hong Kong by its most stunning route, Victoria Harbour, unless you are very rich and on a cruise liner.

Salisbury Road — and nearby side streets — is permanently thronged with pedestrians, especially so on weekends when the pavements are completely packed with tourists, strollers, window-shoppers and the younger local see-and-be-seen crowd. Along this strip, more serious spenders are very well catered to, with every possible variety and price tag of designer product and service available. Salisbury Road is definitely *not* the place to come on a Sunday afternoon if you cannot stand crowds.

1 'Star' Ferry

Salisbury Road

The world-famous 'Star' Ferry, one of Hong Kong's most iconic sights, has shuttled across Victoria Harbour for over a century. The first regular ferries were started by a prominent local Portuguese businessman named Delfino Noronha. Among other enterprises, Noronha's company had the Hong Kong government printing contracts for many years. The initial ferry operation was little more than a weekend pleasure launch to his country house in Yau Ma Tei.

A few paying passengers were allowed on and in due course, Noronha's private launch became a successful business. Eventually, this was sold to a Parsee businessman named Dorabji Naorojee, who also owned successful bakeries on Hong Kong Island and was involved in the colony's hotel business. The 'Star' Ferry Company was subsequently acquired by the Kowloon Wharf and Godown Company. As Kowloon continued to expand and develop in the late nineteenth century, by the 1920s the double-ended 'Star' Ferries were as much as part of commuter life for Kowloon and New Territories residents as the Mass Transit Railway and Kowloon-Canton Railway are today.

Today's green-liveried ferries were all built in the 1960s at the now closed Kowloon Docks in Hung Hom. A trip across Victoria Harbour on the 'Star' Ferry has been an essential part of the Hong Kong experience for generations of residents and visitors, and remains one of the few aspects of local life that has not significantly changed with the passage of time.

(2) *Former Kowloon-Canton Railway Station clock tower*

Tsim Sha Tsui's Kowloon-Canton Railway Station clock tower stands as a lingering reminder of former times and epitomizes the largely failed attempt to legislate effective heritage conservation in Hong Kong in the 1970s. Built from 1915 to 1916, and demolished in 1978, the waterfront Kowloon-Canton Railway Station was a colonnaded, red-brick and granite building adjacent to the 'Star' Ferry. Railway tracks ran along the harbour-side of Salisbury Road, where the Space Museum, Museum of Art and hotels and shopping complexes now stand.

In the 1920s it was possible to board a train in Kowloon and, with changes at Canton, Hankow, Peking, Mukden, Moscow, Berlin and Paris, disembark ten days or so later at London Victoria. Trains departed for the border crossing at Lo Wu every hour, with more frequent departures on weekends and public holidays. The Kowloon-Canton Railway made commuter journeys possible from the New Territories, and even in the 1920s some passengers came to town on a daily basis from their homes in Fan Ling, Tai Po and Sha Tin.

The Kowloon-Canton Railway terminus station was relocated to Hung Hom in 1975. After a sustained, at times impassioned, battle between conservationists

Salisbury Road

and the Urban Council, the original station buildings were demolished in 1978. The waterfront site then stood empty for nearly a decade before the Hong Kong Cultural Centre was built.

This decision proved to be a short-sighted example of town 'planning', as less than thirty years later another main line station in Tsim Sha Tsui was deemed necessary and subsequently built underground, only a few hundred metres further up the road from the original site.

The original Kowloon-Canton Railway Station's clock tower is now, belatedly, a gazetted monument, and features prominently on tourist pamphlets that aim to promote an awareness of Hong Kong's built heritage. The clock tower sustained some damage to the brickwork and granite detailing around its base during

Japanese air raids in December 1941. The repairs made after the war can still be seen.

The dusty pink, lavatory tile-encrusted Hong Kong Cultural Centre commands one of the world's most stunning views. Designed by local architects, it was built with no windows. The area where the main station buildings once stood is now open space, surrounded by clumps of spindly, salt-bitten Cuban Royal Palms (*Roystonea regia*).

(3) *Old Marine Police Headquarters*

Situated on the top of a low hillock at the corner of Canton and Salisbury Roads, the former Marine Police Headquarters was built in 1883. Before Salisbury Road was reclaimed in the early twentieth century, the Water Police Station, as it was then known, had its own harbour front slipway. The buildings overlooked a clean sandy beach to the east, where the YMCA and the Peninsula Hotel now stand. The original time signal tower can still be seen on the harbour-side of the complex, a squat, round whitewashed tower with porthole-like windows.

Salisbury Road

In the 1970s the Marine Police Headquarters lost a large section of its garden when the hillside was partially levelled to create Kowloon Park Drive. This once prominent Tsim Sha Tsui waterfront landmark now seems incongruous and marooned some distance inland, and is almost completely surrounded by newer, taller buildings.

In late 1996 the Marine Police Headquarters was relocated to Sai Wan Ho, at the eastern end of Hong Kong Island. The attractive, colonnaded building is now a gazetted monument and cannot be demolished or significantly altered. Unfortunately the same cannot be claimed for the site itself. Developers have stripped away almost all of its trees; many were several decades old and as monumental as the buildings they once helped shade.

4 *Former Tsim Sha Tsui Fire Station*

Tsim Sha Tsui's old fire station is one of Kowloon's more unexpected relics. Partly obscured by a pedestrian underpass which leads towards the Hong Kong Cultural Centre and 'Star' Ferry piers, these buildings are passed by thousands of people every day. Built in 1904 and renovated a number of times since, this small, red-brick building still features the old fire station doors along the Salisbury Road frontage. In Hong Kong's early years fire-fighting was a responsibility of the Hong Kong Police, which is why the fire station was built just below the police compound.

Thousands of visitors to Hong Kong walk past every day on their way to and from the 'Star' Ferry and for over thirty years, the old fire station building housed

Salisbury Road

a social welfare charity shop very popular with generations of tourists, which sold handicrafts and other items. Attractively folded paper greeting cards made particularly pretty, economical small gifts, and items on sale here numbered among Hong Kong's last remaining real tourist bargains. The welfare shop has recently closed down, and the future preservation and use of the century-old building is somewhat uncertain.

5 *Peninsula Hotel*

Salisbury Road

Fondly known to generations as 'The Pen', the Peninsula Hotel was built in 1926 and officially opened for business in 1928. In the intervening period the building had been requisitioned for emergency military accommodation. Erroneously described in some promotional literature as being situated in the middle of nowhere when first built, this choice of location was a very shrewd business decision on the part of its Sephardic Jewish owners, the Kadoorie family. Only a few minutes' walk from the docks and just across the road from the railway station, the new luxury hotel was perfectly poised to get a generous share of the booming tourist business generated by the worldwide prosperity of the 'Roaring Twenties'. By the 1930s the Peninsula Hotel had become one of Hong Kong's premier hotels.

On Christmas Night 1941 the formal British surrender to the Japanese took place in Room 336. During the Japanese occupation period the Peninsula was renamed the Tōa ('Great Eastern'). Other hotels were also renamed: the Repulse Bay Hotel, appropriately perhaps, was redesignated the Midori-hama ('Green Bay'), and Central's Gloucester Hotel became known as the Matsubara ('Pine Field'). All reverted to their prewar names after the Japanese surrender in 1945.

A tower block extension behind the original building was added to the Peninsula in 1994. Sympathetically coloured and designed, this modern addition complements, rather than overpowers, the earlier structure. In addition to extra hotel rooms, the Peninsula Tower houses an office block and one of Hong Kong's most eclectic restaurants, the Phillipe Starck-designed Felix at the top of the tower, named in honour of Felix Bieger, the Peninsula's popular, long-serving general manager.

6) Signal Hill

Signal Hill, with its attractive garden and red-brick and granite tower, built in 1907, should be much better known than it is. Landlocked now and hidden away behind modern tower blocks, Signal Hill was once one of Tsim Sha Tsui's most prominent landmarks.

The signal tower was built to replace an earlier facility at the Marine Police Headquarters on Salisbury Road (still visible there today), which was obscured when the Kowloon-Canton Railway Station was built. A replacement location on higher ground was found nearby.

Shipping in Victoria Harbour relied on the signal tower at Blackhead Point for accurate timekeeping until time signals shifted to radio in 1933. At exactly 1300 hrs (1 p.m.) every day, a bronze ball was slowly lowered down the pole at the top of the tower. This visual indicator enabled mariners to synchronize and adjust their chronometers; accurate readings were essential for navigational purposes in the days before radar and satellites.

Salisbury Road

On most early maps of Victoria Harbour and Kowloon, Signal Hill was known as Blackhead Point. This name was derived from a German trading firm, F. Schwarzkopf and Co. During the Second Anglo-Chinese War (1856–60), the company were provision contractors for the British forces bivouacked at Kowloon Point, as Tsim Sha Tsui was then generally known.

In due course, F. Schwarzkopf and Co. anglicized their name to Blackhead and Co. Like other German businesses in Hong Kong, the firm was forced out of business during the First World War. Blackhead Point is occasionally found marked on old maps as Tai Tau Mai, which means 'Big Bag of Rice'. The origin of this Chinese name is obscure, and predates the construction of the signal tower.

How To Get There

By MTR:	Tsim Sha Tsui Station.
By Ferry:	'Star' Ferry from Central.
By Taxi:	尖沙咀梳士巴利道 (*Jeem Saa Choy, Sor See Ba Lei Doh*).

STREETS

Nathan Road
彌敦道

Nathan Road was named after the thirteenth governor of Hong Kong, Sir Matthew Nathan, the only bachelor, and the only Jew, to hold the office. When first surveyed in the late 1860s, the lower section was named Coronation Road. It was subsequently realigned at the northern end near Austin Avenue and renamed Robinson Road, after Sir William Robinson (governor of Hong Kong, 1891–98). Robinson Road was redesignated as Nathan Road in 1909, two years after its new namesake's departure from Hong Kong.

In the early years, construction of a thoroughfare as broad as Nathan Road was considered completely unnecessary, as Kowloon was sparsely populated with very little in the way of vehicular traffic. With the passage of time, however, Nathan Road's width has proven invaluable, as it is one of the few major roads in Kowloon never prone to serious traffic jams.

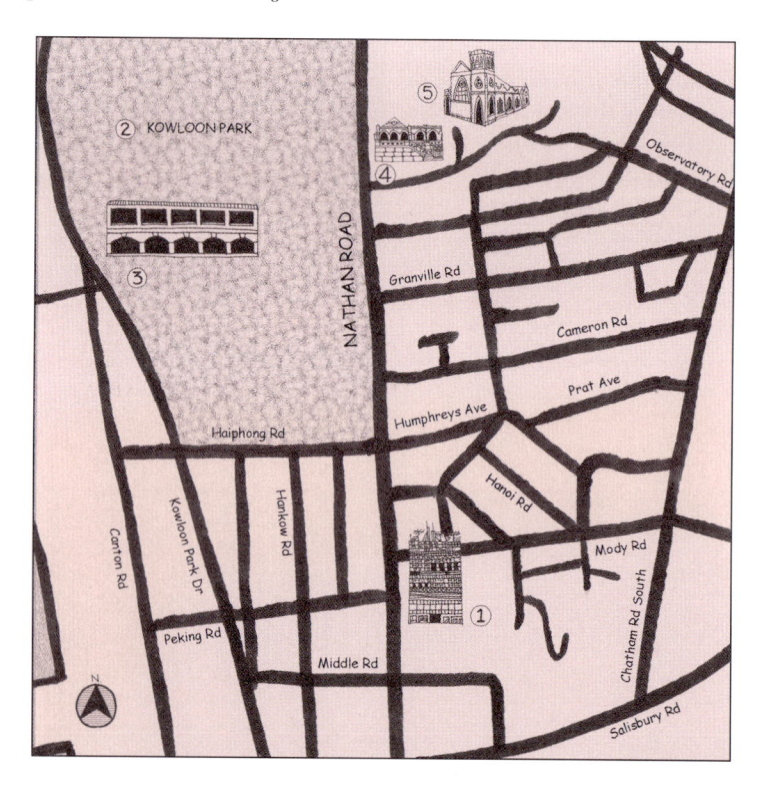

❶ Chungking Mansions
❷ Kowloon Park
❸ Former barrack buildings, Kowloon Park
❹ Antiquities and Monuments Office
❺ St Andrew's Church

STREETS

Nathan Road

Since the late 1950s the entire length of Nathan Road has been completely transformed by rapid redevelopment; some would say it has been totally ruined. Prior to that decade, Tsim Sha Tsui was a relatively quiet district, with numerous low-rise buildings, shady tree-lined streets and a few cinemas, restaurants and hotels. These days, the Tsim Sha Tsui stretch of Nathan Road is popularly known as the 'Golden Mile', due to its stratospheric commercial rents, hundreds of tourist-oriented shops, dozens of hotels and their unfailing collective ability to suck large sums of money out of visitors' pockets.

1 Chungking Mansions

Internationally famous after the release of Wong Kar-wai's 1994 film *Chungking Express*, the dingy corridors and lower alleyways within Chungking Mansions are well-known to the world's backpackers. For many years, the building has been one of the principal stops on the international budget travel route through Asia and is noted as such in every guidebook that mentions Hong Kong.

Chungking Mansions was constructed in the early 1960s by a Filipino-Chinese businessman, on the site of a prewar cluster of shops known as Chung King Arcade. When it first opened, Chungking Mansions was one of the most upmarket residential developments in Tsim Sha Tsui. A number of local film stars lived in the complex; at sixteen stories, it was then the highest building in Kowloon, with magnificent harbour views in every direction.

Chungking Mansions gradually declined in popularity through the 1970s as its view was blocked by new construction. By the early 1980s it had become a dirty, crime-ridden tenement with little to distinguish it from dozens of others like it in lower Kowloon — but with one major difference. Indians, Nigerians, Nepalese, Pakistanis, Filipinos, Hong Kong Chinese and all manner of other nationalities somehow mingle here in the mutual search for profit, and for the most part co-

Nathan Road

exist peacefully and without inter-ethnic problems. Occasional violent incidents reported in the local press are invariably related to disputes over drugs, money or sex, rather than issues of religion or race.

Contemporary Hong Kong is often touted, quite erroneously, as some sort of uniquely cosmopolitan 'melting pot'. In many respects and in most areas, however, the city remains a functionally monolingual place, and very often a chauvinistic, monocultural one as well. Grubby, smelly and periodically dodgy though parts of the complex undoubtedly are, Chungking Mansions is nevertheless one of the most genuinely cosmopolitan, polyglot corners of Hong Kong, as well as a superb place to enjoy an authentic, reasonably priced curry. Recent renovations have done much to improve overall appearances, and part of the complex has even been renamed as — you guessed it — Chungking Express.

② Kowloon Park

For well over a century Kowloon's most popular public park was a substantial British Army camp. Known as Whitfield Barracks, the camp was named after a former general officer commanding in Hong Kong, Major-General H. T. Whitfield, who also served as acting governor at various times during the 1860s and early 1870s.

Whitfield Barracks was one of several British Army camps found in the urban area of Kowloon; others were located nearby in Austin Road, further north at Sham Shui Po, in Kowloon Tong and near Kai Tak Airport. Like Victoria Cantonment across the harbour (now Hong Kong Park), Whitfield Barracks

Nathan Road

remained a military site long enough for its potential for open public space to be recognized and utilized.

With numerous mature trees, relative quiet, superb swimming facilities and that rarest of Kowloon features — ample space to move about — Kowloon Park remains a pleasantly unexpected open area in the middle of densely crowded Tsim Sha Tsui. The park has very old spreading trees which, as they came under the protection of the military, both British and Japanese, managed to survive the twin perils of war and constant redevelopment. Now safely incorporated into Kowloon Park, their spreading branches provide one of the few substantial areas of natural street side shade in modern Tsim Sha Tsui.

In addition to mature trees, the visitor to Kowloon Park can enjoy ornamental ponds, a bird garden, swimming pools and numerous pleasant open areas. Kowloon Park is also extremely clean at all times, a solid tribute to the legions of ever vigilant Leisure and Cultural Services Department employees, and a marked contrast to the often squalid streetscapes found just outside the gates.

③ *Former barrack buildings, Kowloon Park*

For many years the Hong Kong Museum of History was located in temporary premises that survived when Kowloon Park was created out of Whitfield Barracks in the late 1970s. The museum was relocated to its brand new, purpose-built premises at Chatham Road in 1998, and eventually reopened to the public in 2001. The buildings have now been converted into an excellent heritage resource centre for research into various aspects of Hong Kong history, culture and society.

Nathan Road

(4) Antiquities and Monuments Office

This ecclesiastical-looking building next to St Andrew's Church was built in 1900 to accommodate the Central British School (CBS), which opened in 1902. The Central British School was the forerunner of what, in later decades, became the English Schools Foundation (ESF).

Before the CBS was established, those European children who were not sent overseas to school — in practice, this meant the children of the less well-to-do — attended Queen's College on Hong Kong Island or else the church-run schools such as St Joseph's College, the French Convent, the Italian Convent or the Diocesan Boys and Girls Schools. In these institutions their classmates were either Chinese, local Portuguese or Eurasians. In the 1890s widespread complaints by parents about poor educational standards in these schools led to a drive for a new school, which more closely adhered to the British curriculum.

Funds for the construction of this school were donated by prominent Eurasian millionaire Robert (later Sir Robert) Hotung, on the understanding that the new institution was to admit a multiracial student population. Instead, the school was established to provide an education solely for British children resident in Hong Kong. Despite the fact that Hotung had put up the money, his daughters — as local Eurasians — found themselves unable to attend and went to the nearby Diocesan Girls' School instead.

In the 1920s schoolchildren from Taikoo dockyard and sugar factory workers at Quarry Bay came across the harbour by a special company launch — one of the most pleasant memories for these now elderly ex-CBS students. For a few months in early 1945, the CBS buildings on Nathan Road were used as a military hospital, after the closure of the British Military Hospital at Bowen Road.

Nathan Road

The senior section of Central British School moved to new buildings in Ma Tau Wai in 1935, and was renamed King George V School (KGV). The primary section was renamed Kowloon Junior School and moved to adjacent premises after the war. Both are still in the same locations today.

Perhaps appropriately for a designated historical building, the original CBS buildings on Nathan Road now provide a home for the Antiquities and Monuments Office, the government body responsible — as far as Hong Kong's toothless, loophole-festooned heritage legislation allows — for the designation and protection of built heritage and sites of historic interest in Hong Kong.

⑤ *St Andrew's Church*

While St Andrew's Church seems somehow out of place in modern Tsim Sha Tsui, it nevertheless remains a striking reminder of what much of the southern Kowloon peninsula once looked like.

Hidden away behind mature trees on its small hill, many casual passers-by would never even know that this pleasant, small red-brick church even exists. The foundation stone for St Andrew's Church was laid in 1904 by J. C. Hoare, the Anglican bishop of Victoria. Two years later, Bishop Hoare was tragically drowned during a catastrophic typhoon that claimed thousands of lives in and around Victoria Harbour in September 1906.

Along with the adjacent church hall (redeveloped in the late 1970s) and a vicarage in similar style (opened in 1909), St Andrew's Church was a gift to the Hong Kong community from Calcutta-born Armenian businessman Sir Catchick Paul Chater. The co-founder of Hong Kong Land, the Kowloon Wharf and Godown

STREETS

Nathan Road

Company and numerous other prominent local enterprises, Chater was probably the single most significant business and community figure in late nineteenth and early twentieth-century Hong Kong.

Chater's principal local residence was the palatial Marble Hall on Hong Kong Island's Conduit Road, but he also had a house next to St Andrew's Church, which was sold and demolished a few years after his death in 1926. Sir Paul Chater was possibly that rarest of Hong Kong species, an entrepreneurial, yet genuinely community-minded business figure, whose visionary plans for the city where he made his home and fortune are still clearly recognizable today.

A number of blocked-up air raid tunnels extend into the hillside behind St Andrew's Church. First built by the Hong Kong government in 1940 and later extended by the Japanese, these are silent reminders of sustained American air raids over Hong Kong near the end of the Pacific War.

How To Get There

By Bus:	No. 2, 6, 6A from Tsim Sha Tsui 'Star' Ferry.
By MTR:	Tsim Sha Tsui Station.
By Taxi:	尖沙咀彌敦道 (*'Jeem Saa Choy, Nei Don Doh'*).

Haiphong Road
海防道

Haiphong Road links Canton Road, with its popular shopping centres and harbour access, to Nathan Road, Tsim Sha Tsui's main thoroughfare. The road takes its name from the sizeable port city at the mouth of the Red River in northern Vietnam, greatly expanded by the French in the late nineteenth century. Haiphong Road has a number of frequently overlooked places of interest, and both pedestrian and vehicular traffic is fairly heavy along this road at whatever the hour.

In the 1970s the western end of Haiphong Road was bisected by the construction of the Kowloon Park Drive flyover, along which an endless stream of traffic roars towards Yau Ma Tei and beyond. But only a few metres away from all this noise and bustle the relative tranquillity of Kowloon Park can be enjoyed.

Numerous Indian merchants opened shops along Haiphong Road in the 1920s and 1930s. Mostly Hindu merchants from the province of Sindh, now part of modern Pakistan, they initially made a living by supplying Indian foodstuffs and clothing to the soldiers stationed in the Whitfield Barracks adjacent to Haiphong Road. These shopkeepers and their businesses were the precursors of the large and highly visible local Indian commercial presence in Tsim Sha Tsui today.

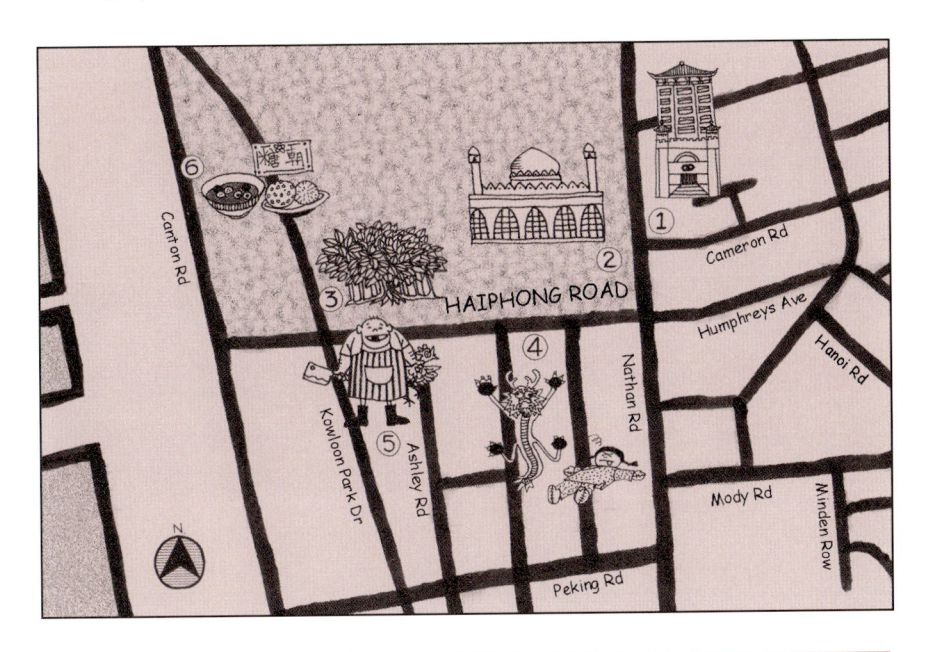

❶ 'Chinoiserie' building (Wayfoong House)
❷ Kowloon Mosque and Islamic Centre
❸ Banyan trees
❹ Chinese souvenir alley
❺ Haiphong Road Temporary Market
❻ Sweet Dynasty

STREETS

Haiphong Road

Many members of the Sindhi community branched out into the garment industry in the 1950s (most of Tsim Sha Tsui's Indian tailors are Sindhi) as well as into other businesses. Probably the most well-known Sindhi family in Hong Kong are the highly visible Harilela clan. This family are the owners of numerous hotels including the Holiday Inn chain, and live in an expansive multi-generational compound on Kowloon Tong's Waterloo Road.

① 'Chinoiserie' building (Wayfoong House)

Directly opposite the Kowloon Mosque, this interesting, eclectically styled building was originally built as an apartment block. Chinese-inspired roof detailing has been tacked on to a thoroughly functional Western-style high-rise building. The general impression, rather odd at first glance, nevertheless seems to work and this building remains one of the most distinctive buildings in Tsim Sha Tsui. Several of its lower floors are now used by the Hongkong and Shanghai Banking Corporation.

Culturally syncretic decoration is not as common in Hong Kong as one may at first suppose. What architectural fusion exists is usually found in ecclesiastical buildings or other structures with a quasi-religious function. The Chinese YMCA on Hong Kong Island's Bridges Street, built during the First World War, is one of the best surviving earlier instance of this trend. St Mary's Anglican Church in Causeway Bay and Holy Trinity Church in Kowloon City, are other attractive examples.

② Kowloon Mosque and Islamic Centre

Kowloon's first mosque was originally built to cater to the spiritual needs of Indian Army soldiers stationed in Hong Kong, as well as the substantial Punjabi Muslim contingent in the Hong Kong Police. There were usually two Indian Army

STREETS

Haiphong Road

battalions garrisoned in the colony at any time before the Pacific War; one was usually a Muslim regiment. While the Muslim soldiers did not bring their families with them to Hong Kong, those who served in the Hong Kong Police did; in time their descendants formed the nucleus of today's sizeable local Pakistani community.

Located near the barrack gates on the corner of Haiphong Road, the original mosque was far smaller and much more basic than the present substantial building. The Kowloon Mosque and Islamic Centre was built in 1984. An Arabian, rather than South Asian, influence is immediately noticeable due to the sleek white domes and soaring minarets. Most regular attendees at the mosque live and work nearby in Tsim Sha Tsui. A surprising number of Hong Kong's Muslims are ethnic Chinese, and therefore invisible among the wide community.

③ Banyan trees

With their dangling aerial roots, these venerable, leafy old Chinese banyans (*Ficus retusa*), known in Cantonese as *yung shue*, are welcome reminders of the not-so-far-off days when many roadsides in Tsim Sha Tsui and other parts of Hong Kong were lined with similar trees.

A very hardy species, Chinese banyans will grow in precarious positions and can survive poor soils, exposure to wind and salt air, and long periods of extended wet or dry conditions. *Yung shue* are also very tolerant of air-borne pollution; just as well, too, as prolonged exposure to Kowloon's unrelenting traffic exhaust would seriously hurt the average human being. Most ornamental

Haiphong Road

plantings attempted along the roadsides in Tsim Sha Tsui, soon blacken with diesel fumes, sicken, and die. Swiftly thereafter they are replaced — in true Hong Kong fashion — by yet more of the same species, which just as rapidly suffer a similar fate to their predecessors.

Just inside the Haiphong Road entrance to Kowloon Park, a row of very substantial old camphor laurel trees (*Cinnamomum camphora*) completely overhang the road outside and provide pedestrians with year-round shade.

(4) Chinese souvenir alley

Chinese souvenirs and oriental *objets d'art* have been favoured tourist purchases for decades, and there are several distinct areas where less expensive items can be found; one of the most famous is Hong Kong Island's Stanley Market. As Tsim Sha Tsui steadily developed into Hong Kong's major tourism and nightlife district in the 1950s and 1960s and more hotels were built, numerous small curio shops catering to the booming visitor trade opened as well. Crowded, atmospheric little alleyways such as this one off Haiphong Road have come to epitomize the 'authentic' backstreet Kowloon experience for many tourists.

Despite the widespread availability of similar items in Chinatowns all over the world, and often at prices similar to Hong Kong, many visitors still want to take back some distinctive, personalized reminder of their time in the fabled Orient. Many of the items on offer in Kowloon's souvenir alleys are, well, certainly very

Haiphong Road

distinctive. Along these curio-choked lanes one can find just about anything you may, or may not, want to display in your home.

Bamboo and bone-backed mah-jong sets are stacked next to ingeniously carved, Indonesian and Thai statues and wooden items, which nestle against pot-bellied laughing Buddhas and luridly coloured sheaves of oil-on-black-velvet paintings. Most of these 'artworks' seem to feature heavily stylized bat-winged junks sailing against a glittering Hong Kong harbour backdrop. All these items are perennially popular, market-proven staples; the basic souvenir alley stock never seems to change. Occasional better quality pieces lurk among the tat and junk.

5. Haiphong Road Temporary Market

'Temporary' is something of a misnomer here; the Haiphong Road Temporary Market has been situated under the Kowloon Park Drive flyover for many years. How many more decades this *gai see* (Cantonese for 'wet market') will 'temporarily' occupy this space is anyone's guess. The section closest to Haiphong Road, directly under the flyover, sells a wide variety of fresh flowers and various types of elaborate floral bouquets, while further back there is a well-stocked fresh produce market.

In an interesting localized twist, the Haiphong Road Temporary Market — unlike most other wet markets in Hong Kong — has several flourishing *halal* stalls selling beef, chicken and mutton slaughtered according to Islamic ritual. Given the significant numbers of Indian Muslims and Pakistanis who live and work in Tsim Sha Tsui, these butchers' stalls provide an everyday convenience to these communities, and thus their presence not as unlikely as would seem at first.

Haiphong Road

(6) Sweet Dynasty

One of Tsim Sha Tsui's most popular venues for late-night *tong shui* (Chinese sweet soups), Sweet Dynasty has been around for years and packs in the crowds, especially on weekends when the queue for a table can easily stretch out into the street. Like many quintessentially Hong Kong culinary phenomena that newcomers either love or loathe, Chinese *tong shui* must be tried at least a few times before a firm 'like-it-or-not' decision can be reached. Even hardcore aficionados of European-style desserts often come to prefer *tong shui*; much lighter, they say, and just the right thing after a Chinese meal.

As well as more traditional varieties of sweet soups such as *hong dau saa* (red bean soup), *fah sang* (peanut), *hup toh* (walnut) and *jee mah* (black sesame) pastes, numerous newer innovations have been devised in recent years. Various confections involving shaved ice, barely ripe mango, ice-cream, lurid-coloured syrups and diverse beans and seeds enjoy intermittent popularity. Many of these concoctions only last a season or so, and become all the rage when they are promoted in various Chinese-language magazines and endorsed by the most popular Canto-pop stars at that point in time.

How To Get There

By Bus:	No. 1, 1A, 2, 6, 6A, 7, 9 from Tsim Sha Tsui 'Star' Ferry.
By MTR:	Tsim Sha Tsui Station.
By Taxi:	尖沙咀海防道 (*'Jeem Saa Choy, Hoi Fong Doh'*).

STREETS

Chatham Road South
漆咸道南

Tsim Sha Tsui

Named after William Chatham, a former director of public works, Chatham Road was originally named Des Voeux Road in honor of Sir William Des Voeux, governor from 1887 to 1891. In the late nineteenth century, a number of street names in Kowloon replicated others on Hong Kong Island. All were standardized in 1909 and those with pre-existing duplicates were renamed. Thus Robinson Road became Nathan Road, Chater Street became Peking Road, and MacDonnell Road became Canton Road.

Originally bordered by railway tracks and the shores of Hung Hom Bay, contemporary Chatham Road epitomizes modern Tsim Sha Tsui: overcrowded, unlovely in places, yet enjoyable and full of surprises. Beyond the non-stop traffic, persistent touts and dubious-looking karaoke dens that colour most immediate impressions of the area, numerous significant elements of the past, such as the century-old Rosary Church, still wait to be better explored.

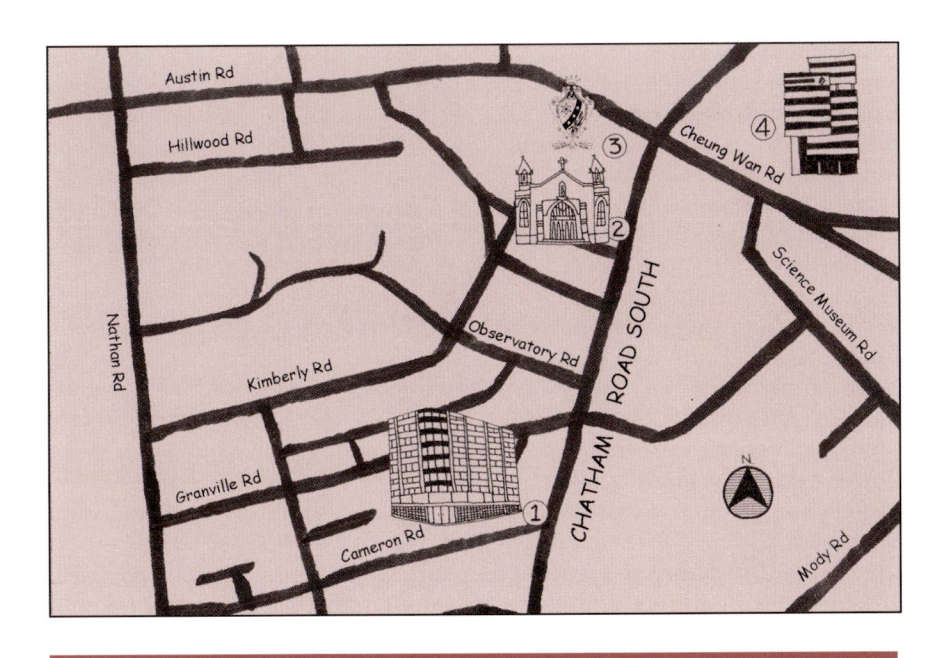

❶ Park Hotel
❷ Rosary Church
❸ St Mary's Canossian College
❹ Hong Kong Polytechnic University

STREETS

Chatham Road South

In the early 1970s Hung Hom Bay was fully reclaimed and the new land area beyond Chatham Road was designated as Tsim Sha Tsui East. Popularly known as *Jeem Tung*, the district is now filled with glitzy hotels, shopping malls, large restaurants and nightclubs of various types and descriptions. Many of these establishments are closely orientated towards the tastes and expectations of Japanese tourists and businessmen. Most do not welcome, or indeed in some instances permit, visitors of other ethnicities — so much for Hong Kong's much vaunted 'cosmopolitan' outlook.

1 Park Hotel

A pleasant survivor from Hong Kong's 1960s tourist boom, the Park Hotel, on the corner of Chatham and Cameron Roads, relies heavily on the packaged tour trade and has recently been revamped for a new generation of visitors. Numerous other tourist-class hotels were built elsewhere in Tsim Sha Tsui during these years, due to Kowloon's proximity to Kai Tak Airport. While some long-established hotels, such as the Kowloon and the Imperial have been demolished and rebuilt, many others from this era, such as the Park, the Mirador and the Shamrock survive and prosper.

In the interwar years, a pleasant private building with a large garden stood exactly where the Park Hotel is located. Informally known as the 'Punjab Mess', this was not a curry house — as one might suspect in contemporary Tsim Sha Tsui — but a Mess for Indian Army officers stationed up the road at Whitfield Barracks.

Even by liberal British Garrison standards, Indian Army officers were well-known for their generous hospitality. Invitations to their Mess guest nights were eagerly coveted by young women out for a good time, much as invitations to Brigade of Gurkhas Officers' Messes in the New Territories were enjoyed seventy years later by a fresh generation of husband-hunters.

STREETS

Chatham Road South

② *Rosary Church*

Rosary Church was donated to Hong Kong's Roman Catholic community in 1904 by Dr A. S. Gomes. Like many 'China Coast' Portuguese of his generation, Dr Gomes was born in Macao. He trained in medicine in Bombay (now Mumbai), London and Edinburgh and in 1867, became the first local Portuguese doctor admitted to practise in Hong Kong. As well as the Rosary Church, Dr Gomes opened the Wan Chai Hospital for the aged and infirmed, and devoted his later years to numerous charitable works.

By the early years of the twentieth century, many of Hong Kong's local Portuguese had moved across the harbour to Tsim Sha Tsui from 'Matto Moro', the area around the mosque on Central's Shelley Street, where many had settled from the 1850s onwards. Rosary Church became very popular with local Portuguese families who lived in Tsim Sha Tsui. By the 1930s the better-off members of this community had moved to new residential developments around Ho Man Tin in the vicinity of St Teresa's Church in Kowloon Tong, but Tsim Sha Tsui retained a distinct local Portuguese flavour until the 1960s.

Rosary Church is very quiet and peaceful, in spite of the near-constant traffic outside along Chatham Road, and is locally well-known for an attractive series of religious paintings on the western wall, which depict the 'Mysteries of the Rosary'.

Chatham Road South

(3) St Mary's Canossian College

The attractively arcaded St Mary's Canossian College contains some of the oldest buildings still extant in this part of Tsim Sha Tsui. Along with the Rosary Church next door, the older buildings at St Mary's Canossian College was donated to the community by Dr A. S. Gomes. As well as a school, there was also an orphanage adjacent to the church; this has long since closed.

St Mary's was initially operated as a Kowloon branch of the Canossian Order's main school and convent on Caine Road on Hong Kong Island. In its early years a number of young boys also attended the school as part of a Kowloon branch of Hong Kong Island's St Joseph's College. As student numbers expanded, a separate Roman Catholic boys' school was opened in Kowloon. This later moved to Kowloon Tong and was renamed La Salle College.

Like the Rosary Church, St Mary's Canossian College is an enduring link with the largely vanished local Portuguese presence in Tsim Sha Tsui. Not all students, however, lived in the local area. In the 1920s at least one young local Portuguese girl came down to school every day on the train from Fan Ling in the New Territories.

Contemporary St Mary's Canossian College remains one of Kowloon's most prestigious girls' schools, and entry is highly competitive. The surrounding backstreets are full of rowdy young schoolgirls in uniform at lunchtimes; as with other long-established elite schools, the overwhelming majority of students these days are Hong Kong Chinese.

Chatham Road South

④ Hong Kong Polytechnic University

It may seem strange for a polytechnic to be also styled a university, but Hong Kong is a city where outward contradictions and signpost solecisms — even in the realm of higher education — are both accepted and expected. Awarded university status in 1994, the Hong Kong Polytechnic University evolved over several decades from the earlier Hong Kong Polytechnic, the Hong Kong Technical College and the Government Trade School. The Government Trade School first opened in 1937. Until the early 1970s, these early institutions provided almost the only formal vocational training available in Hong Kong.

PolyU, as the institution is generally known, is locally well-known for its striking red-brick buildings which, unusually for Hong Kong, manage to combine functionality with a clean-lined aesthetic appeal. Unlike some of the other recently upgraded polytechnics in Hong Kong, which have attempted to reinvent themselves as world-ranking research institutions, Hong Kong Polytechnic University remains strongly committed to teaching the professionally orientated courses for which it was originally established, and to that end maintains firm links with Hong Kong's business community and industrial sectors.

How To Get There

By Bus:	No. 5 from Tsim Sha Tsui 'Star' Ferry.
By MTR:	Tsim Sha Tsui Station.
By Taxi:	尖沙咀漆咸道 ('*Jeem Saa Choy, Chut Haam Doh*').

STREETS

Observatory Road 天文臺道

The low hill on which the Hong Kong Observatory (formerly known as the Royal Observatory) stands was originally named Mount Elgin in commemoration of Lord Elgin, British Envoy Extraordinary to China at the time of the Second Anglo-Chinese War.

On 19 January 1860 Lord Elgin took possession of the Kowloon peninsula north as far as what is now Boundary Street, as one of the terms of the Treaty of Tientsin. Unhappily, Elgin is best known in modern China for allowing the pillage and subsequent destruction by fire of the Yuan Ming Yuan, or Summer Palace, outside Peking (Beijing), in 1860.

Whilst Mount Elgin is marked as such on early maps of Kowloon, this designation has not been in general use since the late nineteenth century. After the Royal Observatory opened in 1883, the more informal Observatory Hill came into general use. Once a prominent landmark just above St Andrew's Church, the Observatory, like Mount Elgin which it surmounts, is now completely surrounded by tower blocks.

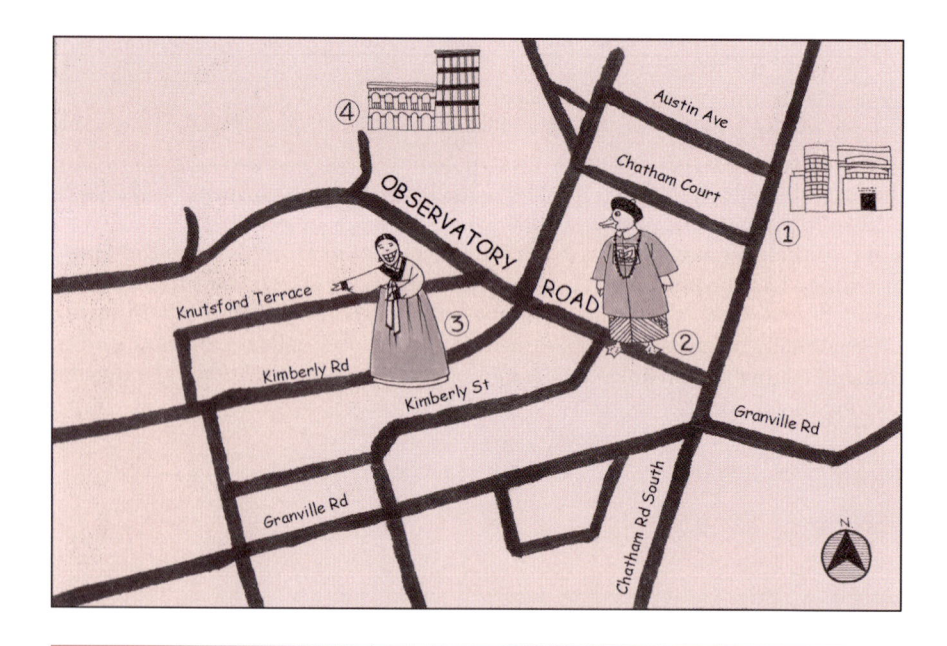

❶ Hong Kong Museum of History
❷ Shanghai Peking Restaurant
❸ Korean grocery shops, Kimberley Street
❹ Hong Kong Observatory

STREETS

Observatory Road

1. Hong Kong Museum of History

Those who dismissively suggest that modern Hong Kong gives no attention to its own past should visit this substantially sized, purpose-built, excellent museum. The Hong Kong Museum of History moved here from its long-established 'temporary' premises at Kowloon Park in 1998. Contemporary Hong Kong's unfortunate architectural love affair with dust-pink tiles is well in evidence from the roadside, but once you go inside, the Museum has much to commend it.

The Hong Kong Story is justifiably one of the museum's most popular permanent exhibits, and remains one of the best ways to gain a broad overview of Hong Kong's past. Well-curated thematic galleries take the visitor through various stages of Hong Kong's development from prehistoric times to the early Chinese era, on to the so-called 'Opium Wars', the British settlement of Hong Kong, and subsequent acquisition of Kowloon and the New Territories.

The Japanese occupation period from 1941 to 1945 is well covered, as are various politically motivated disturbances such as the Nationalist-orchestrated 'Double Tenth' riots in 1956 and the Communist-fomented 1967 riots. Even the last governor Chris Patten receives an honourable mention in Hong Kong's post-handover storyboards; his portrait is displayed along with all of Hong Kong's other British governors.

One very obvious shortcoming is the museum's narrative structure which emphasizes Hong Kong's British-Chinese roots, at the expense of almost everyone else. Little attention is paid to the role played by such disparate groups as the Sikhs and Punjabi Muslims (in the Hong Kong Police), the Parsees and Sephardic Jews (in business), the Eurasians (early progenitors of much of Hong Kong's old-money 'Chinese' elite), the Portuguese (in many respects Hong Kong's first true

Observatory Road

'locals'), and the White Russians (who started the colony's best early cafes). These varied ethnicities that together made early Hong Kong the strikingly cosmopolitan place that it was and whose influences still linger, often in surprising, unexpected corners of local life, should be better documented and displayed.

As with Hong Kong's other museums run by the government's Leisure and Cultural Services Department, admission to the Hong Kong Museum of History is highly affordable (HK$10 before concessions), and free to the general public one day a week.

② Shanghai Peking Restaurant

The short uphill stretch from Chatham Road to the Hong Kong Observatory boasts five Chinese restaurants on either side, three of which profess to be specialists in Shanghainese cuisine. These can be distinguished by the dusty white net curtains strung over doors and windows, shabby 1960s décor, retirement-age waiters and excellent, reasonably priced, near-authentic Northern and Central China-style food. Restaurants that served Shanghainese fare proliferated in Hong Kong in the early 1950s, as the émigré population from Shanghai steadily grew after the communist 'Liberation' of that city in 1949.

The former proprietor of Shanghai Peking Restaurant, Mr Wong Hing-tak, was hailed as the 'King of Pork Rib Noodles' before he sold the restaurant and moved to Australia in 1999. In the days when he ruled the kitchen, Mr Wong insisted on using the freshest ribs and would never use chilled or frozen ones. Such discernment apparently accounted for the distinctive taste.

Chue kwat meen (pork rib noodles) are still the restaurant's *pièce de résistance*. Equally well-known are the *siu loong bau* (steamed pork dumplings) made with lip-blistering, tongue-scalding broth bubbling inside their skins, and the soybean milk made — so it is said — from Mrs Wong's 'secret' recipe. Some of these old-style Shanghainese restaurants, along with others elsewhere in Hong Kong, even

Observatory Road

have palmists who can tell your fortune — for a fee, of course — from nine to eleven every night.

③ Korean grocery shops, Kimberley Street

Hong Kong has a surprisingly large Korean expatriate community, many of whom live and work in Kowloon. Many residents originally from the 'Land of the Morning Calm' have lived in Hong Kong for decades, and have established thriving grocery businesses to cater to the needs and tastes of the local Korean contingent.

Assorted varieties of freshly made and prepackaged *kimchi*, the pungent Korean pickles without which no Korean meal would be complete, are on offer. All manner of other Korean items are available, and stocks of fresh items come down daily from Seoul.

Various aspects of Korean popular culture, especially popular songs, television dramas and films, have become as popular in Hong Kong in recent years as their Japanese counterparts once were. The annually increasing local desire for anything Korean astutely translates into increased business opportunities for Hong Kong's Korean entrepreneurs.

④ Hong Kong Observatory

Hong Kong's weather forecasters are often criticized for failing to accurately predict the local weather — a notoriously difficult undertaking in a mountainous, island-studded place with many distinct microclimates. Localized weather conditions in Hong Kong can vary greatly within a few miles, thus making accurate territory-wide predictions very difficult and sometimes impossible.

The Observatory eventually built in Kowloon was subject to numerous controversies during the planning stages. Sir John Pope-Hennessy (governor of

Observatory Road

Hong Kong, 1877–82) was dissatisfied with plans originally drawn up for an observatory in 1880, and requested that a much 'better' one be built.

Delays inevitably ensued, and more elaborate plans were put forward the following year. Pope-Hennessy initially wanted to name the observatory the K'ang-hsi (Kangxi) Observatory after the one built by that emperor in Peking. This was heavily criticized by members of the Legislative Council who considered the liberal-minded governor already far too pro-Chinese for their liking, without also naming the colony's observatory after a long-dead Chinese ruler. When the building was declared open in 1883, Pope-Hennessy had long since left for his next posting as governor of Mauritius, and the 'K'ang-hsi Observatory' notion was quietly dropped. It became known instead as the Royal Observatory.

The Royal Observatory buildings on Observatory Road was a prominent local landmark in the 1920s, plainly visible from the sea on its inland hilltop and not, as it is today, surrounded and obscured by tower blocks. The original, late Victorian building — renamed the Hong Kong Observatory in advance of the handover — still survives, tree-shaded and attractively surrounded by broad verandahs, but completely invisible from the road below.

How To Get There

By Bus:	No. 5 from 'Star' Ferry, alight outside Rosary Church.
By MTR:	Tsim Sha Tsui Station.
By Taxi:	尖沙咀天文台道 (*'Jeem Saa Choy, Tin Mun Toi Doh'*).

Austin Road
柯士甸道

Austin Road takes its name from Colonial Secretary J. Gardiner Austin. Austin first came to China as the British government agent responsible for organization of the Chinese emigrant traffic to British colonies, in particular Mauritius and parts of the West Indies such as Trinidad. He was appointed to this post in 1869, nine years after Kowloon had been ceded to Great Britain. Mount Austin, one of the ridges on Hong Kong Island's Peak, is also named for him.

This steepish west-east road indicates just how surprisingly hilly Tsim Sha Tsui really is. When seen from high up, across the harbour, or experienced at ground level, the near-solid mass of high-rise buildings gives the mistaken impression that the peninsula below the Kowloon hills is completely flat. Austin Road has two quite distinct personas. Northeast is an area of prestigious clubs, extensive playing fields, barracks and other military buildings. To the west, where Austin Road slopes down towards the southern end of the old Yau Ma Tei Typhoon Shelter, the densely populated tenement areas run parallel to the old waterfront, just past Gascoigne Road.

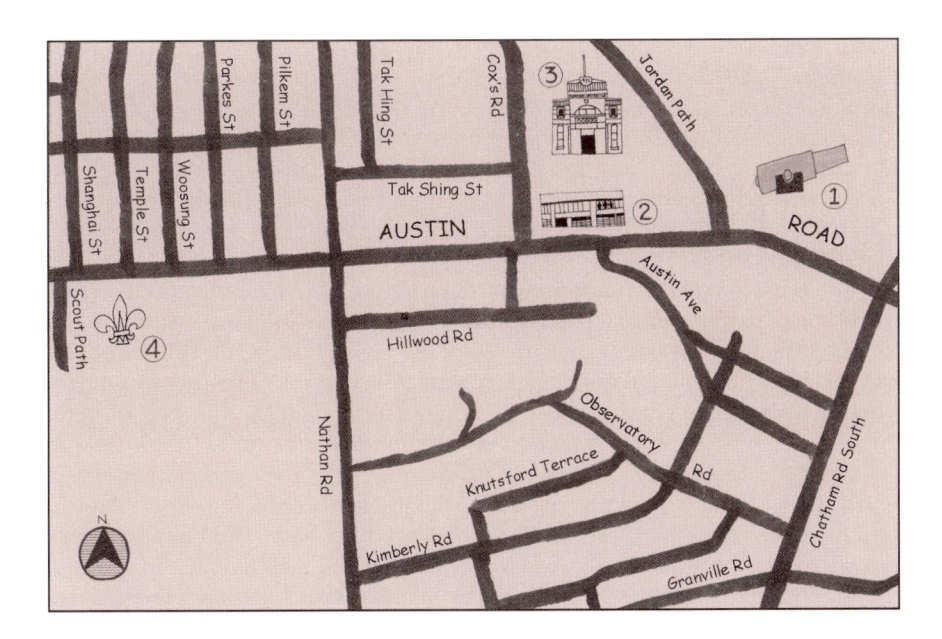

❶ Gun Club Hill Barracks
❷ Kowloon Bowling Green Club
❸ Kowloon Cricket Club
❹ BP International House

STREETS

Austin Road

1 Gun Club Hill Barracks

Gun Club Hill Barracks covers a large area that extends as far north as Jordan and Gascoigne Roads. Buildings within the military complex are an eclectic, sometimes dissonant blend of late Victorian and late twentieth-century architectural styles. The name is derived from two nineteenth-century rifle ranges located on what was then referred to as Gun Club Hill. In operation by 1887, one firing range was used by the military and the other by the Hong Kong Police. By the outbreak of the First World War, both were relocated elsewhere as urban development spread steadily northwards.

For its last few years as a British Army camp before 1997, Gun Club Hill Barracks was home base to the Gurkha Transport Regiment. The attractive, white-painted former Officers' Mess stands more or less at the crest of Gun Club Hill. This solid late Victorian institutional building, very similar in style to contemporary military structures at Lyemun Barracks on Hong Kong Island, can still be glimpsed through the trees near Austin Road's junction with Chatham Road.

Until the 1960s, large sections of Kowloon were in use by the military. As a result, Tsim Sha Tsui's commercial and social life had a distinct garrison flavour, with numerous bars, restaurants, tailor shops and other businesses that specifically catered to the needs and wants of service personnel and their families. In addition to Gun Club, barracks also stood at the harbour end of Chatham Road. The present-day Kowloon Park was used by the military; parts of Kai Tak Airport were used by the Royal Air Force and further north, the British Army occupied sizable sections of both the Sham Shui Po waterfront and Kowloon Tong.

Since 1997 the People's Liberation Army has been stationed at Gun Club — the only original barracks complex that still remains in use by the military in Tsim

Austin Road

Sha Tsui — and just inside the gates, impassive green-uniformed sentries stand near the guardroom motionless all through the day and night under brightly coloured umbrellas.

② *Kowloon Bowling Green Club*

High well-clipped hedges along the roadside conceal the Kowloon Bowling Green Club's immaculately kept lawns from public view. Peer discreetly through the gaps and you may see a few (mostly elderly) white-clad bowlers gently enjoying their game; lawn bowls tends to be an older person's sport in most countries and Hong Kong is no exception. First established in Kowloon in 1900, the present club building was built in about 1950, and subsequently extended in 1994. In addition to lawn bowls, the Kowloon Bowling Green Club also has tennis courts and a swimming pool.

From the outside, the clubhouse building seems completely out of step with present-day Tsim Sha Tsui's high-rise modernity and fashionable crowds. Inside the clubhouse, a pleasantly old-fashioned sense of quiet order and decorum still prevails. In the past members were predominantly British or Australian — lawn bowls is very popular in Australia — but as with other clubs elsewhere in Hong Kong, today's club patrons are predominantly Chinese. The Kowloon Bowling Green Club's premises are fairly small compared to other sporting venues in the area, but it nevertheless remains very popular, with over five hundred current members.

Austin Road

③ Kowloon Cricket Club

The Kowloon Cricket Club's attractive main building is located on Cox's Road, just off Austin Road. Popularly known as the KCC, the present clubhouse, which dates from 1932, replaced a simple wooden pavilion building donated in 1908 by prominent local Parsee businessman H. N. Mody. The Kowloon Cricket Club had been established four years earlier, in 1904.

Mody Road, further to the south in Tsim Sha Tsui, is also named after him. In 1910 he donated the funds for the Main Building of the University of Hong Kong. Mody was subsequently knighted, and died in 1911.

In its early days the KCC was considered a club of equivalent standard to the Craigengower Cricket Club in Causeway Bay. Both were seen to be much less stuffy than the more elite Hong Kong Cricket Club. Kowloon had a substantial lower-middle class European and Eurasian population in the interwar years, who lived and socialized close to home. Many were keen members of the KCC.

During this period, the KCC frequently played Interport sporting matches against other clubs in Shanghai and the Treaty Ports. Numerous faded sepia photographs along the staircase walls recall these long-ago members, events and places. Just inside the door, a Roll of Honour records the names of those who died, either during the Japanese invasion of Hong Kong in 1941, or in the years that followed.

Numerous additions and improvements have been made over the years, but the 1932 clubhouse building retains most of its original features. The KCC enjoys a very multiracial composition with, perhaps unsurprisingly, a strong South Asian and Australasian representation, and its members still consider cricket the number one sport.

④ BP International House

Hong Kong's extremely popular Boy Scout movement first began when Lord Robert Baden-Powell, leader of the relief of Mafeking during the South African War, a leading Freemason and the founder of the international scouting movement, passed through Hong Kong in April 1912. 'B-P', as Lord Baden-Powell

Austin Road

was popularly known throughout the world, suggested to Hong Kong government officials that the colony should form its own scouting movement.

Popular response to the idea was swift and enthusiastic, and in 1913 the colony's first scout group was formed. Hong Kong's first Boy Scouts were mostly local Portuguese students at St Joseph's College on Hong Kong Island. In 1915, a Hong Kong Scout headquarters was established, which existed for some years without a permanent address. Between the wars the local Boy Scout movement, along with the Girl Guides, continued to expand in Hong Kong and in China's Treaty Port cities.

From 1949 onwards, the Scouts headquarters were housed in premises on Garden Road on Hong Kong Island, but before long this building proved too small to cope with the steadily expanding interest. To better cope with demand, a purpose-built Scout headquarters was built in 1954 at Cox's Road in Kowloon.

This site was eventually redeveloped for other purposes and in 1994, the multi-storied Baden-Powell International House was completed on Austin Road. This building combines a Scout headquarters, a drill hall and a popular tourist-class hotel, and has become a popular venue for numerous community activities in this part of Kowloon.

'B-P', who eventually died at Nyeri in Kenya in 1941, would no doubt be very pleased with the movement's continued popularity into the twenty-first century in Hong Kong.

How To Get There

By Bus:	No. 1, 1A, 2, 6, 6A, 7, 9 from Tsim Sha Tsui 'Star' Ferry and alight at junction of Austin and Nathan Roads outside the Tsim Sha Tsui Police Station.
By MTR:	Jordan Station is one block from Austin Road.
By Taxi:	尖沙咀柯士甸道 ('*Jeem Saa Choy, Or See Deen Doh*').

Yau Ma Tei

To many Hong Kong people, and most visitors, Yau Ma Tei is little more than a grotty, grotesquely overcrowded slum district to be visited only if necessary. Despite these initial negative impressions, Yau Ma Tei is one of the most vibrant, concentrated slices of local life in all of Hong Kong. It is also one of the oldest and most historic parts of Kowloon, with numerous aspects of the past that have vanished elsewhere in Hong Kong still extant and readily accessible.

Yau Ma Tei came under British administration, along with the rest of Kowloon peninsula north as far as what is now Boundary Street, following the Treaty of Tientsin in 1860. Yau Ma Tei means 'Oil-Sesame Ground', and in the absence of any other convincing explanation, the area presumably acquired the name because the oil-sesame plant was cultivated and harvested here at some point in the past. Early maps indicate an area just north of present-day Yau Ma Tei then known as 'Ma Tei' or Sesame Ground, which may have marked the site of the original oil-sesame fields.

Prior to 1860, a small hamlet known as Cheng Chin Kok stood near where the present-day Tin Hau Temple stands on Public Square Street. As far as is known, this tiny settlement differed little from various others found elsewhere on the Kowloon peninsula. The area located to the west of present-day Shanghai Street was then under water, and formed a small bay known as Sheung Kok, which was a popular sampan shelter for Tanka and Hoklo boat-families. This anchorage was formed around the mouth of a small stream known as Pak Ho ('North River'). Present-day Pak Ho Street closely follows the northern shore of this long-vanished watercourse, and mostly likely takes its name from it.

One of the first British actions after the occupation of the Kowloon peninsula was to clear out a group of squatters from around the original Tsim Sha Tau village in Tsim Sha Tsui. This removal was done to facilitate military construction work on the southern end of Kowloon. Those villagers who were evicted were offered resettlement in the Yau Ma Tei area in 1864. Most availed themselves of the opportunity and within a few months a new market was established.

The sampan anchorage at Yau Ma Tei had been protected by a small Chinese military post as far back as 1800, but the settled population only increased greatly in size after 1864. Smuggling into the interior of China was a lucrative source of income for boat-dwellers based in and around Yau Ma Tei in the late nineteenth century. Principal contraband goods in those years were opium (the sale of which was legal in Hong Kong at that time) and untaxed salt. A thriving 'thieves' market' also operated at Yau Ma Tei, and accounts of court cases reported in the local press indicate that stolen goods as diverse as sandalwood, copper nails, coal and wire were brought there for sale.

In 1876 the Yau Ma Tei market was redeveloped and by 1900, commercial activity was still largely contained within the boundaries of Station and Temple Streets. In 1904 a major reclamation project was undertaken, which created two major new north-south roads, Reclamation Street and Canton Road, and numerous

- Jordan Road
- Saigon Street
- Gascoigne Road
- Kansu Street
- Reclamation Street
- Shanghai Street
- Portland Street
- Waterloo Road

traverse streets. The reclamation led to a fivefold increase in Yau Ma Tei's land area, which was followed by rapid population growth.

A number of small industries were established in Yau Ma Tei in these early years. Soap and bean curd were both made here in the 1870s, and a match factory opened in 1880. This was followed within a few years by a soy sauce factory, an iron foundry and machine shop, and a sugar-candy factory. By the 1910s factories in Yau Ma Tei produced bamboo and rattan walking canes, preserved ginger, feather products, rice wine and peanut oil.

In these years one of Yau Ma Tei's largest early landowners was a local Portuguese businessman, Delfinho Noronha. Noronha built a substantial home called 'Delmar', on a hill overlooking the Yau Ma Tei waterfront. In the 1870s the extensive gardens at 'Delmar' were a well-known local beauty spot, with numerous rare species of plants imported from as far away as South Africa, Australia and the Netherlands East Indies (modern Indonesia). Noronha sold the property for redevelopment in the 1880s, and the sugarloaf-shaped hillside itself was quarried away to provide landfill for the first phase of harbour reclamation in Yau Ma Tei. No reminder whatsoever of either this early garden or its proprietor — not even a road name — remains in the area today.

Among other business enterprises Noronha was the government printer, and many old Hong Kong government publications bear the Noronha and Co. imprint. Noronha's private launch was an early precursor of the later 'Star' Ferry passenger service established between Hong Kong Island and Kowloon.

Yau Ma Tei has always had a distinct, visible division of land-use on either side of Nathan Road. Relatively open space on the eastern side of Nathan Road accommodates numerous clubs, such as Club de Recreio, India Club, the Kowloon

Yau Ma Tei

Cricket Club and the venerable United Services Recreation Club, as well as a number of churches such as the Kowloon Methodist Church and the Union Church. On Nathan Road's western side, Yau Ma Tei's densely packed tenement streets, which extend towards the typhoon shelter, have very little open public space.

The Tin Hau Temple is probably Yau Ma Tei's best-known historic sight and remains a key focus for Chinese community life. Popularly known as 'the temple of Temple Street' (though it is actually located on Public Square Street), the large open square in front of the temple complex, shaded with numerous old banyan trees, faced the Yau Ma Tei waterfront in the nineteenth century. Popularly known as Yung Shue Tau (Banyan Tree Head), this square is now marooned almost three kilometres inland.

During the 1950s and 1960s, as Hong Kong became annually more crowded with refugee arrivals from China, Yung Shue Tau was one of the few open public spaces in Yau Ma Tei, permanently thronged at whatever hour with dozens of people seeking some respite from nearby tenement life. Yung Shue Tau still has numerous amblers these days, mostly old single men. Martin Booth's evocative semi-autobiographical books *Hiroshima Joe* and *Gweilo* provide vivid descriptions of how parts of Yau Ma Tei appeared to the author (then a small European boy) in the early 1950s; some scenes he describes have changed little in the past half century.

Various Christian missionary organizations such as the London Missionary Society and the Wesleyan Mission became involved with the Chinese community in and around the Yau Ma Tei area from the 1870s onwards. The Wesleyan Mission was particularly active, and a large Methodist church still functions in Yau Ma Tei today. The Roman Catholic presence also dates from the same period; the Italian Canossian sisters, active in education on Hong Kong Island, opened a school in Yau Ma Tei in 1880. They were subsequently followed by a number of Irish Jesuit priests.

Further large-scale reclamation work in west Kowloon was undertaken from 1904 onwards, and the large typhoon shelter finally opened, after various delays, in 1915. Yau Ma Tei continued to expand after Nathan Road was extended north to Boundary Street in 1917, and by the early 1920s the district had approached full development capacity for that period.

A popular night market eventually grew up on Temple Street, and by the 1960s and 1970s had become one of Kowloon's more popular tourist attractions. On a seedier note, Temple Street and surrounding back alleys are some of the most notorious brothel areas in Kowloon. At any hour of the day or night, numerous haggard looking prostitutes loiter just within darkened tenement doorways, while their superannuated sisters tout for trade from the street outside. Numerous heavily muscled, dragon-tattooed 'protectors' stand guard at various strategic points along the road.

Yau Ma Tei

Yau Ma Tei's relatively low-rise character remained largely unchanged from the late 1950s. Strictly enforced height restrictions due to the approaches to Kai Tak Airport ensured that no buildings in northern Kowloon could be taller than twelve to fourteen stories. After the airport's closure in 1998 these regulations have gradually been eased, and Yau Ma Tei seems set to experience considerable changes in the coming years. Numerous new buildings have already gone up since then, mostly on reclaimed land; many are over forty stories high.

At first glance, Yau Ma Tei is one of the most homogeneously Chinese districts in Kowloon, with little apparent ethnic diversity. Nevertheless, the area houses a surprisingly large number of Hong Kong's ethnic minority groups, with significant Indian, Pakistani and Nepalese populations, and various businesses and services that cater to their specific needs and wants.

STREETS

Jordan Road
佐敦道

Jordan Road was named for Sir John Newell Jordan, the long-serving British minister to China. In 1908 a stone obelisk was unveiled at the junction of Jordan and Gascoigne Roads in memory of French sailors drowned in the massive 1906 typhoon. It has since been removed to a remote corner of the Colonial Cemetery at Happy Valley, where it can still be seen today. Jordan Road was a relatively quiet, tree-lined suburban street at that time, and balconied houses and apartment blocks lined both sides of the road between the Diocesan Girls' School and the waterfront.

Once one of the harbour's most common sights, double-ended vehicular ferries were the only way to get a car or truck from Kowloon to Hong Kong Island before the Cross-Harbour Tunnel opened in 1972. Further to the east, beyond the junction with Nathan Road, Jordan Road extended towards a pleasant open area of clubs, schools, barracks and a church. Some of these original buildings can still be seen today.

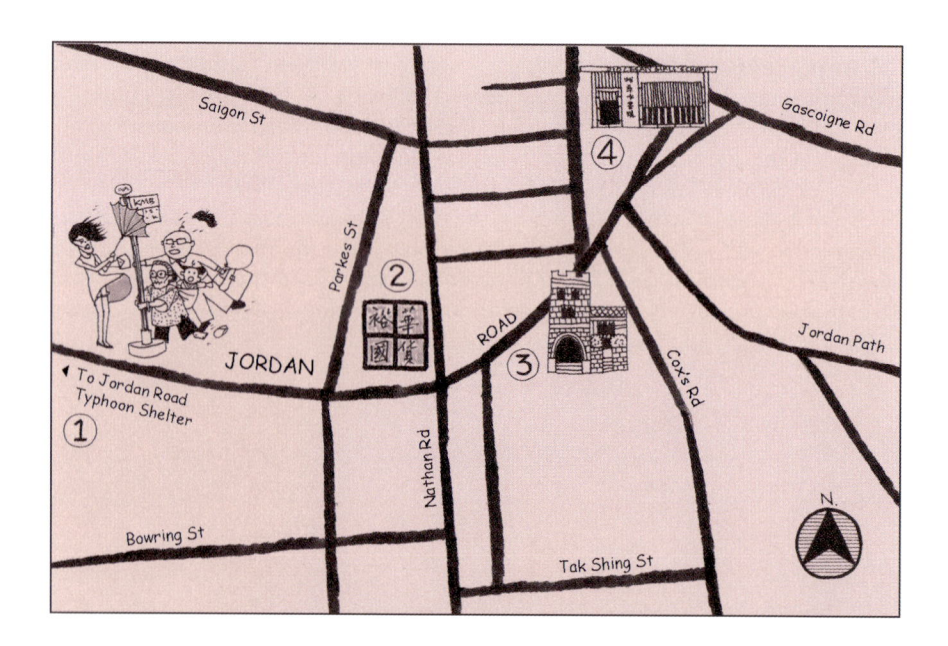

❶ Yau Ma Tei Typhoon Shelter
❷ Yue Hwa Department Store
❸ Kowloon Union Church and Manse
❹ Diocesan Girls' School (DGS)

Jordan Road

Drastic changes started in the 1950s, and these days Jordan Road and its surrounding backstreets are among the most grossly overcrowded parts of Kowloon, fume-choked and squalid by day and seedy and sleazy after dark. Despite these obvious shortcomings, there is much of interest to be found along here, but do try to explore the area at a relatively quiet time; the sheer number of people that mill along here on an average Sunday afternoon would deter all but the keenest backstreet ambler.

① Yau Ma Tei Typhoon Shelter

For several decades one of Yau Ma Tei's best-known features has been its large typhoon shelter, formally declared open in 1915. This secure all-weather anchorage was built in direct response to a massive typhoon in September 1906, during which an estimated 10,000 people drowned in and around Hong Kong waters.

Proposals for a permanent all-weather anchorage had been repeatedly mooted for some years before this disaster struck, but these were persistently opposed by Unofficial members of the Legislative Council on grounds of cost and, as far as they were concerned, questionable necessity. No one *forced* the sampan-dwellers to come to Hong Kong, the legislators' arguments went, and as a result the Hong Kong government had no responsibility for their safety and well-being while they were in local waters. Then tragedy struck, and the full, at least partially preventable, horror of this disaster made change inevitable.

STREETS

Jordan Road

Until the late 1970s, large numbers of boat-dwellers still lived permanently within the Yau Ma Tei breakwater. Numerous sampan-borne shops and services catered to this community. Conditions on board were crowded and dangerously unsanitary, and when offered the opportunity to resettle in public estates on land many boat families were only too pleased to leave the typhoon shelter. *Shui Sheung Yan Gaa* ('People Who Live on the Water') were historically despised and distrusted by land-dwelling Chinese, and even today many do not readily discuss their former waterborne lives with outsiders. With this community's dispersal, an entire way of life, once an elemental part of Yau Ma Tei life, had almost entirely disappeared by the end of the 1980s.

Yau Ma Tei's original typhoon shelter was fully reclaimed in the early 1990s as part of airport-related core projects, and no trace of it exists. A replacement typhoon shelter was constructed further out in the harbour to the west of the reclamation. While some sampans and fishing boats still regularly use this anchorage, most of the vessels that now frequent the typhoon basin at Yau Ma Tei are cargo lighters.

(2) Yue Hwa Department Store

Until the early 1950s a grand three-storied Chinese mansion stood on this site, complete with a green-tiled pagoda on the roof. This was eventually demolished to make way for this Mainland-owned *kwok for kung si*, which remains Hong Kong's largest, and probably most popular, China products department store.

Until the late 1970s, Yue Hwa was one of the few open windows that the outside world had on mysterious, forbidding 'Red China'. Trade with Communist China was forbidden in those days and Certificates of Origin were required for Americans to take anything that may have been Mainland-made back to the United States. Impressionable American tourists, in particular, used to get a frisson of excitement when shopping at the China-owned stores.

STREETS

Jordan Road

Until quite recently, Yue Hwa was also the place for Hong Kong people to stock up on inexpensive but durable household goods; some of these items were of very high quality. While the atmosphere was a bit old-fashioned and dowdy, with grave-faced shop assistants politely hovering, those customers who liked shopping at Yue Hwa (such as the present author) went back time and again.

As with other *kwok for kung si* situated elsewhere in Hong Kong, the stock on offer at Yue Hwa has moved steadily upmarket in recent years. Many old China-made favourites have disappeared altogether as local tastes have changed. Yue Hwa's basement supermarket still has many popular bargains, and stocks an incredible variety of Chinese tea of various grades and prices and an array of reasonably priced pickled, dried or salted foodstuffs. Frozen Mainland-reared pheasant is even in stock from time to time, still with heads and feathers intact. Prices are fixed and quality is generally very reliable.

Yau Ma Tei

③ *Kowloon Union Church and Manse*

Union Church on Jordan Road is an attractive red-brick reminder of interwar Kowloon community life. The tree-shaded Manse next door, surrounded by a small patch of garden, is a pleasant reminder of what many houses looked like in Kowloon in the 1930s. The open upstairs verandahs here — essential in the days before air-conditioning — have long since been glazed in to provide more living space.

The foundation stone for the Kowloon Union Church was laid on 27 May 1930 by the then colonial secretary, Sir W. T. Southorn. This government official was cruelly, though some suggest accurately, caricatured by W. Somerset Maugham in his Hong Kong–China Coast-themed novel *The Painted Veil*. Southorn Playground in Wan Chai is named after him.

Southorn's wife Lady Bella wrote a number of amusing, anecdotal memoirs of her life as the wife of a colonial civil servant as well as a well-researched, entertainingly written history of the Gambia. Probably the best known was the atmospherically titled *Under the Mosquito Curtain*. Maugham and Lady Bella were

STREETS

Jordan Road

not Southorn's only encounters with the literary world. Lady Bella's brother was the former colonial civil servant-turned-publisher Leonard Woolf; his wife was Virginia Woolf, leader of the influential 'Bloomsbury Set' of writers and artists, and patron saint of gender studies programmes the world over.

Many churches elsewhere in Hong Kong have found that redevelopment of their premises allows them to do more 'good works' with the money they receive. A number of local congregations have eventually conceded to property developers incessant demands and surrendered their buildings to 'progress'. But for now, at least, the Kowloon Union Church has resisted the temptation to demolish and rebuild.

④ Diocesan Girls' School (DGS)

The Diocesan Girls' School, popularly known as DGS, originally opened in 1860 as the Diocesan Girls' Training School. It has been one of Hong Kong's premier local girls' schools for well over a century. DGS was established by the Anglican Church to provide an education for Eurasian children who, in Hong Kong's rough-and-tumble early years, were often more or less abandoned by their putative fathers. Deprived of any adequate education or career training and complicated by an unpromising family background, many early Eurasians got involved in petty crime, or drifted into prostitution.

In 1869 the Diocesan Girls' Training School expanded to include boys and in 1878 was given grant-in-aid by the Hong Kong government. In 1900 the boys' section was separated and an independent Diocesan Boys' School was formed. Substantial new premises for the Diocesan Girls' School were built on the Jordan Road site in 1913. These buildings were eventually redeveloped in the early 1980s.

Jordan Road

In the early years, teachers at DGS were usually either spinster missionaries or clergymen's wives, generally engaged due to their willingness to help rather than any formal academic or professional qualifications. By the 1930s, however, more properly trained teachers were recruited and standards steadily rose.

Until the 1950s most of the girls at DGS were either Eurasians or girls from anglicized Chinese families; today most students are Hong Kong Chinese. A strong *esprit de corps* still prevails amongst DGS 'Old Girls', as with other elite schools elsewhere in Hong Kong, and its alumni are well represented at senior levels in academic life, government, business and the professions.

The school's long-serving Eurasian headmistress, the late Mrs Joyce Symons, was a pre-war graduate of the University of Hong Kong. She also served as a legislative councillor for many years and in her retirement wrote a slim memoir of her time at the school, *Looking at the Stars*, which provides numerous interesting glimpses into the now largely vanished Hong Kong and Treaty Port Eurasian world of her generation.

How To Get There

By Bus:	No. 1, 1A, 2, 5A, 6, 6A, 7 from Tsim Sha Tsui 'Star' Ferry.
By MTR:	Jordan Station.
By Taxi:	油麻地佐敦道 (*'Yau Ma Dei, Jor Don Doh'*).

Saigon Street
西貢街

Saigon Street is remarkably quiet for the depths of Yau Ma Tei. But turn the corner into Nathan Road, and you are back into the realm of double-decker buses, blue-painted, open backed delivery vans, minibuses and taxis by the thousand. Turn into nearby Temple and Shanghai Streets, and there are plenty more of the same.

In spite of being located only a few blocks away from popular tourist destinations such as the Jade Market, Temple Street Night Market and the Tin Hau Temple, Saigon Street is one of those corners of Kowloon that nevertheless remains little known except to those who live and work nearby. The sights and sounds found here are typical of numerous other Kowloon backstreets, but as with all the others, a few facets are unique to here.

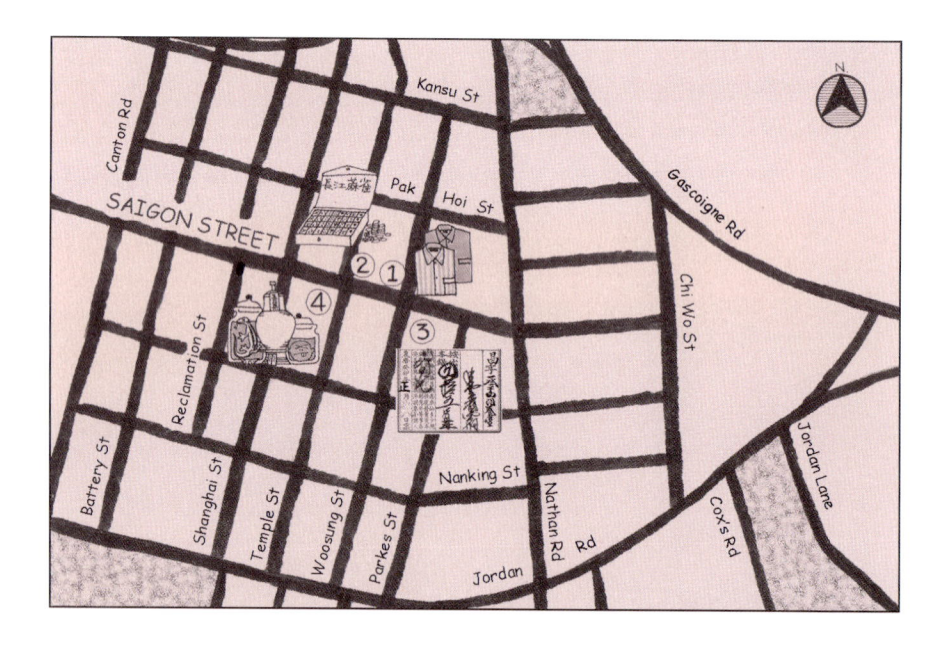

① Europe Tailor
② Cheung Kong Majong
③ Pawnshops
④ Chun Wo Tong herbalist's shop

STREETS

Saigon Street

① *Europe Tailor*

Dozens of tiny tailor shops can be found right across Kowloon's backstreets. Sindhi and Pakistani entrepreneurs dominate the customized garment business in Tsim Sha Tsui, several blocks further south; these little places in Yau Ma Tei are all Chinese-run.

Some of the older Kowloon tailors came down from Shanghai after the end of the Chinese Civil War, and one can still discern a faded hint of that city's pre-Liberation style in this small shop's décor; it obviously has not changed much in decades. Like many such places, Europe Tailor is dominated by a treadle sewing machine in the middle of the shop, highly polished and lovingly tended. The friendly owner 'doesn't remember how long' he has used it now.

Come by here at about noon and the homely lunch-time smell of rice steaming on the side cupboard permeates the entire shop, and the owner's slinky tabby cat will purr round your legs if you let it. In addition to the usual clothing items, Europe Tailor does a good line in attractive, well-made waistcoats, with prices varying depending on size and material. There are always several on display in the glass cases near the doorway.

Everyday, reasonable quality clothing is the norm in shops such as this one; those looking for really high-end tailoring are probably best advised to stick to the arcades of the city's international hotels in Tsim Sha Tsui or Central.

② *Cheung Kong Majong*

The enduring Chinese mania for mah-jong is much in evidence at various points along Saigon Street. A number of small, well stocked shops sell brightly coloured tiles, counters, tables and game-related paraphernalia. There are also a number of mah-jong parlours where you can play by the game, or the hour, or the day, or the night.

Do not bother looking for signs telling you where to go, the mere sound alone will guide you straight there. And of course, as

Saigon Street

open gambling on mah-jong, or cards, or the stock or property markets, or indeed anything other than horse races at the Hong Kong Jockey Club is *completely* illegal in Hong Kong, none of the patrons in these places has ever been known to place a bet.

Beautifully crafted bone tiles backed with polished bamboo make attractive purchases, but are not really suitable for the serious mah-jong fiend. Tiles made of this material do not respond kindly to the essential banging and pounding and soon split, crack and fall apart. Sets like these are fine for a genteel game played before afternoon tea by four old ladies in Bournemouth or Cheltenham, but for everyday Hong Kong-style usage, far more durable plastic tile sets are essential. Counters, dice and other items all cost extra when bought individually, but you can get the whole lot combined with a set of mah-jong tiles in a vinyl carrying case, for a lower overall price.

③ Pawnshops

With grilles on all openings, no windows and interior screens to shield the identity of customers, *dong poh* (pawnshops) are still very much a feature of backstreet Kowloon life. Pawnshop businesses enjoyed a resurgence in the late 1990s when the local economy faltered, and a quite a few *dong poh* operate in this area of Yau Ma Tei.

As illegal gambling is totally prohibited in Hong Kong, the presence of so many pawnshops in this area must, of course, be completely coincidental to the large number of commercially run mah-jong parlours located in the street nearby.

Pawnshops all over Hong Kong can yield some remarkable bargains on unredeemed watches and jewellery. Prices quoted for gold rings, jade pendants, diamond earrings and similar items at a pawnbroker's shop can be quite low when compared to new items of similar style purchased from one of the jewellery shops just round the corner on Nathan Road.

But the purchaser must not have any superstitious qualms. Second-hand items obtained from unknown persons are often considered unlucky and, even worse, they may have belonged to the dead. As a result, most traditionally minded Chinese do not want to have second-hand personal items in their possession at any price. This, in turn, perhaps explains why so little demand exists for second-hand goods

Saigon Street

in Hong Kong, unless of course they are considered antiques — and therefore have re-sale potential — or have fashion brand names emblazoned across their surfaces; these items, somehow, are exempt from the usual 'second-hand equals bad luck' formula.

④ Chun Wo Tong herbalist's shop

This little herbalist's shop has been here on Saigon Street for decades. Chun Wo Tong manufactures and retails their own proprietary brands of popular herbal medicines, some of which are also brewed (or otherwise concocted) and then sold by the bowl or vial from the open counter in front. Tan Ngan Lo Medicine Ear Drop Oil is bottled on the premises and, according to the graphic enclosed leaflet, it effectively and harmlessly clears away 'wax accumulations, pus and foul smelling secretions' from inside the ears.

Chun Wo Tong's colourful packets of brew-it-yourself *fu cha* ('bitter tea') herbs are the shop's most popular purchase. Just the thing, according to the staff, to clear out the body's *yeet hei* ('heatiness') and *yeet dook* ('heat poison'). These 'complaints' are usually brought on by too much alcohol, rich or spicy food, lack of sleep or the weekend's general overindulgence, but can be easily remedied.

Briskly boil the contents for an hour and twenty minutes with two bowls of water, cool it down, strain, hold your nose and swallow. At times like these it is best to think of Ernest Hemingway's immortal line, 'What does not kill me makes me stronger', but a great many people in Hong Kong — the present author included — swear by these potions as a general remedy.

How To Get There

By Bus:	No. 1, 1A, 2, 6, 6A, 7 from Tsim Sha Tsui 'Star' Ferry and alight on Nathan Road.
By MTR:	Jordan Station Exit A.
By Taxi:	油麻地西貢街 (*'Yau Ma Dei, Sai Kung Gaai'*).

Gascoigne Road
加士居道

Gascoigne Road was laid out after 1901 and named after Major-General W. J. Gascoigne, general officer commanding in Hong Kong when the New Territories was pacified in 1899. During this period, the moderately hilly upland area east of Nathan Road was, for the most part, still relatively open country. Large tracts were gradually surveyed off for government and military use, and to provide land for recreation and sporting facilities.

This land-use pattern eventually turned the Gascoigne Road area into Kowloon's 'club land'; a large number of sporting facilities and recreational associations have been located in the area for decades. This part of Kowloon was once considered so quiet that if a car passed along the road it was almost an event — a far cry from today's arterial road, so busy that a parallel flyover was built for much of its length.

Popularly known as King's Park, though the name only refers to a small section, the expansive area around Gascoigne Road also takes in Queen Elizabeth Hospital, King's Park Government Quarters, the former British Military Hospital site on Wylie Road and several schools and colleges.

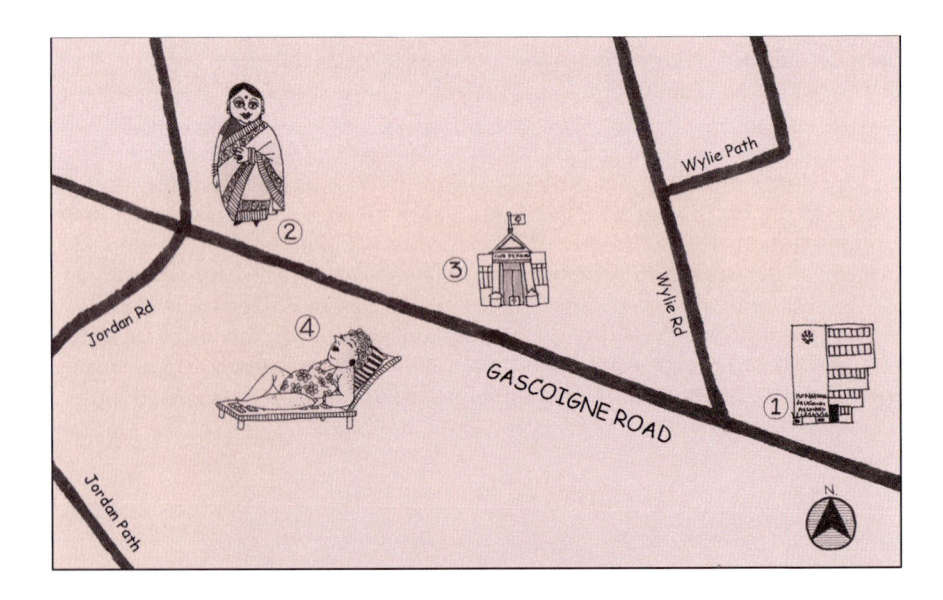

❶ Girl Guides Association
❷ India Club
❸ Club de Recreio
❹ United Services Recreation Club

STREETS

Gascoigne Road

① *Girl Guides Association*

Like the Boy Scouts Association, headquartered nearby on Austin Road, the Girl Guides Association has a long history in Hong Kong. The Girl Guide movement was established as a direct counterpart to the Boy Scouts; Lady Olave Baden-Powell became World Chief Guide and visited Hong Kong in 1958 and 1962. The first Girl Guides Company in Hong Kong was formed in 1916 from students drawn from the Central British School, and the Hong Kong Branch of the Girl Guides Association was formally registered in 1919. The first colony commissioner, appointed in 1926, was Lady Bella Southorn, wife of the then colonial secretary Sir William Southorn (and, coincidentally, the sister-in-law of novelist Virginia Woolf and a published author in her own right).

Successive governor's wives from Lady Maurine Grantham (in Hong Kong from 1947 to 1957) onwards have served as presidents of the Girl Guides Association; Mrs Betty Tung, wife of former chief executive Tung Chee-hwa, also served as president after the handover in 1997.

Thousands of girls, both in Hong Kong and all over the world, have learnt self-reliance and team skills through membership of the Girl Guides, and formed friendships that endured for the rest of their lives. As in other parts of the world, the Girl Guides Association in Hong Kong relies heavily on the enthusiasm of former Girl Guides who give generously of their time, energy and expertise to lead and train new troops. There are long waiting lists to join a troop.

The Hong Kong Girl Guides Association's symbol is a stylized Blake's Bauhinia (*Bauhinia blakeana*), the Hong Kong Special Administrative Region's floral emblem, combined with the Chinese character 光 (*kwong*) which means light.

Gascoigne Road

② *India Club*

A steep flight of steps between the trees at the junction of Gascoigne and Wylie Roads leads up to the India Club, for many years a popular gathering place for Kowloon's local Indian community. India Club was originally known as the Kowloon Indian Tennis Club, and commenced operations in 1924–5. The first postwar president was Dr H. Mohan Singh. A pre-war Hong Kong University medical graduate from a prominent local Sikh family, Dr Singh's father was president of the Gurdwara (Sikh Temple) in Wan Chai for many years. India Club was formally incorporated as a separate entity in 1967.

Among other functions, India Club organizes an annual ball to celebrate Divali (the Hindu Festival of Lights), Dashera festivals and a popular Miss India Hong Kong pageant. Prominent guests to the club over the years have included former Indian prime minister Mrs Indira Gandhi, Mother Teresa of Calcutta and leading Indian political figures.

Numerous club members both live and work in nearby Tsim Sha Tsui, which makes this a very convenient organization to join for many local Indian families. Like many other clubs in Hong Kong, India Club now has an international membership contingent, but as in the past, most of its contemporary members have some ethnic origins on the Indian subcontinent.

Unsurprisingly perhaps, given the enormous popularity of cricket on the subcontinent, many members of India Club are keen cricketers and active supporters of the game elsewhere in Hong Kong. After a long period of refurbishment which started in 2000, India Club has reopened and serves excellent curry lunches, catered by one of the restaurants from — where else — Tsim Sha Tsui's Chungking Mansions.

STREETS

Gascoigne Road

③ Club de Recreio

Established in 1906, for over half a century Club de Recreio was one of the premier sporting clubs in Hong Kong, and permanently thronged with games players, spectators and their families at weekends. This attractive, porticoed building has decayed considerably in recent years, a reflection in some ways of the decline of Hong Kong's once substantial local Portuguese community. Club de Recreio has facilities for lawn bowls, tennis, badminton and hockey.

During the heyday of the local Portuguese community, before migration overseas accelerated in the early 1950s, Club Lusitano on Central's Ice House Street was where the older generation went to relax and socialize, while Club de Recreio became the Kowloon sporting arm for younger members of the community. Many lived nearby in Tsim Sha Tsui, Kowloon Tong or Ho Man Tin, and the club was convenient for sporting fixtures at weekends, and games and gatherings after office hours.

A memorial tablet in front of the entrance to the main building records the names of many local Portuguese in the Hong Kong Volunteer Defence Corps and those who were killed during the Japanese invasion. Every Liberation Day on 30 August (no longer celebrated in the rest of Hong Kong) a small remembrance ceremony is held here, attended by members of the local Portuguese community, and a memorial wreath is laid.

For most of its history, membership of Club de Recreio was restricted to members of the local and expatriate Portuguese community resident in Hong Kong. Along with other clubs in Hong Kong, the club has been forced to internationalize somewhat in recent years. As with other clubs in the area, Club de Recreio does not own the property it occupies but operates on a series of renewable ten-year leases. A nearby building houses the Little Flower Club, a charity-orientated Roman Catholic association whose membership is principally composed of local Portuguese ladies.

Gascoigne Road

(4) United Services Recreation Club

Originally built as a social and sporting club for officers of the British Garrison, for many years the United Services Recreation Club, popularly known as the USRC, had a policy of admitting a limited number of civilian members to help balance the more transient military members. In recent years the USRC has become entirely civilianized, but retains the old title and at least some of the Mess-like ambience.

First established in 1911, its attractive old buildings have changed little over the years. Expansive grounds with huge mature trees and well-maintained gardens and lawns make the USRC one of Kowloon's more popular clubs — for those who know that it even exists. Remarkably, a great many people in Hong Kong, even Kowloon residents, have never even heard of the place.

Service members used to remark that while the club was very convenient for shopping and a good place to park the car during a day down from the New Territories, the food on offer at the USRC was nothing to rave about. Recent comments seem to indicate that this situation has changed for the better. Perhaps this improvement has been brought about by the new entirely civilian management committee, and the need to actively compete for membership subscriptions with the many other social and sporting clubs in the vicinity.

How To Get There

By Bus:	No. 1, 1A, 2, 5, 5A from Tsim Sha Tsui 'Star' Ferry.
By MTR:	Jordan or Yau Ma Tei Stations (Gascoigne Road is roughly equidistant).
By Taxi:	油麻地加士居道 (*'Yau Ma Dei, Gah See Gui Doh'*).

STREETS

Kansu Street
甘肅街

Kansu Street extends from Nathan Road down to the former typhoon shelter. The general vicinity of Kansu Street is one of the oldest parts of Yau Ma Tei. Settled in the early 1860s, the area is distinguished by the interesting cluster of buildings and markets mostly located around the junction of Gascoigne and Nathan Roads.

Towards the Jade Market, numerous small shops sell padded quilts, Chinese wedding costumes, suitcases and luggage, and various plant and animal-derived items destined for inclusion in traditional Chinese medicines. One small shop stocks various varieties of dried lizard skins; the reptiles are still clearly recognizable and come mounted on cross-sticks. Open cardboard boxes are stacked high with dried seahorses and other less immediately obvious forms of marine life.

Around Temple Street's junction with Kansu Street, one can see some of Hong Kong's annually increasing numbers of mainland Chinese prostitutes, two-way permit holders who come to Kowloon to work in the local sex industry for a couple of months at a time.

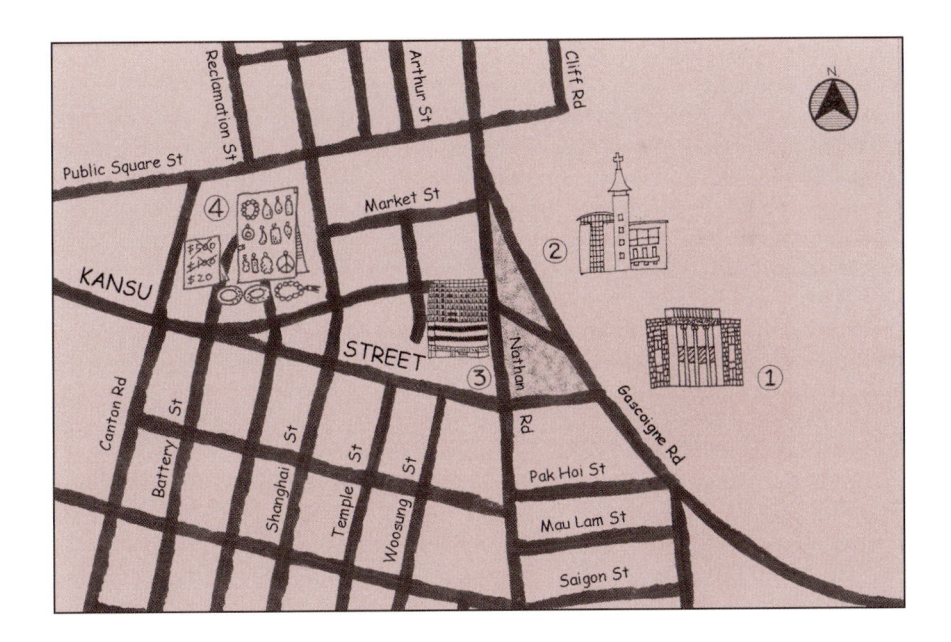

Yau Ma Tei

❶ South Kowloon Magistracy
❷ Kowloon Methodist Church
❸ Alhambra Mansions (old Alhambra Theatre)
❹ Jade Market

STREETS

Kansu Street

① South Kowloon Magistracy

This austere red-brick and concrete pillared building was built in 1936. For years it was used as the South Kowloon Magistracy. An imposing flight of stone steps leading up from the road is now partly obscured by the flyover over Gascoigne Road. The South Kowloon Magistracy building was used as the Kowloon Headquarters of the Kempeitai during the Japanese occupation of Hong Kong. The Kempeitai were the Japanese secret police, very similar in organizational structure and function to the Nazi Gestapo, and feared even by the Japanese themselves. For a few months immediately after the war ended, the building housed the Kowloon Standing Military Court. After Hong Kong had returned to civilian administration in 1946, the complex reverted to its former use as a magistracy and government offices.

The South Kowloon Magistracy was also used by the New Territories administration as the District Office, South. Most of this district was quite remote and difficult of access; it included Lantau, Sai Kung and most of the Outlying Islands. In spite of this wide geographical spread, the District Office responsible for this area was located right in the middle of Yau Ma Tei.

The South Kowloon Magistracy closed down on 1 July 2000, and the building now houses the Lands Tribunal.

Kansu Street

② *Kowloon Methodist Church*

The first Methodist Church to be established in Hong Kong opened in 1881 on Wellington Street in Central. From the very earliest days of British settlement many Methodists, both in Hong Kong and elsewhere in China, were active in medical missionary work. The drug rehabilitation centre at Shek Kwu Chau, which opened in the 1960s, was the work of Methodist missionaries who had to leave China in the late 1940s.

A prominent landmark on a low hill next to the South Kowloon Magistracy, the Kowloon Methodist Church's foundation stone was laid in December 1951. Despite being partially obscured by a busy flyover, the Kowloon Methodist Church remains a distinctive feature and, at a little more than half a century old, is one of the older extant buildings in the Yau Ma Tei area. Reverend Arthur Bray, the father of former senior Hong Kong government administrator, the late Denis Bray, was responsible for the construction of this church. As with most other churches in Hong Kong, the Kowloon Methodist Church has a school attached to its premises.

③ *Alhambra Mansions (old Alhambra Theatre)*

The attractive Moorish-styled cinema that once stood here used to be one of the most popular entertainment venues in Kowloon. Former Hong Kong prisoners-of-war often remark that when they passed by the Alhambra Theatre on their way to internment at Sham Shui Po in late December 1941, the hoardings in front displayed posters for the John Wayne film *The Long Voyage Home*. Many viewed this as somewhat prophetic as they were subsequently locked up by the Japanese for almost four years. The theatre was demolished in the 1960s and Alhambra Mansions was built on the same site.

Kansu Street

For many years the new building housed a very popular nightclub of the same name that has since closed down. *Cheongsam*-clad *moh lui* (taxi dancers) were a well-known feature at the Alhambra, as in many other venues elsewhere in Hong Kong at that time. Tickets for a dance in the early 1960s cost one Hong Kong dollar, with ten cents extra added on as government tax.

A few ballrooms from this period still survive in some corners of backstreet Yau Ma Tei, and it is still possible to waltz, foxtrot and tango the afternoon and evening away. For most part though, Kowloon's surviving dance halls have become very tired looking and decayed, like many of their remaining *moh lui*, and are often little more than a front for vice-related activities.

Dancing has experienced a resurgence of popularity in recent years among a new generation of Hong Kong people, and ballroom dance schools have become a feature of many urban areas, including Yau Ma Tei.

4) Jade Market

STREETS

Kansu Street

From the early 1950s, numerous refugee jade dealers from Canton's Changshu Road Jade Market set up stalls on Canton Road in Yau Ma Tei. In these years quite a lot of good quality jade could be found on sale in markets in Hong Kong. Many refugees from China brought jade and other jewellery items into Hong Kong because these items were lightweight, portable, easily concealed and could be readily disposed of for cash if necessary.

By the early 1970s there were more than a hundred jade stalls in business on the section of Canton Road between Jordan Road and Saigon Street. Jade jewellery and decorative items enjoyed a burst of international popularity after President Richard Nixon's visit to China in 1972, when numerous jade items were presented as official gifts.

Kansu Street's Jade Market, which opened in 1984, has gradually evolved into one of Yau Ma Tei's most popular, 'authentically flavoured' tourist sights. A surprising number of visitors, however, never venture much further than the confines of its covered market. It is still possible to find the occasional good piece at the Jade Market, but these days really valuable jade is only sold in high-end jewellers' shops. The best quality, the dealers say, mostly comes from southwest China and Burma.

The Jade Market now has over four hundred stalls, and is always worth a wander for the atmosphere, if not the goods on offer. Stallholders are generally friendly, but as in markets everywhere else in Hong Kong a strong sense of *caveat emptor* must be applied around here. If the price of a particular piece of jewellery or jade carving seems just too good to be true, then it almost certainly is. A number of jade shops along Canton Road in Yau Ma Tei — descendents of some of the early postwar jade stalls — sell more expensive items of more reliable quality than the Jade Market.

How To Get There

By Bus:	No. 1, 1A, 2, 5, 5A from Tsim Sha Tsui 'Star' Ferry.
By MTR:	Either Jordan or Yau Ma Tei Station (Kansu Street is roughly equidistant).
By Taxi:	油麻地甘肅街 (*'Yau Ma Dei, Gum Sook Gaai'*).

STREETS

Reclamation Street
新填地街

Generally known, when first built, as the Yau Ma Tei Praya, Reclamation Street extended along the waterfront until 1904. A further large-scale reclamation project started in that year, which extended to the present Ferry Street and north to Tai Kok Tsui. Development on the newly reclaimed land commenced in 1910, and the Yau Ma Tei Praya was renamed Reclamation Street. Yau Ma Tei's present-day seafront is now almost two kilometres west of the original anchorage, and Kowloon peninsula is now joined to the once-remote Stonecutter's Island.

The area around Reclamation Street was extensively redeveloped in the years after the Pacific War due to Hong Kong's massive increase in population. A few original arcaded pre-war shop houses along Reclamation Street still survive; most are now very dilapidated. Shops along here sell a wide variety of everyday furniture, kitchen goods, and other domestic items. There are also quite a few idol carvers, religious goods sellers and all manner of other small shops, all of which add to Yau Ma Tei's perennially appealing 'Chinese backstreet' colour and atmosphere.

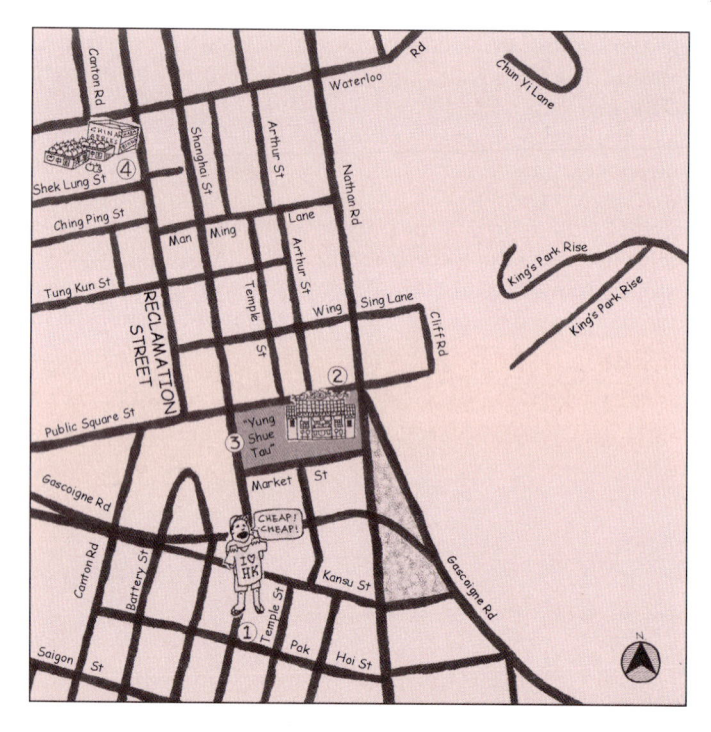

❶ Temple Street Night Market
❷ Tin Hau Temple
❸ Yung Shue Tau
❹ Kowloon Wholesale Fruit Market (Gwo Laan)

STREETS

Reclamation Street

① *Temple Street Night Market*

Yung Shue Tau, the banyan tree-shaded square in front of the Tin Hau Temple, became known from about 1920 onwards as a 'poor man's nightclub', the Kowloon answer to Western District's popular *Dai Daat Dei* (*'Big Piece of Ground'*), night bazaar, originally located at Possession Point. Acrobats, soothsayers, peddlers, quacks, hawkers and harlots all plied their trades here, and an evening spent wandering about Yung Shue Tau was as inexpensive a night out as it was possible to get anywhere in Hong Kong. Over the next two decades, the hawker stalls gradually spread into the surrounding streets, and by the late 1940s the nucleus of what became the internationally known Temple Street Night Market was already well established.

In 1968 the Hong Kong government decided to redevelop the area around Yung Shue Tau for recreational purposes, and as a result over two hundred stalls were moved to Shanghai Street. For several years, this became a 'temporary' night market. The present Temple Street Night Market precinct opened in early 1975, and then there were over six hundred registered stalls in operation. In 1998, in an attempt to shore up Temple Street's flagging tourist appeal, the market's opening hours were brought forward to noon.

Well-known for all manner of cheap and cheerful items, from inexpensive clothing and copy watches to plastic toys and gadgets, Temple Street is still a lot of fun to wander around for an evening, and is as popular with locals out for a low-cost evening in Kowloon as with visitors to Hong Kong from abroad. A word of warning: expect most goods purchased here to last about as long as it takes to walk back to the MTR station.

Reclamation Street

(2) Tin Hau Temple

Probably Hong Kong's most well-known Tin Hau Temple, this large religious complex at Yau Ma Tei was originally located on the waterfront. A tablet preserved in the temple regarded the establishment as 'ancient' in 1870; this description indicates that the temple had been established at least a generation before that date. By this reckoning, the date of foundation can be estimated around the 1840s at the very latest.

By the early 1870s a well-established leadership structure had evolved in Yau Ma Tei, with the Tin Hau Temple Committee and the local *kai fong* association at its core.

Yau Ma Tei's Tin Hau Temple is dedicated to other gods and goddesses as well as the Goddess of Fishermen and Seafarers. The temple celebrates the birthday festivals of ten other deities, including Judge Pao (perhaps best known in Hong Kong from a popular Cantonese television serial screened in the 1990s), Wong Tai Sin (the 'Refugee God'), and Kuan Yin (the Goddess of Mercy). The Tin Hau Temple complex is made up of five separate 'chambers'. The one on the extreme right was originally a book repository (*shue yuen*), which now houses a courtyard and eight fortune-tellers who rent their tiny cubicles from the temple authorities.

Beware of these fortune-tellers; some are quite fierce and will tell you in no uncertain terms exactly what to do with your immediate female antecedents if they realize you do not plan to put some business their way.

Reclamation Street

Spiral incense coils promoted as 'long-term offering to the gods' that 'lasts for ten days, wishing you and your family good luck, good health and good fortune' are on sale at the temple. And at a hundred dollars or so per coil, they are some of Hong Kong's more reasonable spiritual offerings. Perhaps surprisingly for a completely Chinese shrine, Yau Ma Tei's Tin Hau Temple attracts quite a few devotees from Hong Kong's other ethnic groups. Many Nepalese residents in the area quite frequently visit; some say that the atmosphere here reminds them of the temples found back in Kathmandu.

③ *Yung Shue Tau*

Yung Shue Tau, the 'Banyan Tree Head', is the popular local Cantonese name for the large open square in front of the Tin Hau Temple. Shaded with numerous old banyan trees, Yung Shue Tau faced directly onto the Yau Ma Tei waterfront in the late nineteenth century. For decades a popular night market — precursor to the Temple Street Night Market — was located here. It has now been marooned almost three kilometres inland by successive land reclamation projects.

The sitting-out area here is one of the few relatively open, freely available public spaces in this part of Yau Ma Tei, and there are always plenty of people walking about, chatting to friends on benches and playing chess, card games or draughts. From time to time an itinerant letter writer sets up a stall at Yung Shue Tau, to process paperwork of various kinds for the dwindling number of elderly illiterate clients who have no family members in Hong Kong to write a letter or fill in a form for them. A few itinerant barbers offer haircuts as well, and Yau Ma Tei's numerous, mostly mainland Chinese street prostitutes look for trade at most times of the day and night.

Reclamation Street

4) Kowloon Wholesale Fruit Market (Gwo Laan)

By 1910 the site of today's Gwo Laan (Wholesale Fruit Market) had become a thriving daily market, and was conveniently close to the wharves where junks that brought fresh produce from the Pearl River Delta districts and further afield docked and unloaded. Even at that time the market's distribution was predominantly wholesaler-to-wholesaler, and by the 1920s Reclamation Street market had become the centre of Kowloon's wholesale commercial life.

In 1926 the Kowloon Fruit and Vegetable Operator's Guild was established to reinforce co-operation between various parties within the market. The vegetable section left the guild in 1946 when the Government Vegetable Marketing Organisation was established, but the name of the Guild remained unchanged.

From 1946 onwards the market dealt in vegetables, poultry and fish, as well as fruit. By the late 1950s the vegetable *laan* (monopoly) had moved most of their operations to Cheung Sha Wan where, along with live poultry traders, it is still based today. After that time, Yau Ma Tei Market became the sole preserve of fruit traders.

In the early postwar years the volume of operations was quite low compared to today. Fresh fruit was considered a luxury item in Hong Kong and very few families could afford to buy it on a regular basis. Almost everything sold in those

Reclamation Street

years was grown in the New Territories or brought in from China. Availability for most locally produced items, such as lychees and longans, was highly seasonal.

One exception was oranges; these were imported into Hong Kong in large quantities, mostly from the United States, even before the Second World War, and generally used as religious offerings. With increased general affluence, fresh fruit is now affordable for most people. Air-freight has made the seasons irrelevant; produce comes from all over the world, and Chilean grapes, Australian melons, Philippine mangoes, Thai durians and rambutans, Egyptian oranges, South African apples and pears, American strawberries and New Zealand blueberries are all readily available all year round.

Very busy in the early hours of the morning, like Hong Kong's other wholesale markets, Yau Ma Tei's Gwo Laan is a very quiet place in the afternoon. Most stalls have closed and workers departed by late morning, and after lunch the wholesaler's count the day's takings and workers sit about playing cards or mah-jong or sprawled out on top of the palettes sleeping. Many fruit dealers will happily sell a couple of cases to casual retail customers, and prices are much lower here than in the supermarkets; you just have to be prepared to eat a lot of apples, durians or grapefruit within a short space of time!

How To Get There

By Bus:	No. 1, 1A, 2, 6, 6A from Tsim Sha Tsui 'Star' Ferry.
By MTR:	Yau Ma Tei Station.
By Taxi:	油麻地新填地街 (*'Yau Ma Dei, Sun Teen Dei Gaai'*).

Shanghai Street
上海街

Shanghai Street is one of the most varied places to wander in Kowloon, with something of interest on almost every corner. Furniture shops and wholesale knife merchants compete with idol carvers, makers of wooden chopping blocks, split-bamboo *dim sum* baskets and all manner of other locally orientated small businesses. Some items on sale here, such as *mook kek* (wooden slippers), were once common items in every household in Hong Kong, but are now difficult to find elsewhere.

Numerous Kowloon backstreets, such as this one, were named after cities and provinces elsewhere in China. Some of these names, such as Shanghai, are immediately recognizable major cities; others are relatively small towns in the immediate vicinity of Hong Kong or further afield. In many places in China, the Wade-Giles romanization system used in Hong Kong has long since been superseded by pinyin, and the old forms are increasingly unrecognized and largely unknown. For example, pinyin-rendered names like Beijing and Guangdong have replaced the earlier Peking and Kwangtung, which are still commonly used in Hong Kong.

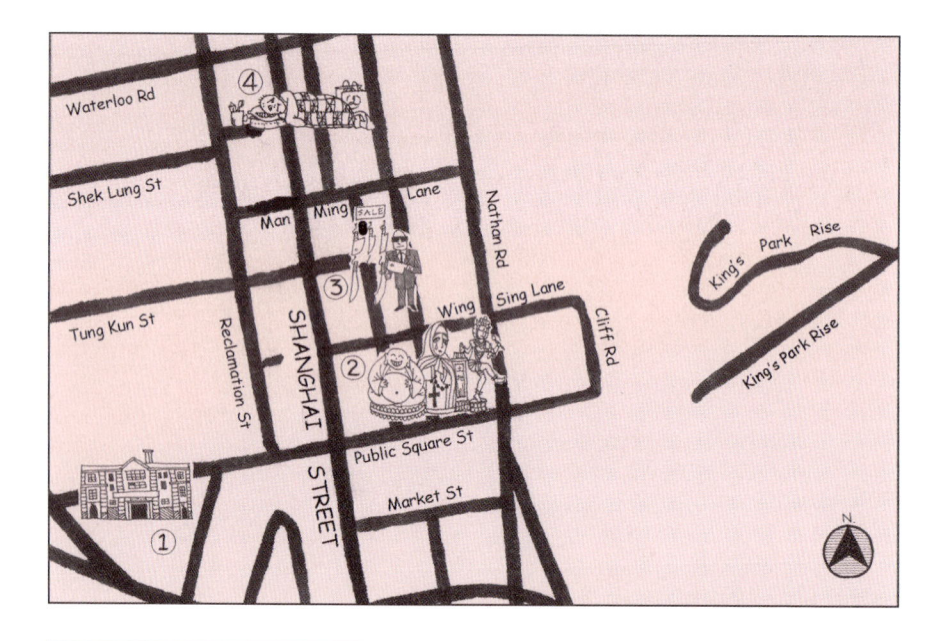

❶ Yau Ma Tei Police Station
❷ Chinese gods and idols shops
❸ Kitchenware and chopper shops
❹ Salvation Army Street Sleepers' Shelter

STREETS

Shanghai Street

Pedestrians should be especially careful when attempting to negotiate Shanghai Street's notorious one-way traffic system. Yau Ma Tei's maniacal minibus drivers set new standards for reckless motoring, even by Hong Kong's fast paced standards, and despite the high police presence red lights are by no means universally respected. Be warned!

1 Yau Ma Tei Police Station

The first Yau Ma Tei Police Station was built in 1873 at the junction of Shanghai and Public Square Streets. In 1922 the station moved to the present attractive premises then close to the waterfront. Police stations elsewhere in Hong Kong have frequently survived the pattern of demolition and reconstruction so prevalent in the private sector; continuous use seems to favour long-term conservation.

Kowloon has a number of well-preserved police stations; Mong Kok and Sham Shui Po both have similarly styled buildings of roughly the same age. As it has survived in more or less original condition, Yau Ma Tei Police Station is frequently used as a backdrop for locally produced films, especially at night. Evocative 'Old Hong Kong' atmosphere shots are mostly unobtainable elsewhere in Hong Kong and Kowloon these days, and filmmakers either have to take what they can get locally, or else go to Guangzhou, Macao or even further inland in China and Southeast Asia.

Shanghai Street

② Chinese gods and idols shops

Fancy 'inviting' a Goddess of Mercy into your house but don't know where to look for one? Nearby Shanghai Street, just around the corner from the Tin Hau Temple, is dotted with small shops which sell images of just about every Chinese deity in existence, as well as all sorts of other Chinese religious paraphernalia.

Shops such as Hop Keung Cheong Kee, along with many others, have almost the entire pantheon of Chinese divinities displayed in their shop windows. Any other gods or goddesses that you may want to worship and are not readily available in their shop can be custom-made in their factory in China. They can even produce non-Chinese ones, if you need them. Armed with a photograph, descriptions and dimensions, these shops can manufacture a Ganesha, Shiva, the Virgin Mary or St Anthony, either plainly finished or in full Technicolor splendour. Cute, hand-painted, ten-inch high Monkey Gods carved from camphorwood cost several hundred dollars, though most items on offer are much cheaper than that.

③ Kitchenware and chopper shops

Unlike many other large, densely packed cities elsewhere in the world, random, violent crime is, fortunately, a relative rarity in Hong Kong. The average resident can walk the streets in complete safety at all hours of the day or night, in almost all areas, including the backstreets of Yau Ma Tei.

Despite this welcome fact, gruesome chopper attacks and oddly performed murders are surprisingly common in Hong Kong. A day seldom passes that one such incident is not luridly reported in the Chinese-language press with highly coloured descriptions and gory accompanying photographs. Almost inevitably, it transpires, the attack was either Triad-related — and therefore ultimately about money — or happened when family members or others living in closely confined, hopelessly overcrowded locations have finally had *enough* of whatever has been

Shanghai Street

bothering them and let fly with the sharpest, closest, most convenient implement to hand. All too often, this was the kitchen cleaver.

But where do the more premeditated go to get the means to exact their revenge? From shops such as these on Shanghai Street, of course! A virtual armoury of cleavers, meat axes, and knives, both large and small, can be found in any one of them. While their principal business is as suppliers to the local restaurant trade, prices are very reasonable and quality is high. Most kitchenware shops will take orders to produce anything that is not readily available in stock.

4) Salvation Army Street Sleepers' Shelter

'Asia's World City' may have the second highest per capita income in the region after Japan, but there are still a large number of impoverished, sometimes desperately poor people in Hong Kong. The gap between the city's 'haves' and 'have-nots' has continued to widen since the 1997 handover to China and is now one of the largest in the 'developed' world. Older parts of Kowloon, such as Yau Ma Tei, Mong Kok and Sham Shui Po, are home to Hong Kong's most visible concentrations of urban poverty.

Shanghai Street

While most of the truly impoverished residents in Hong Kong can at least find some form of permanent shelter, however basic, quite a number cannot. Organizations such as the Salvation Army are renowned the world over for providing front-line aid to those who need it most, and their operations in Hong Kong's poorer districts are both extensive and much needed. This street sleepers' shelter, located in one of the most rundown corners of Yau Ma Tei, is open every day of the year to those in need. The Salvation Army headquarters in Yau Ma Tei is located nearby at Wing Sing Lane.

How To Get There

By Bus:	No. 1, 1A, 2, 6, 6A from Tsim Sha Tsui 'Star' Ferry.
By MTR:	Yau Ma Tei Station.
By Taxi:	油麻地上海街 (*'Yau Ma Dei, Seung Hoi Gaai'*).

Portland Street
砵蘭街

Portland Street is one of the long roads that broadly parallel Nathan Road. It extends northwards from near the Tin Hau Temple until well into neighbouring Mong Kok. For the moment, Portland Street still offers an interesting amalgam of Yau Ma Tei's past and present, and provides a vivid glimpse of what large tracts of Kowloon may look like within the next decade or so. With a few exceptions, the main fascinations of a wander along Portland Street are the glimpses that it affords of the hard edged, life-is-where-you-live-it existence common to so many Kowloon residents.

Much like Kowloon Tong and for very similar reasons, Portland Street and the various images its name brings forth are known to anyone who has ever watched Cantonese films and television dramas, even if they have never been to Hong

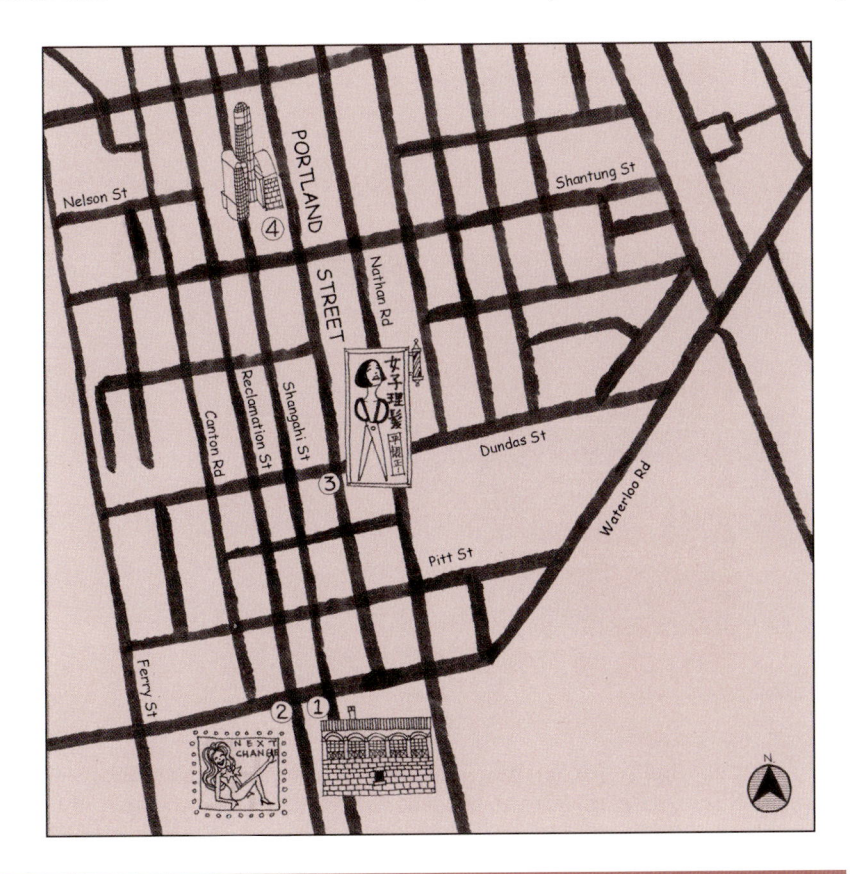

❶ Yau Ma Tei Pump Station ❸ Brothel signs
❷ Yau Ma Tei Theatre ❹ Langham Place Hotel

Portland Street

Kong. Portland Street is the exact Kowloon counterpart to Wan Chai's famed Lockhart Road, but with far less neon and nothing of tawdry *The World of Suzy Wong* romanticism. And like Lockhart Road, in amongst the working girls and Triad boys, there are plenty of shops selling bathroom tiles, taps, pipes, bathtubs and sanitary fittings. Somehow the two go together in Hong Kong.

Aspects of the Triad element so often glimpsed in and around Portland Street were romanticized in a popular Cantonese film, *Portland Street Blues*, released in 1998. The Hong Kong film industry, in its way, is a tremendous supporter and advertiser of the Triad lifestyle, as films such as this one — among dozens of others — play up the loyalty, enduring friendship and support for society's underdogs that make Triad associations appealing to many disenfranchised youths from Kowloon's sprawling 'Housing Estate Heartland', spread out along the MTR lines and thundering expressways to the north and east. Recruitment to the ranks of 'secret' societies seems as widespread today as at any point in the past, and is a burgeoning international problem for law-enforcement agencies.

(1) Yau Ma Tei Pump Station

The first pump house for Yau Ma Tei's freshwater supplies can still be seen on Shanghai Street. The modest two-storied, red-brick building was spared by the Urban Renewal Authority and sympathetically restored, and is now incongruously situated right next to a forty-storied high tower block. At the moment the pump house stands empty and unused, not the best of all possible fates for an old building in Hong Kong, even one that has been renovated. It is now Grade One listed, which means it cannot be demolished.

Portland Street

The continued existence of this small, fairly unremarkable building does give hope to those who would like to see an imaginative use put to the neighbouring Yau Ma Tei Theatre and the increasingly dilapidated old buildings within the nearby Gwo Laan. Local architects and planners have acknowledged — very belatedly — that the incorporation of some original structures or features within new developments allows a sense of memory and continuity from previous buildings and times to come forward into the modern day. With gradually increased awareness, the trend should become more widespread elsewhere in Hong Kong.

② *Yau Ma Tei Theatre*

Built in the early 1920s, the old *Yau Ma Dei Hei Yuen* (Yau Ma Tei Theatre) is the oldest remaining cinema building in Hong Kong, and remained in regular use until 1998, when it finally closed down. During the last stages of its existence the cinema showed *haam peen* (soft porn films); the posters can still be glimpsed near the boarded-up box office on Waterloo Road.

During the 1990s the decaying, smelly cockroach-infested auditorium always had a mid-afternoon contingent of *haam sup lo* ('salty and wet' old men), who leered and lurked in its darkened recesses and presumably, when the show was over, crossed the road to Portland Street in search of the real thing.

Various new uses for the crumbling building have been mooted since its closure. With sympathetic renovation the Yau Ma Tei Theatre would make a wonderful community theatre or art-house venue. One imaginative suggestion involved the building's conversion into a venue to show classic Hong Kong-made films from the 1950s, 1960s and 1970s.

STREETS

Portland Street

Periodic calls for the Yau Ma Tei Theatre's preservation continue, but given Hong Kong's generally dismal heritage conservation record it is almost certain that the semi-derelict building will eventually be demolished.

③ Brothel signs

From the very earliest years of British settlement, Hong Kong has been home to legions of prostitutes of various nationalities who generally worked either in brothels or on the streets. Census figures from the late nineteenth century indicated that approximately one in four Chinese women in the colony were prostitutes. Most of the brothel keepers during this period were also Chinese women; whether feminists would consider this a form of female empowerment or simply the exploitation of women by women for the ultimate benefit of a patriarchal society is, of course, open to endless circular debate.

For decades Yau Ma Tei's typhoon shelter had dozens of floating brothels, euphemistically known as 'flower boats'. Macao and Canton also had a large number of these vessels — some were very large and ornate. The last remaining water-borne prostitutes relocated on land in Yau Ma Tei after the typhoon shelter was reclaimed and redeveloped in the early 1990s.

Prostitution is one of contemporary Hong Kong's ongoing contradictions. It is illegal to own or operate a brothel, to live on the proceeds of 'immoral earnings', or to solicit for custom. But it is, nevertheless, *completely* legal under Hong Kong law to be a prostitute! Work *that* one out!

Brothels along Portland Street, and other streets in the vicinity, operate quite openly, despite their illegality. Brothels are indicated by signs including the characters 女子理髮, which mean 'Lady Barber Shops'. Legitimate barber shops are for men, and are staffed by male barbers; they are not generally staffed by women for men unless other services are implied.

The Hong Kong Police regularly shut these places down, and within days a new one has opened a few doors away. As in other parts of northern Kowloon the advertising hoardings, usually a lurid yellow, leave little to the imagination. Yau Ma Tei's backstreets must surely be home to more 'pretty girl students' than anywhere else in Hong Kong, with the possible exception of some parts of Wan Chai.

Portland Street

(4) Langham Place Hotel

A sign of changing times in Yau Ma Tei and Mong Kok, the Langham Place Hotel provides an enormous new marker towards the way large tracts of northern Kowloon are heading in the near future. This enormous new development encompasses an entire block, and — for now at least — provides a vivid contrast with the surrounding area.

Vast expanses of glittering marble, chrome and glass dominate one side of the street, while family-run dry-cleaners, open fronted *ng kam poh* (metal goods shops), bathroom shops and small cafés selling *wonton* and noodles operate much as they have for decades. Rows of minibuses stand along the pavements; as in other parts of Mong Kok, their engines idle for hours on end and no one ever seems to be prosecuted.

The Langham Place Hotel and shopping complex was closely designed with the tastes, desires and aspirations of Hong Kong Chinese consumers in mind. Some may find the décor and fittings vulgar, pretentious and completely over-the-top. But for the majority of those who flock here every weekend and public holiday, this is exactly how they would decorate their own homes, if they had the cash and space to do so. Afternoon tea at the hotel is remarkably good, and quite reasonably priced for this part of Kowloon.

How To Get There

By Bus:	No. 1, 1A, 2, 6, 6A from Tsim Sha Tsui 'Star' Ferry.
By MTR:	Yau Ma Tei Station.
By Taxi:	油麻地砵蘭街 (*'Yau Ma Dei, Boot Laan Gaai'*).

Waterloo Road
窩打老道

One of Kowloon's principal thoroughfares, Waterloo Road was laid out in the early twentieth century. At this time it extended from the then waterfront at Canton Road towards Kowloon Tong. The western stretch of Waterloo Road, which leads down to the now reclaimed typhoon shelter, passes through densely packed tenements with almost no open space. A broad nullah ran down the middle of the road; most of it was not covered until the early 1970s. Parts of this odoriferous drainage ditch still remained open until the early 1980s.

To the northeast, Waterloo Road passes through Kowloon Tong, first developed as a garden suburb in the 1920s and still one of modern Kowloon's more affluent residential areas, before ending just below the Lion Rock Tunnel.

The lower section of Waterloo Road in Yau Ma Tei has numerous areas of interest, especially along the side streets.

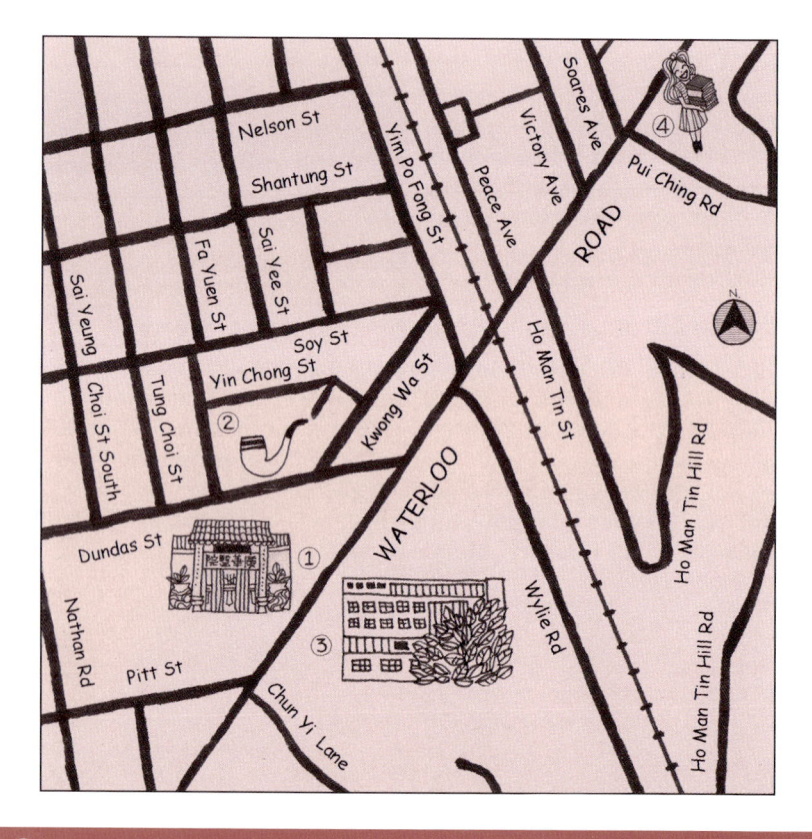

❶ Kwong Wah Hospital
❷ Yin Chong Street
❸ Kowloon Wah Yan College
❹ Kowloon Central Library

Waterloo Road

Waterloo Road passes through and over the remnants of Kowloon's formerly hilly profile, traces of which still remain. Waterloo Hill, an exclusive residential area near King's Park with a number of high-profile recent developments, has long been one of Kowloon's more favoured addresses.

From 1967, King's Park was the site of the British Military Hospital, which was surrounded by military quarters and spacious civil service apartment blocks. Significant sections of this area were sold to commercial interests in the late 1990s and redeveloped into yet more luxury private housing. Apartments here enjoy some of central Kowloon's most sweeping views and are among the most expensive on the entire peninsula. The contrast between the relative space and comfort these residents enjoy, and the grotesquely overcrowded tenements only a few hundred metres away, could hardly be more stark, and does much to illustrate Hong Kong's steadily widening wealth gap.

① Kwong Wah Hospital

Kowloon's original Kwong Wah Hospital was established on this site on Waterloo Road in 1911. *Kwong Wah Yee Yuen*, loosely translated, means 'Chinese-people-from-Guangdong Hospital'; most of the Chinese population then resident in Hong Kong in those years were Cantonese migrants from the neighbouring province. The Kwong Wah Hospital has been closely affiliated with Yau Ma Tei's Tin Hau Temple since its establishment, in much the same way that Hong Kong Island's Tung Wah Hospital maintains close historical links to the Man Mo Temple on Hollywood Road.

Kwong Wah Hospital has an interesting exhibition hall with a number of well curated displays. These feature the history and development of the Tung Wah Hospital, Hong Kong's original Chinese-oriented hospital, which was established in Western District in 1870. In 1931 the Tung Wah Hospital, the Kwong Wah Hospital, and the Eastern Hospital in Causeway Bay, all merged to form the Tung Wah Group of Hospitals.

A large, elaborately decorated meeting hall in the Kwong Wah Hospital is used by the Board of Directors for ceremonial activities. Every morning a ritual offering of three sticks of lighted incense is made to Shen Nong, the legendary Sage-Emperor traditionally believed to be the inventor of medicine and the patron saint of medical practitioners.

Waterloo Road

② Yin Chong Street

Yin Chong Street ('Smoke Factory' Street) recalls the Orient Tobacco Factory, a large tobacco processing plant that operated here in the 1920s. Although the factory has long since closed, like many other elements of heritage interest in Hong Kong, the name of the street remains as a tenuous link with what went before.

In the interwar years a number of cigarette factories, such as Orient Tobacco, had large-scale operations in Hong Kong. These were mostly owned by either British American Tobacco (BAT), which operated extensively in China during this period, and the Chinese-controlled Nanyang Brothers. Nanyang Brothers, as the name *nan yang* ('South Seas') implies, was a Southeast Asian-owned concern.

Both companies processed dried leaf tobacco, most of which was imported into Hong Kong from northern Sumatra, the Philippines and western provinces of China. The majority of locally rolled cigarettes were re-exported to Southeast Asia and China. As labour costs in Hong Kong steadily rose in the postwar years, the tobacco industry declined and all locally consumed nicotine products are now imported or smuggled.

③ Kowloon Wah Yan College

Hong Kong has two Wah Yan Colleges; the other institution is on Wan Chai's Queen's Road East, opposite the Ruttonjee Hospital. The Hong Kong Wah Yan College was established by Tsui Yan Sau, a Chinese-language teacher from St Joseph's College, who opened the original Hong Kong Island school under the supervision of teachers from the Jesuit order. He later opened Kowloon Wah Yan College to cater to students on the northern side of the harbour. One of his sons, Paul Tsui, was the first Chinese administrative officer in the Hong Kong government. His appointment was made

STREETS 98

Waterloo Road

after years of distinguished service with the British Army Aid Group (BAAG) in wartime China.

Kowloon Wah Yan College has moved addresses a number of times since its founding in 1924. The school was first located at Portland Street, somewhat further north in Mong Kok, then moved to premises in nearby Nelson Street. Kowloon Wah Yan College finally moved to its present premises on Waterloo Road in 1952. The school's chapel, which is of considerable architectural interest, opened in 1959.

The Roman Catholic-run College has extensive well-maintained grounds and playing fields (a rarity for most schools in Hong Kong), and for decades has continuously enjoyed high academic standards.

4 *Kowloon Central Library*

To many local and overseas observers, the recently built Hong Kong Central Library in Causeway Bay is one of the worst architectural eyesores to blight Hong Kong in recent years. Few, then, can have witnessed this Kowloon-side example of Urban Council-approved design and aesthetics without at least some strongly negative feelings.

The Kowloon Central Library's dark chocolate brown walls are clearly visible for a great distance, and the building is hard to miss for its sheer, unremitting ugliness. The heat-absorbing colour scheme most surely help ramp up the building's electricity bills; but then, environmental concerns have never been a Hong Kong strong point.

Exterior design horrors aside, the Kowloon Central Library, like public libraries elsewhere in Hong Kong, is well laid out within, extremely well stocked with excellent resources, and has reasonably helpful staff all contained within an easily accessible, central Kowloon location.

How To Get There

By Bus:	No. 7 from Tsim Sha Tsui 'Star' Ferry to Lok Fu; No. 208 from Tsim Sha Tsui East to Broadcast Drive.
By MTR:	Yau Ma Tei Station.
By Taxi:	油麻地窩打老道 (*'Yau Ma Dei, Wor Dah Loh Doh'*).

STREETS

Mong Kok

For many years this central section of the Kowloon peninsula, sandwiched between the Tsim Sha Tsui tourist strip to the south and the factories and housing estates just to the north and east, has been locally renowned, or notorious, as a venue for all manner of illicit undertakings.

Most contemporary images of Mong Kok, both within Hong Kong and overseas, have been created and fuelled as much by cinema and television as first-hand experience. For decades, Mong Kok — at least in the popular imagination — was second only to Kowloon City as Hong Kong's hotbed of organized crime, flagrant vice, several species of *haak she wui* (Triad gangs), general immorality and permanently sleazy, down-at-heel general ambience.

This highly coloured if somewhat superficial perception is an easy one to arrive at in most corners of modern-day Mong Kok. Throughout the district, legitimate businesses operate right next door to all-too-obvious covers for Triad activity. Honest, long-established features of local life stand next to shop-fronts that change form and function every other month, or so it sometimes seems. This constant state of transience helps make Mong Kok one of Kowloon's most interesting areas to wander around, as there is always something new to see, explore and experience.

Mong Kok

'Mong Kok' is a modern mispronunciation and subsequent mistransliteration of 'Wong Kok', meaning Prosperous Corner. On some of the earliest detailed maps of the Kowloon peninsula drawn in the early 1860s, Mong Kok is rendered 'Mong Kong'. The road across the northern Kowloon peninsula that later became Argyle Street was laid out at this time. In the late nineteenth century, this road passed through scattered fields, small villages and low hills towards present-day Ma Tau Wai and Kowloon City. A number of small creeks drained the area; the mouth of the largest was found at Mong Kok Tsui, slightly to the south of present-day Argyle Street. A small inlet extended across from Mong Kok Tsui to Tai Kok Tsui, which was periodically used by sampan-dwellers in need of shelter.

Major reclamation work north of Yau Ma Tei was undertaken from 1904 onwards, which greatly extended Mong Kok's land area and joined Mong Kok Tsui and Tai Kok Tsui. Nathan Road was extended northwards in 1917 to link up with the newly completed Castle Peak Road into the northwest New Territories. By the early 1920s, the north Kowloon reclamation was largely completed, and by the end of the decade most of the area west of Nathan Road had been completely developed.

For decades, the northern Kowloon peninsula districts have become some of the most densely crowded places in the world. One of the most frequently quoted Mong Kok statistics proclaimed that if everyone inside came down from all the buildings at the same time, there would be no room on the streets for all the people to stand, even on each other's shoulders. Even when most of the district's residents are still *in* their buildings, Mong Kok's streets can sometimes feel that way.

• Peace Avenue	• Prince Edward Road West
• Argyle Street	• Boundary Street
• Kadoorie Avenue	

While other parts of modern Kowloon, such as Tsim Sha Tsui, are large-scale shopping districts firmly orientated towards the international tourist trade, the backstreets of Mong Kok are where local Hong Kong people come to browse — for anything and everything. Entire streets here are given over to the sale of a particular item; Fa Yuen Street is the place to come for cut-price women's garments and accessories; Tung Choi Street stocks everything that one could possibly want in the way of fish-tanks, goldfish, water plants and other aquarium items, as well as bicycles and spare parts, while Flower Market Road, unsurprisingly, sells every possible variety of indoor and outdoor plant, and cut flowers imported from as far as Malaysia, the Netherlands, Kenya and Columbia.

A few hours spent wandering around the backstreets of Mong Kok epitomizes a vital chunk of the *real* Hong Kong experience: densely clotted, kaleidoscopic, challenging and very much alive, there is always something to see and experience, and never a dull moment whatever the time of day. This part of Kowloon is also home to some of the wealthiest people in Hong Kong — and many of the poorest; both live at very close quarters, and the contrast between their living standards alone provides a great deal of the area's interest.

Ho Man Tin

Ho Man Tin was one of ten villages documented in a land survey made in 1861, shortly after the Kowloon peninsula's transfer to British rule. Sometimes rendered Homantin or Homuntin, the village was then populated mostly by recent Hakka settlers to the Hong Kong region. As was the case in other parts of Kowloon at that time, these tough, hardy migrant labourers worked extensive quarries which supplied building stone to Hong Kong Island and further afield.

Within a few decades Ho Man Tin had its own impressive Kwun Yam Temple (or Shui Yuet Kung Temple) which, in the late nineteenth century, stood near the site of the present China Light and Power building on Argyle Street. This popular, well supported temple was removed to Shantung Street in 1926 and still stands there today, dwarfed by tower blocks on all sides, and still well attended by crowds of devotees.

German missionary groups worked among the Hakka villagers of Ho Man Tin in the late nineteenth century, and as a result of their sustained efforts, the Ho Man Tin area became locally known for a time as 'the Christian Valley'. Christian churches of various denominations are still a noted feature of modern Ho Man Tin.

The eastern side of Mong Kok, around Ho Man Tin, started to be developed by private interests in the late 1920s. By 1941 the area had developed into a pleasant suburb known locally for its spacious low-rise apartment blocks and attractive garden villas. Some fragments of these pre-war developments still remain, though most have been demolished. During the interwar years this part of Mong Kok was known to many European residents as Argyle (from Argyle Street), or simply as Kowloon.

STREETS

Mong Kok

One Hong Kong businessman who saw the potential of Ho Man Tin was Francisco (Frank) Paulo de Vasconcelos Soares, a prominent local bill and bullion broker who turned his hand to property development after the First World War. Due largely to the success of his enterprises, Soares became known as 'the Father of Ho Man Tin'.

As Ho Man Tin continued to develop, its appearance further changed. The hillside near the present Waterloo Hill Road and the Ho Man Tin and Oi Man Estates had been a cemetery area for the Indian, Muslim, Roman Catholic and Chinese communities since the 1900s. All these cemeteries were removed in the early 1950s, and swiftly replaced by squatter settlements. By the 1960s, most of the huts that had crowded around Ho Man Tin since the late 1940s had been cleared to make way for modern housing developments and resettlement estates.

Certain parts of Mong Kok, such as Ho Man Tin, Yau Yat Chuen and Kadoorie Hill, have long been very desirable residential areas. Formerly grotty, seedy corners between Yau Ma Tei and Mong Kok, such as Portland Street, have undergone considerable reconstruction and revitalization in recent years, and the trend towards urban improvement seems set to continue for many years to come.

Stonecutter's Island

Stonecutter's Island, located in the western harbour just off Yau Ma Tei, was ceded to Great Britain, along with the rest of Kowloon peninsula north as far as what is now Boundary Street, under the Treaty of Tientsin signed in 1860. Stonecutter's Island was always a military zone, and the island remained completely off-limits to the general public for many years.

Although once one of Victoria Harbour's most prominent natural features, Stonecutter's Island is no longer even an island. It was completely joined to the rest of Kowloon peninsula by massive reclamation work in the mid-1990s, as part of airport-related core projects.

For decades Stonecutter's Island has been locally renowned as a bird and wildlife haven. With no cars and relatively few people to disturb them, various species with a limited habitat elsewhere within the urban area found some sanctuary among the heavy vegetation and abandoned gun emplacements.

Recent high density developments in western Kowloon ended the island's geographical isolation. Lower Kwai Chung's massively expanded container port, just to the north, has probably also had a negative effect on local bird populations.

Gun batteries and barracks were built on Stonecutter's Island in the 1860s, and further additions were made in the late nineteenth century. For over a century the Hong Kong Garrison stored their ammunition, mines and ordnance at an underground depot on the island. For decades the British Army employed a contingent of specially recruited Sikhs as guards at the ordnance depot. Forbidden by their religion to smoke, *khalsa* (orthodox) Sikhs were considered just the people

Mong Kok

to have around large quantities of high explosives. For many years one of Hong Kong's more popular urban myths maintained that if the contents of the magazines ever exploded, most of Kowloon would be wiped out — though of course no one really knew that for sure!

In the interwar years, Stonecutter's Island was home to one of the largest British military SIGINT (signal intelligence) installations in the Far East. Known as FECB (Far East Combined Bureau), the complex opened in the early 1920s and expanded through the 1930s. This strategically important 'listening post' facility, along with most of its key staff, was relocated to Singapore long before the Japanese invasion of Hong Kong, and was not reinstated on Stonecutter's Island after the war.

Stonecutter's Island is probably best known these days as the place where the majority of Kowloon's sewage is given primary treatment before being discharged further out at sea. Due to technical and other problems, the treatment plant project has been delayed for years, and as a result the overwhelming proportion of human waste generated in Hong Kong is still simply discharged into the harbour.

By international standards the treatment of effluent in Hong Kong is still fairly minimal and can be fairly described as of 'Third World' standard. Hundreds of tonnes of you-know-what are sieved every day to lessen the visual impact, but the end result is the much same. Victoria Harbour's *E. coli* count has been millions of times beyond internationally acceptable limits for decades, especially in the western sections, and only a complete fool would eat any fish — much less shellfish — that were obtained from Hong Kong's grossly polluted waters.

Cross-harbour swimming races were discontinued for health reasons in the late 1970s, and some thirty years later the water is still too foul for most sensible bathers to contemplate. Some hardy individuals still swim in some parts of the Victoria Harbour, in particular through the Sulphur Channel between Kennedy Town and Green Island, and occasionally bathers can be seen around the rocky Lyemun coast.

Until the early 1960s, most cargo shipped to or through Hong Kong was either unloaded at harbour-side wharves, mostly at North Point or along the western Kowloon waterfront between Tsim Sha Tsui and Sham Shui Po, or off-lightered into smaller vessels from elsewhere in the harbour.

The mid-1960s saw an annually increasing volume of shipping that used containerization, and Hong Kong rapidly adapted to meet the demands of this global trend. The port of Kwai Chung was developed on mostly reclaimed land at that time, and continued to expand until full capacity was reached there in the late 1980s.

A decision was made in 1990 to reclaim the area of harbour between Kwai Chung, Stonecutter's Island and Sham Shui Po as part of the Port-Airport Development Strategy (PADS) and so provide more land for container terminal expansion. Stonecutter's Island was finally joined to mainland Kowloon in 1996, and at the northern end, at least, the island now differs little from the rest of the nearby container port.

Peace Avenue
太平道

Peace Avenue was laid out in the early 1920s as part of a substantial residential development initiated by Francisco (Frank) Paulo Vasconcelos Soares, the prominent local Portuguese businessman also known as the 'Father of Ho Man Tin'.

Peace Avenue was named to commemorate the end of the First World War. Nearby thoroughfares were called Victory and Liberty Avenues to mark the same event. Soares Avenue was named for the developer's family, and neighbouring Emma and Julia Avenues were named after female members of the Soares family. Soares successfully floated the Ho Man Tin residential project against considerable local scepticism. At that time the area was surrounded by paddy fields and was considered too remote from 'urban' Kowloon for many people to want to move there.

As well as being a successful businessman Frank Soares was also a great lover of flowers and plants, and a pillar of the Hong Kong Horticultural Society for

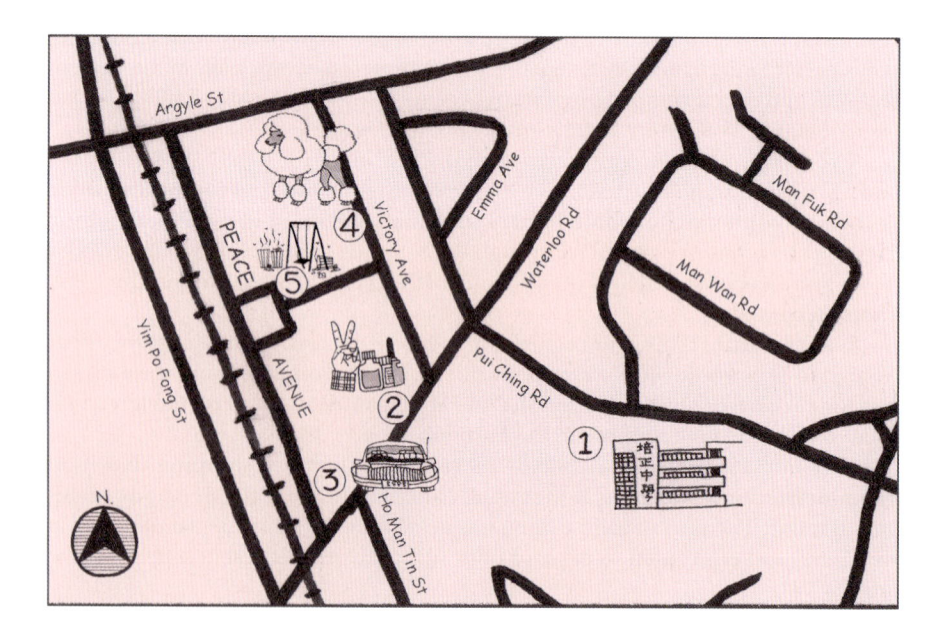

① Pui Ching Middle School   ④ Pet shops
② Victory Dispensary   ⑤ Refuse collection point and playground
③ Car shops

STREETS 104

Peace Avenue

decades. Along with his father Matthias Soares, he did much to introduce new and unusual plants from all over the world into various private gardens. Many of these species are now widely planted all over Hong Kong. From 1937 until the end of the Pacific war, Soares accepted the difficult appointment of honorary consul of Portugal in Hong Kong. He died in 1953 and is buried in the Roman Catholic cemetery at Happy Valley.

In the years before the Pacific War, Ho Man Tin, along with neighbouring Kowloon Tong, was very much a local Portuguese enclave, populated by more middle-class members of this community who wanted houses with gardens, rather than flats in Tsim Sha Tsui.

As in most other parts of Kowloon, the spacious garden villas once found around here have long since been replaced with apartment blocks.

① *Pui Ching Middle School*

One of Hong Kong's most prestigious Chinese-medium schools, *Pui Ching Chung Hok* (Pui Ching Middle School) was first established in Canton in 1889 by a group of Chinese Baptist converts. At that time the school was known as Pui Ching College. In 1908, management of Pui Ching College was given over to the Baptist Association of Kwangtung and Kwangsi.

In 1933 a Hong Kong branch of Pui Ching College was opened at Ho Man Tin by the Anglican bishop of Hong Kong, R. O. Hall. This was followed in 1938 by another branch in Macao. Pui Ching Middle School ceased operations in Hong Kong between 1941 and 1946. According to some sources, the hill behind the

Peace Avenue

school (where the secondary section is now located) was used as an execution ground by the Japanese during their occupation of Hong Kong. For years after the war ended, human remains were periodically dug up there.

In 1950 both the Hong Kong and Macao Pui Ching Schools became independent of their Mainland counterparts, and in 1958, the Hong Kong school came under the general authority of the Hong Kong Baptist Association. In 1978 Pui Ching Middle School became a Grant-in-Aid School while the Pui Ching Primary School and Kindergarten remained independent. It remains one of Kowloon's most sought-after Chinese-medium schools.

2 Victory Dispensary

Victory Dispensary, like hundreds of similar *yeuk poh* (chemists' shops) right across Kowloon, stocks a little of just about everything. Black, potent smelling *chau shui* (Jeyes Fluid) and bars of fragrant B-brand soap are stacked next to rolls of bandages in different sizes, several dozen brands of Chinese cough mixture and rubbing oils, and various sized bottles of washing-up liquid and scouring pads — everything is on open display. Almost anything in terms of medicinal and household products can be found in little shops like these, often at prices substantially lower than charged by the larger chain stores.

No advertising expenses and relatively low overheads is part of the explanation for reasonable prices in shops like this one, and businesses like Victory Dispensary are often family-owned and operated. Another comparative advantage is parallel importation, which allows shops like this one to source the same proprietary item at considerably less than is charged in chain pharmacies. And another big plus: these shops are open at practically all hours, and can be found everywhere.

Peace Avenue

③ Car shops

Peace Avenue is well-known locally as Kowloon's 'Street of the Car Shops' due to the number of motor vehicle establishments found here. Mong Kok has several other 'themed' streets as well, selling goods as diverse as Taiwan goldfish, vehicle parts, nylon-and-lace women's knickers and freshly cut flowers. A number of long-established car dealerships around Ho Man Tin sell the (mostly) Japanese brands so popular with middle-class Hong Kong families, and staff are generally both helpful and knowledgeable.

Despite the ready availability of safe, clean, reliable and reasonably cheap buses, one of the best Mass Transit Railways in the world, and an abundance of affordable taxis, the Hong Kong public's passionate love affair with the private car shows no signs of abatement. Local roads are often badly congested; fuel prices are high by international standards; registration fees are expensive and the cost of both temporary parking and permanent garages are exorbitant.

Yet despite these issues, it seems that practically anyone who can afford a car in Hong Kong — and more than a few who probably cannot — desperately wants to own one! The net result is that with every passing year air pollution benchmarks steadily worsen, and traffic levels all over Hong Kong and Kowloon become more and more untenable. And the official solution to the problem is — you guessed it — simply build more roads!

Peace Avenue

(4) Pet shops

In the early 1990s cute little doggies, or well-bred large ones, became one of Hong Kong's most desirable must-have fashion accessories and status symbols. The trend for pedigree canines has continued to grow annually up to the present day. Never mind the complete inappropriateness of keeping a full sized Rottweiler or Doberman Pinscher in the average poky Hong Kong flat, or the lifelong discomfort endured in a subtropical climate by a Siberian Husky or St Bernard; if a particular breed of dog was the latest must-have accessory, then — like a live, overpriced handbag — of course plenty of local fashion victims simply *had* to have one. Until, of course, the next latest must-have breed came onto the market.

Local demand for cuddly and furry baby animals peaks, unsurprisingly, in the lead-up to Christmas and Valentine's Day. Sadly, and perhaps predictably, Hong Kong's animal shelters report increased numbers of generally young discards being brought in the weeks following these festivals, as new owners realize that successful house training and socialization take up much more time and effort than did the initial purchase, rapidly lose interest, and then abandon the creatures.

More unscrupulously, many Hong Kong pet shops give their animals steroid injections to make them appear 'cuter' (read 'more lively') in the shop environment, and therefore more attractive to a potential customer. When the puppy is bought and taken home, many are found to suffer withdrawal symptoms, and get very ill and often die. Treatment may leave their new owners liable for thousands of dollars in veterinary bills. Like many such trades in Hong Kong, official regulation and enforcement is — at best — minimal, abuses are commonplace, and much of the local population fails to see the problem as 'a problem'. And so it continues.

STREETS

Peace Avenue

Many of the dogs sold in pet shops all over Hong Kong are produced on breeding farms on the Mainland. The 'doggie industry' has caught on massively in China in recent years as well, though some much more expensive breeds imported from Australia, the United Kingdom and the United States are also available at shops around Hong Kong.

5) *Refuse collection point and playground*

Few more glaringly negative examples exists of what so often passes for urban 'planning' in Hong Kong than this one along Peace Avenue. In their wisdom, some presumably intelligent, and no doubt well-paid and handsomely pensioned government officials have seen fit to locate a well-equipped children's playground directly above a malodorous skip.

With the permanent stench of rotting garbage and strong disinfectant hanging in the air — never mind the possible health risks from aerosol-borne germs —is it any wonder that many other playgrounds such as this one remain relatively underpatronized in all seasons by both children, parents and domestic helpers. One glance sadly illustrates yet another example of public resources mindlessly, albeit well-meaningly, wasted with little wider community benefit — an all-too-common occurrence across Hong Kong.

How To Get There

By Bus:	No. 7 from Tsim Sha Tsui 'Star' Ferry to Lok Fu, alight on Waterloo Road.
By KCR:	Mong Kok Station.
By Taxi:	旺角太平道 (*'Wong Kok, Tai Ping Doh'*).

Argyle Street
亞皆老街

One of Mong Kok's busiest thoroughfares, modern Argyle Street contains a few pleasing architectural surprises, such as the Art Moderne-style CLP Power Headquarters, as well as a few lingering reminders of the Japanese Occupation period towards its eastern end.

Densely packed tenement buildings along the western end of Argyle Street eventually give way to spacious garden bungalows and substantial houses along Kadoorie Avenue and Braga Circuit. The 'garden suburb' look that is still a noted feature in this part of Kowloon formerly extended towards Ho Man Tin, but most of those houses located further east have been demolished and replaced by substantial middle-class apartment blocks.

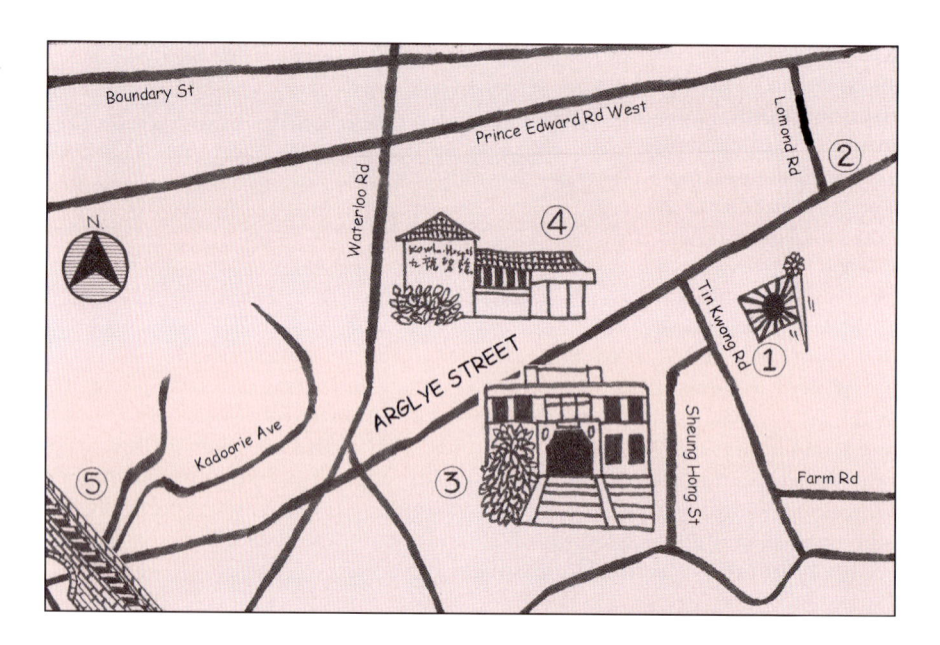

❶ Argyle Street Officer's Prisoner-of-War Camp
❷ Former Commandant's House, Argyle Street Officers' Prisoner-of-War Camp
❸ King George V School (KGV)
❹ Kowloon Hospital
❺ Argyle Street Railway Bridge

STREETS 110

Argyle Street

1) Argyle Street Officer's Prisoner-of-War Camp

Argyle Street Camp was laid out in 1938, along with another temporary prisoner-of-war camp in North Point on Hong Kong Island, to accommodate Nationalist troops who had escaped to the colony from the Japanese and been subsequently interned by the Hong Kong government until repatriation to China could be arranged.

Argyle Street Officer's Prisoner-of-War Camp was set up in April 1942 after three Royal Artillery officers and a Hong Kong Volunteer Defence Corps sergeant successfully escaped from Sham Shui Po Prisoner-of-War Camp. There had been a number of successful escapes from Sham Shui Po in the first few months of imprisonment and the Japanese authorities considered, rightly as it turned out, that there was no possibility of escape from this completely surrounded urban location. A number of Allied officers remained behind with their men at Sham Shui Po. The majority were concentrated at Argyle Street until late in 1944, when the camp was closed and the officers returned to Sham Shui Po.

In the late 1970s, Argyle Street Camp was used to house Vietnamese boat people awaiting resettlement in third countries. The camp closed in the 1980s, as the Vietnamese were gradually resettled overseas or repatriated to Vietnam. All the original buildings, with the exception of a single remaining hut, now used to store maintenance equipment, have since been demolished. Unlike Sham Shui Po, where some small memorials exist, there is currently no plaque or marker anywhere here to indicate that a prisoner-of-war camp once existed on the site.

Argyle Street

(2) Former Commandant's House, Argyle Street Officer's Prisoner-of-War Camp

This sadly decayed Art Deco-style house on the corner of Argyle Street and Forfar Road is almost the last remaining link with the wartime Officers' Prisoner-of-War Camp. Colonel Tokunaga Isao, the Camp Commandant for both Argyle Street and Sham Shui Po Camps, lived in this house for most of the war. Detested by prison camp inmates, who nicknamed him the 'Fat Pig' — among other choice epithets — Tokunaga was tried for war crimes in Hong Kong and eventually executed in 1947.

In addition to its wartime connections, the dilapidated villa is one of the last remaining examples of the substantial garden residences once usual in this part of northern Kowloon. Heavy metal gates, now rusted, are elaborately wrought with a stylized peacock with a spreading tail in the centre.

In the side garden, under a spreading magnolia tree, one can see a Japanese-style stone lantern; whether this garden ornament is a postwar addition or a lingering remnant of the house's wartime role is unknown. How much longer the building will survive is uncertain.

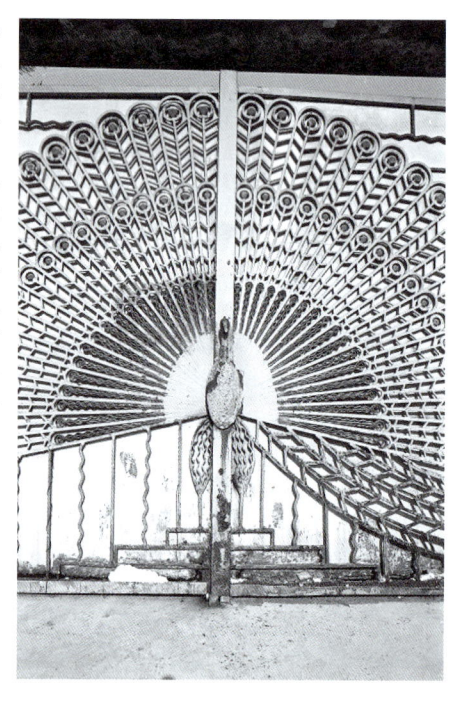

Argyle Street

③ King George V School (KGV)

Located on a hillside at Tin Kwong Road, just off Argyle Street, King George V School is Hong Kong's longest-established English Schools Foundation (ESF) School. Popularly known as 'KGV', the school evolved from the earlier Central British School on Nathan Road in Tsim Sha Tsui, which opened in 1902.

By the early 1930s the school had outgrown these original premises. KGV's main building, which dates from 1936, is one of Kowloon's more substantial pre-war buildings. Designed by prominent local architectural firm Palmer and Turner, KGV has extensive playing fields and numerous mature trees.

Argyle Street Officers' Camp was directly overlooked by the school buildings, which were used for a time during the Japanese occupation as guards' quarters. The pre-war Central British School only catered to British children resident in Hong Kong, but after the war entrance requirements were expanded to include any locally domiciled children who had sufficient English to benefit from instruction in that language. As the years progressed, an increasing number of a number of local Portuguese, White Russians, locally born Indians and Hong Kong Chinese attended the school.

Present-day KGV provides a polyglot snapshot of Hong Kong's surprisingly small, genuinely international community. While some students remain in Hong Kong for tertiary education, the overwhelming majority go overseas for further studies, and remain there after graduation.

④ Kowloon Hospital

Built in 1925, a number of Kowloon Hospital's original buildings still survive, incongruously tucked away among numerous modern additions. These older buildings have numerous attractive Chinese-inspired decorative features, such as curving eaves and an extensive use of Chinese roof tiles. Many other buildings constructed during this period elsewhere in Hong Kong, such as the Kowloon-Canton Railway stations in the New Territories, incorporated similar architectural

Argyle Street

styles; most have since been demolished. Prolonged government occupation would seem to have a relatively benign effect on old buildings in Hong Kong. Continuous use seems to preserve them from the threat of demolition that seems to hang like a miasma over most vintage buildings that remain in private ownership.

Kowloon Hospital, along with Queen Elizabeth and Princess Margaret Hospitals, is one of the busiest government hospitals located within the inner Kowloon urban area, and treats hundreds of in- and out-patients every day of the year.

A number of air-raid tunnels belonged to the Pacific War era are located in the hillside beneath the hospital; some are used to store radioactive materials for use in various medical procedures. More than sixty years after the war ended, dozens of these air-raid tunnels still remain in various corners of the urban area in both Kowloon and Hong Kong Island. Some, such as these at the Kowloon Hospital, have been converted to other uses over the past half century or so; most found elsewhere have been sealed off and abandoned.

5) Argyle Street Railway Bridge

This railway bridge across perennially busy Argyle Street was the site of one of the few active acts of resistance to the Japanese during their occupation of Hong Kong from 1941 to 1945. Most resistance activity within the occupied colony was passive, and consisted mainly of quiet acts of sabotage and defiance; this incident was one of the few exceptions.

In the closing months of the Pacific War, Chinese guerrillas from the Hong Kong–Kowloon Independent Battalion of the East River Brigade mounted a daring raid within the urban area. Popularly known as the East River Column, the Hong Kong–Kowloon Independent Battalion was a branch of a Communist-supported resistance movement which worked closely with the British Army Aid Group (BAAG) elsewhere in southern China.

Argyle Street

During this raid the Argyle Street railway bridge along the Mong Kok section of the Kowloon–Canton Railway line was clandestinely mined and destroyed. While the bridge's destruction did little to seriously disrupt the Japanese war effort and the damage was soon repaired, the guerrilla group's boldness was nevertheless a considerable morale booster to residents of the occupied city during the closing stages of the war.

It has been claimed in post-handover Hong Kong, mostly to further a political agenda, that the wartime role of Chinese guerrillas was not properly recognized in peacetime by the British authorities. Well-documented facts tell a different story; many of the East River Column members were given cash grants and certificates of recognition from the Hong Kong government.

Major Raymond Wong, one of the East River Column's senior leaders and a pre-war student at Queen's College on Hong Kong Island, was awarded a military MBE as a result of his services. He subsequently became an aide to Premier Zhou Enlai. Wong was killed in the 'Kashmir Princess' plane crash in 1955, when Nationalist agents planted a bomb on an Air India plane during its transit through Hong Kong en route to the Afro-Asian Conference in Bandung.

A substantial memorial to the East River guerrillas can be seen at Pak Tam Chung near Sai Kung in the eastern New Territories; this monument is far larger than any other war memorial in Hong Kong.

How To Get There

By Bus:	No. 2, 6, 6A from 'Star' Ferry.
By MTR:	Mong Kok Station.
By KCR:	Mong Kok Station.
By Taxi:	旺角亞皆老街 (*Wong Kok, Ar Gaai Loh Gaai*).

Kadoorie Avenue
嘉道理道

A very affluent stretch of hillside garden suburb located just off Argyle Street, Kadoorie Avenue is perhaps one of Mong Kok's more unusual, unexpected sights. Large houses set in substantial gardens behind high walls seem to be — and are — a world away from the general squalor, gross overcrowding, hawker stalls and backstreet life that — at first glance — dominate the rest of Mong Kok only a few blocks away.

One of Hong Kong's most immediately recognized non-Chinese names is that of the Kadoorie family, a Sephardic Jewish family who settled in Shanghai in the nineteenth century and subsequently established themselves in Hong Kong. The Jewish community that evolved on the China Coast in this period were mostly Sephardic Jews from Baghdad. Like Middle Eastern genies, they embodied fabulous wealth and, for some of them at least, a larger-than-life, almost mythical status.

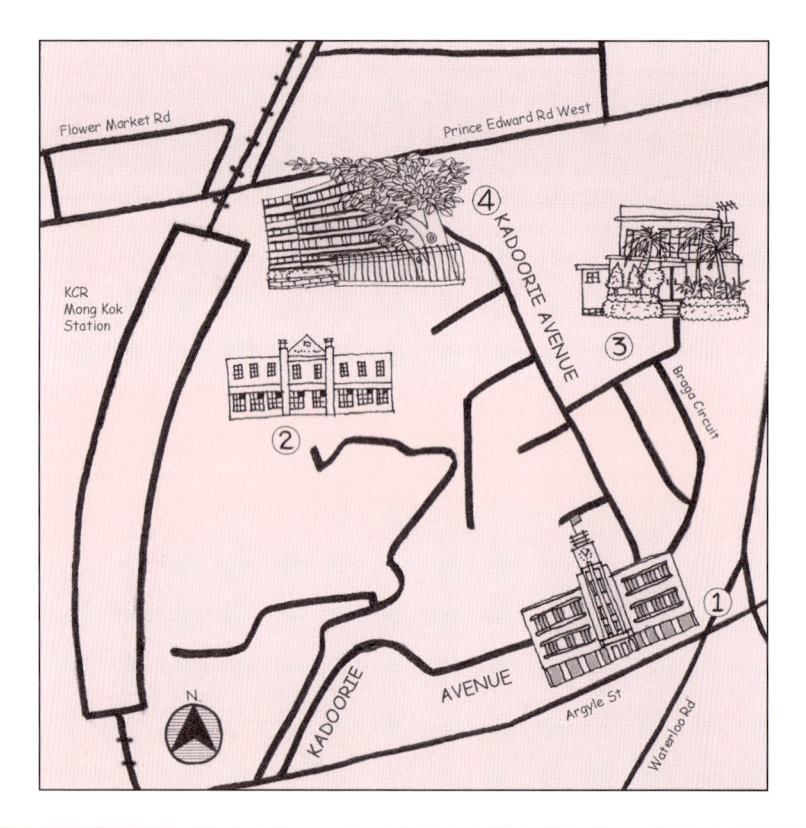

❶ CLP Power Headquarters
❷ Diocesan Boys' School
❸ Houses with gardens
❹ Grand Court

STREETS

Kadoorie Avenue

While a few once influential Sephardic Jewish families, like that of the opium-trading Sassoon clan, have long since vanished from the local scene, various others, like the Kadoories still remain. Now forgotten names such as Abraham, Ezra, Hardoon, Gubbay and Judah were once very well-known in Hong Kong. If overall length of residence in Hong Kong is taken into consideration, the Sephardic Jews and their families, like the Eurasian and Portuguese communities, have considerably *more* claim to be truly local people than do most present-day Chinese residents of Hong Kong.

Braga Circuit, an attractive crescent that runs off Kadoorie Avenue, is named for a once-prominent local Portuguese family. In the late 1920s José Pedro Braga became the first local Portuguese appointed to the Legislative Council, while his son José Maria (Jack) Braga was an enthusiastic local historian who, in a seminal series of publications, such as the wonderfully detailed *China Landfall*, did much to further understanding of the Portuguese presence in China and the Far East.

Kadoorie Avenue has long been one of Hong Kong's most prestigious places to live, except in the minds of some suburban snobs, who disdain any other address than a more prestigious-sounding Hong Kong Island one. This highly affluent enclave's presence right in the middle of Mong Kok says a lot for the levels of personal safety enjoyed in Hong Kong. Access to this obviously very wealthy neighbourhood is not achieved via constantly re-encrypted smart cards or under the watchful eye of armed security guards — as it certainly would be in Shanghai, Jakarta, Manila and many other Asian cities — but simply by walking up the hill from the main road. Close up though, most houses are very well fortified, and bristle with security cameras, intercoms and other electronic apparatus.

① *CLP Power Headquarters*

Kadoorie Avenue

Partially obscured by a flyover, this attractive old building was built in 1940 and is one of the few remaining high quality examples of Art Deco–Art Moderne architecture still standing in Hong Kong. With an annual reported average company profit running into many millions of Hong Kong dollars in recent years, it is to be sincerely hoped that the power company has no need, or desire, to redevelop this attractive building at any point in the future.

China Light and Power Co. Ltd, better known today by the oddly repetitive acronym CLP Power ('China Light and Power Power'), holds the monopoly, under a Scheme of Control agreed with the Hong Kong government in 1958, for electricity generation and distribution in Kowloon, the New Territories mainland and all of the outlying islands except Lamma.

CLP Power was initially established, and is still largely owned, by companies controlled by the Kadoorie family, who also held substantial interests in hotels, 'public' utilities and other businesses in pre-Communist Shanghai.

The company's first electricity generating plant in Kowloon was built in Tsim Sha Tsui, near the harbour end of Chatham Road, in 1903. In the pre-war era China Light and Power built a substantial new power plant at Hok Un, in the developing light industrial area of Hung Hom near the Kowloon Docks. This large facility later closed and another replacement plant was built in Tsing Yi.

This facility was superseded by the present massive power station in Black Point, just below Castle Peak in the northwest New Territories. The company also have a substantial holding in a French-built nuclear generating facility in China, which opened in 1994. The Daya Bay facility is located about fifty miles, as the wind blows, from the Mainland's frontier with the New Territories.

(2) Diocesan Boys' School

Kadoorie Avenue

Established in the days when open land was relatively plentiful in Kowloon and the local population much smaller than it is today, the Diocesan Boys' School has extensive grounds, numerous mature trees and several playing fields — a welcome reminder of the past and a rarity in most other parts of urban Hong Kong.

The Diocesan Boys' and Girls' Schools were initially established to provide an education for the numerous Eurasian children that began to appear on the streets of Hong Kong in the 1850s. Largely unrecognized and uncared for by their putative European fathers, they were generally unwelcome in either Chinese or European communities and grew up in an uncertain, precarious world, with all too often a life of virtual prostitution for the daughters and low-level clerical positions for the sons as the only adult career option.

Early Governor Sir John Bowring pungently if accurately described Hong Kong's early Eurasians as forming 'a potentially dangerous element ripening out of the dunghill of neglect'. The Anglican Church intervened, and the Diocesan schools, then also combined with orphanages, were set up.

Nineteenth and early twentieth-century donor lists for this and other local educational institutions reveal that quite a few then prominent businessmen were regular subscribers to school funds; whether the men's motivation was genuine charity or a sense of guilt — or both — is of course hard to determine from this point in time. The school's chapel has a memorial to various staff and students of Diocesan Boys' School who lost their lives during the Pacific War; many served as members of the Hong Kong Volunteer Defence Corps.

Popularly known as DBS, the Diocesan Boys' School has enjoyed a high academic reputation ever since it was established. The Eurasian presence in the school these days is tiny by comparison with the past, and as in other elite local schools, the overwhelming majority of contemporary students are Hong Kong Chinese.

③ Houses with gardens

Kadoorie Avenue

And now to the inevitable Hong Kong question: What would it cost to actually *live* somewhere along here? The answer to that one — as elsewhere — is that if you genuinely need to ask, then you would probably be better off looking elsewhere! A month's rental here can easily cover the better part of a year's annual household income for many average Hong Kong families.

A brief walk along Kadoorie Avenue really does make one feel like a voyeur to a very different world that exists five hundred metres away in any direction. Birds twitter in the trees that line the roadside or in the aviaries that grace many individual gardens; luxuriantly trailing and brilliantly coloured creepers spill over the fences, and most verandahs are bright with hanging baskets full of flowers or ferns. It all somehow seems a *very* long way from the rest of Mong Kok, just a short distance down the hillside behind.

(4) Grand Court

If any apartment building in Kowloon symbolizes just how easy it is to put up an attractive block of flats — which then begs the question why so many truly ugly apartment complexes get built in Hong Kong — it must surely be this one. In spite of its conceited name, Grand Court manages to be as quietly elegant as the rest of Kadoorie Avenue without, like so many other blocks elsewhere in Hong Kong, being garish and flashy-pretentious as well as shoddily built and finished.

Built in the 1930s, flats at Grand Court have large open verandahs that can be used for outdoor living — not poky balconies fit only for flinging oneself off when

Kadoorie Avenue

life in the overcrowded city all gets too much to bear. The roadsides along Kadoorie Avenue were sensibly planted with trees that eventually grew into today's pleasant shady specimens. Unlike most street-side plantings elsewhere in Hong Kong, considerable thought and care were clearly given to Kadoorie Avenue in the early stages, and the long-term results are obvious and attractive.

How To Get There

By Bus:	No. 1 from Chuk Yuen to 'Star' Ferry; No. 1A from Sau Mau Ping to Tsim Sha Tsui 'Star' Ferry; No. 27 from Shun Tin to Mong Kok (all alight on Prince Edward Road); No. 3C from China–Hong Kong Ferry to Tsz Wan Shan; No. 27 from Mong Kok to Shun Tin; No. 9 from Tsim Sha Tsui 'Star' Ferry to Ping Shek; No. 24 from Mong Kok to Kai Yip (all alight on Argyle Street).
By MTR:	Mong Kok Station, take exit for Argyle Street.
By KCR:	Mong Kok Station, take exit for Argyle Street.
By Taxi:	旺角嘉道理道 ('Wong Kok, Gah Dor Lei Doh').

Prince Edward Road West
太子道西

The area that extends along Prince Edward Road West was opened up to residential development in the early 1920s, at the same time when the neighbouring Kowloon Tong and Ho Man Tin areas were developed as garden suburbs. Mong Kok village, the original settlement in the area, was only finally cleared for redevelopment in the early 1920s, which made it one of the last pre-British-era villages on the Kowloon peninsula to be removed.

The spacious houses and low-rise apartment blocks that once stood along here were built to include large tree-shaded gardens. Cars and buses were a relative scarcity until the postwar era, and a trip across the harbour to Hong Kong in those years was, paradoxically, both a major excursion for many local residents and an everyday commuter journey to some — much as it still remains today.

Prince Edward Road West is one of northern Kowloon's busier main thoroughfares these days, choked with heavy goods trucks and double-decker buses at all hours. Numerous densely crowded side streets, such as the locally renowned 'Lady's Market' on Fa Yuen Street, offer much of local colour and interest, as well as some of Kowloon's best shopping bargains.

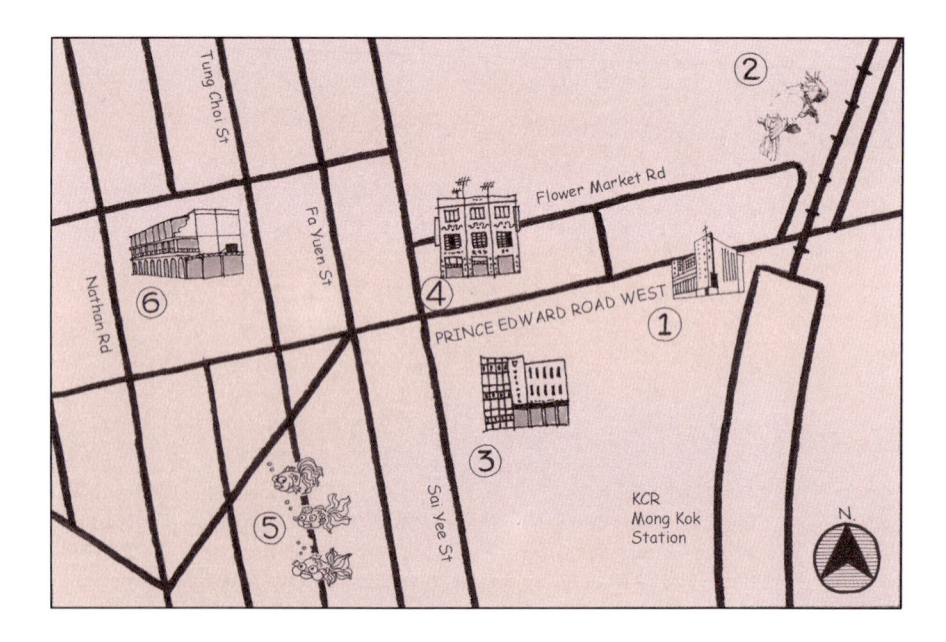

❶ Cheung Lo Church
❷ Yuen Po Street Bird Garden
❸ Queen Elizabeth School
❹ Old shop houses
❺ Goldfish shops (Tung Choi Street)
❻ Mong Kok Police Station

Prince Edward Road West

The eastern end of Prince Edward Road leads on towards the densely packed Kowloon City tenement areas which surround the old Kai Tak Airport complex. Like many other parts of contemporary Kowloon, this area will certainly change dramatically in coming years due to drastic urban renewal plans brought about by the abolition of airport-related height restrictions, and the process of transformation is already under way.

1 Cheung Lo Church

The Cheung Lo Church is a branch of the Church of Christ in China, and has been in operation in northern Kowloon since 1925. Surprising numbers of churches of various Christian denominations operate in various parts of Kowloon. While many, such as this one, have long-established premises, quite a number also operate out of somewhat obscure apartment-sized units in high-rise commercial buildings.

Some offer services in various languages, including English and Tagalog; for the most part, however, churches in this part of Mong Kok cater to Hong Kong's Cantonese-speaking majority, and the Cheung Lo Church is no exception to this general trend.

STREETS

Prince Edward Road West

② Yuen Po Street Bird Garden

This attractive garden was established when the well-known, rather grubby 'Bird Street' just off Argyle Street was closed down and the surrounding buildings redeveloped in the early 1990s. Many of the vendors of birds, cages, seeds, bugs and grasshoppers were helped to move here by the Hong Kong government. While some enthusiasts may decry the consequent loss of such 'atmosphere' as the old site had, the purpose-built surroundings here, shaded by heavily fragrant *kwai faa* (*Osmanthus fragrans*) trees, are much more pleasant for both humans and birds. All sorts of avian food items, such as American sunflower seeds, millet and sorghum can be purchased in any quantity necessary. General surroundings are much cleaner than in the old location, and the risk of insanitation-caused disease, both for the birds and the people who care for them, has been greatly reduced.

Many of the tropical birds for sale here (especially the Australian cockatoos, rosellas and galahs, various Indonesian or South American parrot varieties, such as vividly coloured Eclectus parrots and different species of Macaws and other Amazon birds) are victims of the rampant illegal trapping and smuggling trade. Most of those birds smuggled into Hong Kong have been jammed into cardboard tubes for over twenty-four hours in transit. As a direct result, a high proportion — one in four — die before they eventually reach their destination. And despite this well-known, disgraceful fact, the Mong Kok Bird Market is *still* featured on official tourist literature as one of Hong Kong's must-see destinations.

More responsible dealers source their birds from established breeders in the United States, the Philippines and South Africa; as these captive-bred birds have been hand-reared since they were chicks, they are much tamer than wild-caught birds, and are also far less susceptible to avian diseases. Most, but by no means all, of the cockatoos, macaws and parrots on sale in Hong Kong are now reared in this way.

Prince Edward Road West

(3) Queen Elizabeth School

Officially opened in 1954 and named after the then recently crowned sovereign, Queen Elizabeth School was the first government-run co-educational school in Hong Kong. Later in the same year, a scheme was initiated through which five scholarships per year were awarded to bright and needy pupils so that they might attend the school.

Until Queen Elizabeth School opened, all other government schools in Hong Kong had been single sex only, though a few grant-in-aid schools, such as St Paul's Co-Educational College on Hong Kong Island, had admitted both girls and boys before then. When first attempted, the co-education experiment was considered quite radical for what was then (and in many respects still remains) a very conservative Chinese society. After the success of this and other pioneer establishments, co-educational schools are now the norm right across Hong Kong.

(4) Old shop houses

Between the wars, Prince Edward Road and the surrounding roads were a pleasant area of three and four-storied shop houses and apartment blocks. A few examples still remain here and there among more recent developments. These now face out on an ever busy urban thoroughfare and a towering flyover, instead of a quiet suburban road.

Prince Edward Road West

In the 1930s a number of similar residential buildings in northern Kowloon were built by the Franco-Belgian construction firm Credit Foncierre d'Extreme Orient. This development company was also responsible for numerous ecclesiastical buildings in Hong Kong in the interwar years, such as Stanley's Carmelite Convent, Causeway Bay's St Mary's Anglican Church and The Little Sisters of the Poor at Ngau Chi Wan. Belfran Road, located just off Prince Edward Road, was the site of one of the firm's major residential developments; the name is an abbreviated acronym for Belgium and France.

5 Goldfish shops (Tung Choi Street)

Tung Choi Street, a lengthy thoroughfare which runs between Prince Edward Road and Argyle Street, is known throughout Kowloon as Gum Yue Gaai — the 'Street of the Gold Fish'. Dozens of shops sell every conceivable variety of *gum yue* (goldfish). These range in price from small fish which cost a couple of dollars each to white-and-gold *koi* (Japanese carp), on to flamboyant *sze jee tau* (lion-headed) specimens with trailing gossamer-like tails, which can sell for hundreds of dollars apiece.

Goldfish have been prized by the Chinese for hundreds if not thousands of years. The average space-constrained Hong Kong flat means that for many people, fish are often the

Prince Edward Road West

only really viable pets. Watching fish swim about an aquarium is considered relaxing by many Chinese, who also believe that a strategically placed fish tank can do wonders for a room's *fung shui*, and consequently the prosperity and general well-being of those who frequent it.

As well as freshwater species, saltwater aquariums along Tung Choi Street sell various varieties of colourful tropical fish. Much like many of the birds on sale at nearby Yuen Po Bird Garden, most of the species are obtained from Southeast Asia, the Indian Ocean and the Western Pacific. Tropical reefs there continue to be depleted at an alarming rate due to massive overfishing and uncontrolled trapping for the pet trade.

Along with goldfish, fish tanks and aquariums, Tung Choi Street is also locally well-known its large number of bicycle shops. Anything that the cycling enthusiast could possibly want or need — and quite a few items that seemingly fit into neither category — can be easily obtained here.

6 Mong Kok Police Station

Mong Kok Police Station was extensively rebuilt in 1960s and now comprises mostly new buildings. The station previously housed the Hong Kong Police Force's Kowloon headquarters. The first Mong Kok Police Station, constructed early in the twentieth century, stood on the corner of Nathan and Mong Kok Roads, at which time the present station site was used by the Diocesan Boys' School.

Prince Edward Road West

After the Diocesan Boys' School moved from there to its present extensive site off Argyle Street, this location was used for a while as the Police Training School (now situated at Wong Chuk Hang, near Aberdeen on Hong Kong Island).

Part of the old Mong Kok Police Station building, completed in 1925, still remains within the station compound. This complex comprises an attractive colonnaded structure with granite columns and the deep shady verandahs typical of Hong Kong's pre-air-conditioned era. This building was used during the Japanese occupation for the training of local Chinese and Formosan collaborators and informants by the Japanese Kempeitai (secret police); some of these elderly individuals still live on in Hong Kong.

How To Get There

By Bus:	No. 2, 6, 6A, 203 from 'Star' Ferry.
By MTR:	Prince Edward Station.
By KCR:	Mong Kok Station.
By Taxi:	旺角太子道 (*Wong Kok, Tai Jee Dou*).

Boundary Street
界限街

Boundary Street marks what until 1997 was, at least in purely legal terms, one of the strangest international frontiers in the world. This busy road, which passes right through the middle of what is now one of the world's most densely crowded places, marked the exact border between British Kowloon, ceded 'in perpetuity' to Great Britain in 1860 by one of the provisions of the Treaty of Tientsin, and the New Territories, leased to Great Britain from China in 1898 for ninety-nine years under the Convention of Peking.

An arbitrary line was drawn on a map across the northern section of Kowloon peninsula in 1860, following the Second Anglo-Chinese War, and a dividing fence was subsequently erected. The boundary between 'British Kowloon' and what became known as 'New Kowloon' (in effect modern Sham Shui Po and Lai Chi Kok) was eventually marked by a road; hence the name, Boundary Street.

As Kowloon gradually expanded towards the end of the nineteenth century the border distinction gradually eroded, and with the construction of the Kowloon-Canton Railway in the 1910s, and substantial housing development in Kowloon Tong in the 1920s, the actual territorial border as defined by Boundary Street became meaningless to all except diplomats and political agitators of various kinds.

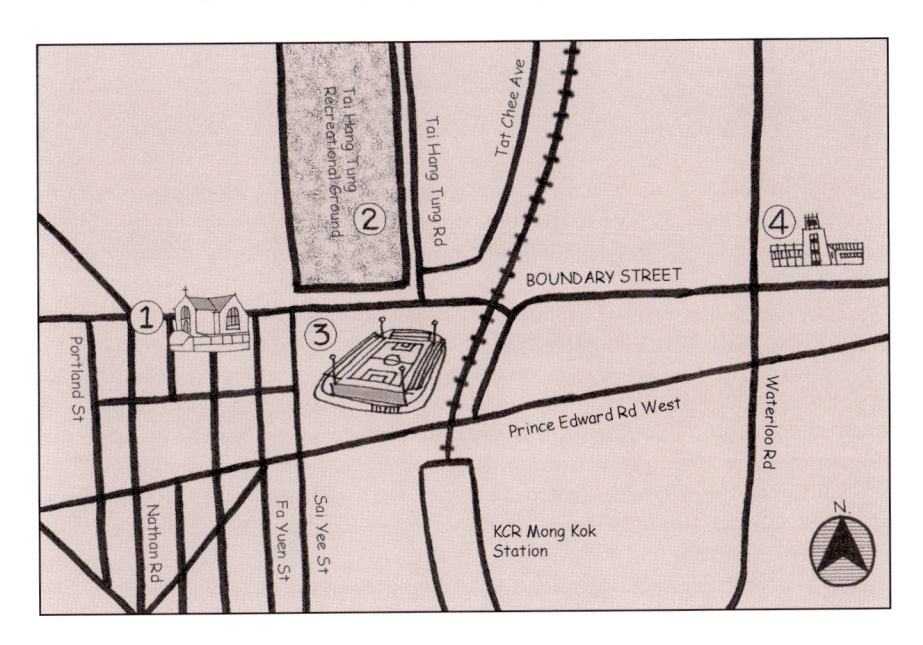

❶ Kowloon Church of Seventh-Day Adventists
❷ Tai Hang Tung Recreation Ground
❸ Mong Kok Stadium
❹ Maryknoll Convent School

Boundary Street

As the colony's handover to China drew closer, this area became a minor tourist draw for people fascinated by quirks of history and geography such as this one. With Hong Kong's return to China in 1997, the only physical reminder of Kowloon's mixed status during the British era is the name of the road itself.

(1) Kowloon Church of Seventh-Day Adventists

The granite-faced Church of Seventh-Day Adventists building looks considerably older than it actually is. The foundation stone was only laid in 1950, yet the church already appears to be one of the more venerable buildings still standing along Boundary Street.

Like many other churches elsewhere in Hong Kong, the Kowloon Church of Seventh-Day Adventists also has a school attached to it. The Kowloon Sam Yuk Secondary School, like the adjacent church, was first established here in 1950. *Sam Yuk* refers to three categories of education, known as *ling-tsi-tai*. *Ling* means spiritual education; *tsi*, refers to the education of the intellect, and *tai* incorporates the physical dimension to learning. *Mens sana in corpore sano*, in other words.

Christian missionaries in China established schools wherever they built churches. Church-funded educational facilities, which catered to those who might never have otherwise had the opportunity to go to school at all, have a very closely linked history in Hong Kong and elsewhere in China since the 1840s.

As with the free charitable kitchens attached to churches that kept many families from starvation, many poorer Chinese parents sent their children to the free mission schools and accepted, or at least tolerated, the religious component that came along with it. Most considered that this was simply part of the price to be paid, one way or another, if their children were to have the chance of any education at all.

Boundary Street

② *Tai Hang Tung Recreation Ground*

Like affluent residential pockets, large recreation grounds are one of Mong Kok's apparent contradictions. The densely crowded, mixed residential-commercial areas in the district nevertheless have a choice of large parks and playing fields quite close by. These days Tai Hang Tung Recreation Ground is a large and very popular complex of playing fields, but in the late 1940s and early 1950s the area was *anything* but a place for pleasure or relaxation.

One of Kowloon's largest postwar squatter settlements extended from Tai Hang Tung to Shek Kip Mei, a sprawling urban emergency zone where tens of thousands of refugee arrivals from China lived in makeshift shanties, in constant danger of typhoons, and fires. In 1952 a massive fire broke out at Tai Hang Tung, which rendered tens of thousands homeless in a matter of hours.

Relief was quickly provided by both private and government agencies, but it was only after a further devastating fire in neighbouring Shek Kip Mei, on Christmas Day 1953, that a public resettlement housing programme became official Hong Kong government policy. By the end of the following decade, over a third of Hong Kong's population lived in early versions of public housing provided by either the government or the Hong Kong Housing Society, or were waiting to move to such accommodation when it was completed.

After the Tai Hang Tung squatter area was cleared for resettlement, part of the area would become public recreational space, in what was, even in the mid-1950s, a very densely populated part of Kowloon. So it remains today, even as the memory of squatter settlements, devastating fires and general hardship gradually fades from memory in contemporary Hong Kong.

Boundary Street

③ Mong Kok Stadium

Hong Kong Chinese have a well-deserved reputation for extreme studiousness at school, with very little opportunity for sports and games during most childhoods. When they finally reach adulthood, most then work very long hours and lead quite sedentary lives. Nevertheless, in recent years there has been a keen and growing interest in sports in Hong Kong, at least from a spectator's perspective. In particular, football has experienced enormous popularity. All this interest was greatly aided by shrewd soccer-related merchandising, such as T-shirts, jackets and other clothing items, and saturation coverage of international sporting events on local terrestrial and cable television channels. In 2002, after some controversy, soccer betting was finally legalized in Hong Kong.

Mong Kok Stadium hosts numerous sporting matches and unlike the controversy-plagued Hong Kong Stadium in Causeway Bay, this venue is very convenient and is untroubled by noise complaints from surrounding apartment blocks. On any fine weekend this facility is packed with people out having a good time which, after all, is what the complex was designed to facilitate in the first place.

④ Maryknoll Convent School

Maryknoll Convent School opened in 1925 and moved into the present substantial premises on the corner of Boundary Street and Waterloo Road in 1936. This

Boundary Street

attractive, two-storied red-brick building, with leaded-light windows and a low tower, was a prominent northern Kowloon landmark before the Pacific War started. For many years, most of the teachers were American nuns from the Roman Catholic Maryknoll Order.

The low slopes which lead up to the school buildings are thickly planted with vividly coloured azaleas, one of the few non-native plants that seem to grow really well in Hong Kong's shallow, nutrient-poor soils. The massed red, pink, white and purple blooms are quite spectacular and many people actually come to the school from other parts of Hong Kong to view them, somewhat like the annual procession that makes its way into the grounds of Government House at about the same time.

With consistently high academic standards, Maryknoll Convent School remains one of the most respected girls' schools in Kowloon. As with other elite local schools, many 'Old Girls' occupy numerous senior positions in government and in community affairs. The primary section is located in the old building and now has over 1,100 students. The secondary section is located in newer premises nearby, at 5 Ho Tung Road.

How To Get There

By Bus:	No. 7 from Tsim Sha Tsui 'Star' Ferry.
By MTR:	Prince Edward Station.
By Taxi:	旺角界限街 (*Wong Kok, Gaai Haan Gaai*').

New Kowloon

To most people in Hong Kong, 'Kowloon-side' means — at least in a geographical sense — the extensive urban sprawl that extends around the shores of Kowloon Bay from Tsim Sha Tsui towards Lei Yue Mun, and northwards to Tsuen Wan. However, the area now generally known as 'Kowloon' was not always defined like that, and some explanations from the past are necessary to help understand how the region has changed and evolved over the last century and a half.

Those segments of the Kowloon peninsula that had remained in Chinese-administered territory after 1860 gradually evolved into a rough-and-ready, extrajudicial extension of the rapidly developing town below the land border. By the 1880s, this area, which comprised much of present-day Tai Kok Tsui, Sham Shui Po, Cheung Sha Wan and Lai Chi Kok, as well as some southern parts of Kowloon Tong, had become known as 'New Kowloon'. The term was used to help distinguish this area both geographically and administratively from 'British Kowloon', south of Boundary Street, when increased development on both sides blurred the distinctions with every year that passed.

Until the lease of the New Territories in 1898 (within which all these areas officially lie), 'New Kowloon' was a haven for illicit businesses and other illegal activities, and a notorious haunt of smugglers on their way to and from the interior of China. Present-day location names in the Kowloon hills — Smuggler's Ridge and Customs Pass — give some indication both of these activities, and attempts at their prevention and suppression.

Many of the 'illicit' activities that took place in 'New Kowloon', such as untaxed or 'sly' grog shops, gambling saloons, opium divans and brothels, operated legitimately under licence on Hong Kong Island and in British Kowloon. In the absence of most other forms of recurrent official revenue in the Crown Colony, registration and licence fees for these enterprises, along with land sales, were one of the only significant sources of government income. It was therefore in the administration's interest to ensure that non-revenue generating forms of these activities were discouraged whenever possible.

In these years press criticism of vice activities just across the harbour was frequent and sustained. As is often the case in Hong Kong, the ultimate cause for these public complaints was as much the loss of potential profit by powerful vested interests as any genuine moral or ethical issue. During this period, Hong Kong Island-owned and operated syndicates even operated launch services across the harbour to vice establishments that they owned in 'New Kowloon', which drew business away from established, 'legitimate' (that is, government-licensed), competitors.

Tai Kok Tsui

In many respects Tai Kok Tsui ('Big Pointed Promontory'), the area closest to the pre-1898 land frontier, epitomizes urban Kowloon at its rawest. This, in turn, makes

• Anchor Street	• Tai Po Road
• Yu Chau Street	• Cheung Sha Wan Road
• Apliu Street	• Lai Chi Kok Road
• Yen Chow Street	

it a very interesting place to wander about. Around here, the sheer contrast between Kowloon's everyday urban realities and the glamour, glitz and hype associated with popular images of 'Asia's World City' could not possibly be more stark.

Like most parts of Kowloon, Tai Kok Tsui has undergone considerable change and redevelopment in recent decades. Amble about here and you will find no visual references to what was, for many years, one of Hong Kong's most important industries — shipbuilding and repairing. Along with other dockyard facilities at Hung Hom and Quarry Bay, the Cosmopolitan Docks at Tai Kok Tsui was a mainstay of the local economy and vitally important for Hong Kong's import-export trade.

Cosmopolitan Docks was inaugurated by a consortium of Eurasian and Hong Kong Chinese businessmen, who chose the name in the hope that the dockyard's clients would include 'the ships of all nations'. The venture was a considerable success until the Pacific War broke out when Hong Kong's volume of shipping drastically declined. The Cosmopolitan Docks and surrounding area was badly damaged by American bombing raids in early 1945, and eventually closed down in the late 1950s. A variety of commercial and residential buildings were built on the site, and no built reminders of the dockyard era still remains in modern Tai Kok Tsui.

Tai Kok Tsui also shows a few unexpected elements of the not-so-distant past as well, in particular the lingering Vietnamese migrant presence in some corners. The Vietnamese flavour is a hangover from the days when Hong Kong was a way station for thousands of 'boat people' from Indochina on their own 'Journey to the West'.

Another well-known local 'attraction' in Tai Kok Tsui, as in Yau Ma Tei further south, are the large numbers of 'barbershops', which offer lady 'stylists' in just about every race, creed, colour and price range one could possibly think of. The sheer variety alone is enough to make your hair curl!

Since the completion of the West Kowloon reclamation project in the late 1990s, Tai Kok Tsui and the surrounding areas have enjoyed a renaissance, and a number of new hotels and shopping complexes clustered around the Olympic MTR station have opened. It seems likely that further improvement of decaying streetscapes in this area will occur as the work of the Urban Renewal Authority steadily gathers pace.

Sham Shui Po

Just to the north of Tai Kok Tsui, Sham Shui Po ('Deep Water Pier') greatly expanded in the years immediately after the First World War from its pre-British-era village origins. A number of light industries set up in the area in the 1920s, which greatly expanded in the 1930s. Many of these industries were originally branches of Chinese industry that moved to the stability of Hong Kong during the warlord-wracked early Republican period (1912–27). Unlike in the postwar

New Kowloon

era, when Shanghainese commercial interests tended to dominate Hong Kong's industrial development and expansion, the overwhelming majority of these earlier enterprises utilized Cantonese capital and expertise, as well as labour.

In the mid-1920s a large-scale reclamation project was undertaken by private enterprise, which was subsequently taken over by the military for barracks. An ambitious scheme to link Tsim Sha Tsui with Sham Shui Po by a tramway system, similar to that which operated successfully along the northern coast of Hong Kong Island was proposed at this time, but plans faltered in the late 1920s and eventually came to nothing.

In addition to its burgeoning light industrial sector, Sham Shui Po life had a distinctive military element during the interwar years and, like Tsim Sha Tsui and Wan Chai, numerous businesses such as bars, cafés and tailors catered to the Garrison's varied needs and wants. Sham Shui Po Camp remained on the Hong Kong government defence estate until the 1970s, and was only completely closed, its buildings demolished and the site redeveloped, in the late 1980s.

Cheung Sha Wan and Lai Chi Kok

As the name implies, Cheung Sha Wan ('Long Sandy Bay') was once a series of long sandy beaches and isolated hamlets that stretched north towards Tsuen Wan. Along with the other beaches located further out along Castle Peak Road, Cheung Sha Wan was a popular sea-bathing spot for residents of urban Kowloon. Sham Shui Po's industrial areas gradually expanded north towards the Cheung Sha Wan area which, in the 1920s, still had most of its beaches. By the 1950s Cheung Sha Wan had become well-known for its shipyards; many pleasure cruisers, as well as fishing junks and larger sampans, were built on commercial slipways here. All these businesses have long since been removed.

Towards Lai Chi Kok ('Lychee Point'), the Standard Vacuum Oil Company had a major petroleum storage facility in the pre-war years. Standard Vacuum Oil had the well-known advertising slogan 'Oil for the Lamps of China', and dealt mainly in kerosene. The petroleum depot was one of the targets of extensive American bombing raids over Hong Kong in 1944 and 1945. Standard Vacuum Oil Company's long vanished presence at Lai Chi Kok lingers in the name of Hong Kong's earliest major middle-class residential estates, Mei Foo Sun Chuen, which was built on the depot site in the late 1960s.

In the postwar era, and for some decades afterwards, Lai Chi Kok was very well-known locally for its amusement park. Lai Yuen had all manner of exciting rides, merry-go-rounds, Ferris wheels, dodgem cars, and a rather sad and pathetic private zoo.

By the early 1990s Lai Yuen was a decaying shadow of its former self, and in 1997–98 the amusement park closed down. When the closure was announced, Lai Yuen enjoyed a short burst of popularity from large numbers of nostalgia

New Kowloon

seekers. This newfound public interest nevertheless failed to save it from redevelopment. Two generations of Hong Kong people remember the place fondly, as a reminder of the days before Ocean Park, Disneyland, mega shopping malls, multiplex cinemas and other more sophisticated forms of entertainment took its place.

By the early 1950s, ramshackle squatter settlements straggled northwards beyond Lai Chi Kok through the dingy factory estates of Kwai Chung, and on towards Tsuen Wan. In these years this stretch of coastline was still deeply indented and dominated by Gin Drinker's Bay. An extensive, ultimately useless defence line was built in 1938 across the Kowloon hills from Gin Drinker's Bay to Port Shelter. It became popularly known as the 'Gin Drinker's Line' after the bay located just below the major defensive emplacements. The line was briefly fought over in 1941, and thereafter abandoned.

As the name would imply, Gin Drinker's Bay was a popular rendezvous point for launch parties and picnics in the pre-war era. Tellingly, the bay was also marked as Laap Saap Wan ('Rubbish Bay') on various older maps; presumably the scraps, empties and other detritus from those junk parties were flung straight over the side of the boat into the bay, much as still happens elsewhere every weekend in contemporary Hong Kong. Gin Drinker's Bay and the surrounding coastline was progressively reclaimed for factory estates in the 1950s and 1960s. Tsing Chau (Pillar Island), the rocky island at the entrance to the bay, is now a hill, and little more than an additional pylon for the bridge across to Tsing Yi.

By the early 1970s, Kowloon's relentless northward expansion had completely subsumed most of what little open country still remained around the hillside fringes at Lai Chi Kok and further out towards Kwai Chung. Small, isolated fragments of a few original coastal Kowloon villages still remain here and there, marooned in among the expansive reclamation work, hillside tower blocks, railway lines and thundering expressways.

Anchor Street
晏架街

For decades the Tai Kok Tsui waterfront, at the northern end of the Yau Ma Tei typhoon shelter, was dominated by the Cosmopolitan Docks. Along with the Cosmopolitan Housing Estate and the recently built, four-star Cosmopolitan Hotel, Anchor Street's name itself is just about the only surviving oblique reference to the vanished dockyards.

Despite its reputation as a rough-edged part of Kowloon, Tai Kok Tsui is completely safe for the average visitor to wander around, although some care should be taken late at night. Reclamation work completed in the 1990s as part of the Airport Core Projects has moved the waterfront several hundred metres to the west, and the older parts of Tai Kok Tsui are now located a long way inland.

Tai Kok Tsui and the surrounding areas are now separated from the western harbour by two railway lines, several expressways and a new typhoon shelter and cargo working basin. In spite of its gritty reputation Tai Kok Tsui is vital and lively, and an intrinsic part of the 'real Kowloon' that very few local people — and almost no visitors to Hong Kong — ever see. For that reason alone, perhaps, a few hours of self-guided exploration rewards the effort made to get there.

❶ Yuet Wong Vietnamese Restaurant
❷ 'Barbershops'
❸ Anchor Street Park

STREETS

Anchor Street

① *Yuet Wong Vietnamese Restaurant*

Tai Kok Tsui and Sham Shui Po are home to a substantial number of ethnic Vietnamese residents, and a surprising number of small shops which cater to their various requirements have opened in recent years. The Vietnamese presence in northwest Kowloon is a legacy of the early late 1970s and 1980s, when many thousands of 'refugees' from Vietnam flooded into Hong Kong on rickety boats. Many were initially accommodated at the then disused, now demolished army barracks at Sham Shui Po, and another smaller camp at Argyle Street, beyond the Kowloon Hospital. Both had also been used to intern Allied prisoners-of-war during the Japanese occupation some forty years before.

In due course, most Vietnamese 'refugees' were either formally classified as political refugees by the United Nations High Commission for Refugees (UNHCR) and resettled in 'third country' destination overseas, or were repatriated, sometimes forcibly, to Vietnam. Some Vietnamese managed to remain permanently in Hong Kong, principally those individuals whom no other country would admit and Vietnam would not accept back. With nowhere else to go, they stayed on in these familiar parts of Kowloon and started new lives.

Like many similar 'ethnic' eateries elsewhere in Hong Kong, the 'Vietnamese' food on offer at Yuet Wong Vietnamese Restaurant has a heavy Cantonese flavour cannily incorporated to accommodate conservative local tastes. Pictorial menus depict bowls of beef *pho* (Vietnamese noodle broth) and plates of *cha gio* (Vietnamese spring rolls) appetizingly surrounded by mint leaves, bean sprouts, dipping sauces and all the usual Vietnamese condiments. Yet when you order a selection of dishes, none of these essential, highly flavored items appear.

'*Heung Kong Yan m'sik sik!*' ('Hong Kong people don't know how to eat them!') explained the friendly owner, who went on to say that serving up such things with every order would just be a waste of his time and money. To enjoy an authentic

Anchor Street

Vietnamese taste here, as with many other eateries elsewhere in Hong Kong that specialize in Southeast Asian cuisines, you really *do* need to ask for the extras.

② *'Barbershops'*

As in Yau Ma Tei further south, the casual visitor to Tai Kok Tsui could easily assume that Anchor Street, nearby Mong Kok Road and a few neighbouring thoroughfares are northern Kowloon's 'Street of the Hairdressers', due to the dozens of multicoloured barber's poles spiralling upwards over darkened staircases. Think again, very carefully, and only head upstairs in one of these places if you are after rather more than a shampoo and set, otherwise you will be in for quite a shock. Almost all these establishments offer substantially more than a quick trim, although the naïve or unwary will quickly find themselves very professionally clipped in other respects.

Nearby Mong Kok, along with many other parts of Kowloon has plenty of 'barber shops', 'massage parlours' and 'short-time' motels, all regularly raided and closed down by the Hong Kong Police. Most reopen a few days or weeks later, in the same locations, but with different signboards and (mostly) the same staff. Tai Kok Tsui has quite a few such establishments and, or at least so it is alleged, the prices charged here are a little lower than elsewhere in Mong Kok and the 'merchandise' on offer is somewhat more varied than that found in other parts of town.

Signs posted outside would seem to bear out this general perception. Most blatantly advertise 'fair skinned Malay girls', 'exotic Eastern European girls', 'willing northern maidens', 'spicy Thai ladies', 'innocent girl students', 'Japanese and Korean air hostesses', 'busty Filipinas' and so on; only the most naïve passer-by could possibly mistake the real function of these places.

Needless to say, Hong Kong's much romanticized, ever-present Triad societies gain a significant amount of their annual revenue both from the operation of these 'businesses', and the trafficking and control of the women who end up employed in them.

STREETS

Anchor Street

③ Anchor Street Park

Anchor Street Park is a typical example of Hong Kong's often inventive use of limited quantities of urban public space. Like the rest of Tai Kok Tsui, it appears overwhelmingly concreted at first glance, but nevertheless this small park is a lively place and something is always happening around about. There is a heavily used playground, a roller-skating rink, pitches for football, basketball and volleyball, and a space intended for *tai chi* exercises.

Like many such places elsewhere in Kowloon, there are always plenty of ordinary people sitting outside; most are only too happy to get away for a few hours from the often impossibly overcrowded apartments nearby where they live. The benches here are especially popular with Kowloon's legions of old men, who play draughts, read the newspapers, chat to their cronies, smoke a few cigarettes or just stare into space throughout the day and late into the night.

Along with neighbouring Sham Shui Po, Tai Kok Tsui has a number of dingy tenements which contain individual 'bed space' dwellings that are literally the size of a single bed. Known as 'cage homes', these bed spaces are stacked up in tiers and caged in for security. In order to enjoy any fresh air, open space, sense of privacy and relative quiet at all, the 'cage home' occupants — mostly elderly single men — must head downstairs and out into the streets. Many of the old men hanging out for hours on end at Anchor Street Park probably live in these grim conditions, an ongoing public reproach in a society as affluent as Hong Kong.

How To Get There

By Bus:	No. 12 from Shum Mong Road.
By MTR:	Olympic Station.
By Taxi:	大角咀晏架街 (*'Dai Kok Tsui, Ngan Gark Gaai'*).

Yu Chau Street
汝州街

This long thoroughfare stocks a wide variety of items, and like other corners of Sham Shui Po, always has much in the way of unexpected, off-hand interest to reward the casual explorer, including one very unique temple. Like many others in Kowloon, Yu Chau Street is named for a small town in the interior of China; Yu Chau is in Hunan, on the border with Guangdong province.

Yu Chau Street is also famed for the number of wholesale fabric merchants; there is even greater variety on offer here than Cheung Sha Wan Road, which is famed all over Hong Kong for its large number of textile outlets. Some of these shops will process a retail order if the quantity is not too small; many vendors along here, though, only want to deal in dozens of bolts of cloth at a time. Brightly coloured boards outside practically every shop display a bewildering variety of colours, prints and fabrics.

❶ Sham Shui Po Kai Fong Association
❷ Bonesetter at Yu Chau Street
❸ Button and beading shops
❹ 'Palace of the Third Prince' Temple

STREETS   142

Yu Chau Street

1. Sham Shui Po Kai Fong Association

Kai fong ('street and squares') associations are found all over Hong Kong. Completely local in orientation and focus, their principal concerns are day-to-day issues which affect everyday life and livelihood in their immediate area. In the past members of local *kai fong* associations across Hong Kong were known as prominent members of the immediate localized community, were often active on temple committees and all too often, many were local fixers and 'bosses' of one form or another as well. It is much the same today.

In the days when the gulf between government and governed in Hong Kong was much wider than today, *kai fong* associations, along with *tung heung wui* ('same native place') associations, performed a very valuable community and social welfare role. These were the organizations that residents turned to in the first instance whenever a localized problem arose. In a district such as Sham Shui Po, where a significant number of present-day residents are poorly educated or else *sun yee mun* ('new migrants' from China), *kai fong* associations still have an important role to play.

Kai fong associations have experienced a general decline in importance and influence within contemporary Hong Kong. The combination of steadily rising general affluence in recent decades, more widespread education, and increased reliance on different forms of political expression, have all meant that their once important roles in local society have diminished.

2. Bonesetter at Yu Chau Street

One of the many small trades that were once so common in Kowloon's backstreets, this tiny business sells homemade medicinal concoctions, including a presumably

Yu Chau Street

potent variety of homemade snake wine. The massage-like skills employed by 'bonesetters' such as this one are commonly used to ease the discomfort of muscular or joint sprains and strains, rather than set and cast actual bone breakages.

Numerous very contented return patients swear by the homemade *tsing kuat shui* (liniments and embrocations) on offer. As with many such establishments, most of the clientele are elderly and as this generation passes on, the businesses that cater to their specific needs, such as this one, may become a thing of the past right across backstreet Hong Kong and Kowloon. Traditional Chinese Medicine (TCM) has experienced a resurgence of interest in recent years and a number of institutions in Hong Kong are actively involved into research into these areas. Most Hong Kong people, however, continue to prefer 'Western' medicine for more serious complaints, and visit herbalists and bonesetters for relatively minor ailments.

③ Button and beading shops

Hong Kong is renowned for the glittering array of beaded garments on sale everywhere from high-end boutiques in Central, Tsim Sha Tsui and Causeway Bay to popular outlets Mong Kok's *nui yan gaai* ('lady's market'). This part of Kowloon is the place to get the beads. Need to buy a few buttons? The great number of shops along here can arrange for any quantity, from half a dozen or a container load if you need them.

Shops such as these along Yu Chau Street are the wholesalers for numerous small retail button shops elsewhere in Hong Kong, such as along Central's Pottinger Street. With steadily rising affluence in Hong Kong in recent decades, most people

STREETS

Yu Chau Street

would not bother to sew on a few new buttons, but would buy a new garment instead. This extravagance would have been unthinkable even a few decades ago when, for want of any alternative, most Hong Kong people mended their clothes until they were practically in rags.

(4) 'Palace of the Third Prince' Temple

Sandwiched in among tall buildings, this small temple is the only one in Hong Kong that honours Sam Tai Jee ('The Third Prince'). The real name of the Third Prince was Ne Zha, the third son of a mythical general named Li Jing. Ne Zha's specialty is getting rid of evil spirits.

During the first major outbreak of bubonic plague in Hong Kong in 1894, in the absence of any understanding of germs, a large number of people blamed the plague on the wrath of malevolent spirits, rather than the general public filth that was the real cause of the epidemic. Hakka residents in Sham Shui Po suggested that Sam Tai Jee be invited down from their home district of Wai Yeung (Huiyang) to help ward off evil spirits. After his image had been paraded around Sham Shui Po, the spread of the disease 'miraculously' stopped. It is, of course, also possible that greatly enhanced, firmly enforced government sanitary measures at that time might have had something to do with it.

In 1898 this small temple was built on Yu Chau Street as a permanent memorial to the event, and to provide a lasting Hong Kong home for Sam Tai Jee. Artefacts within the temple include a bell and drum inscribed with the reign title Guangxu, which indicates their late Qing origins. Extensively renovated a number of times since then, the old temple still retains an incense-blackened, smoky, 'traditional' and very photogenic atmosphere, yet other than worshippers it receives surprisingly few visitors.

How To Get There

By Bus:	No. 2 and No. 6 from Tsim Sha Tsui 'Star' Ferry.
By MTR:	Prince Edward Station, and then walk north towards Boundary Street.
By Taxi:	深水埗汝州街 (*'Sum Soy Poh, Yue Jau Gaai'*).

Apliu Street
鴨寮街

'Duck Coop Street' is one of Sham Shui Po's more intriguing places to wander about. Well-known locally and with much of interest, most visitors to Kowloon, except those from China, are completely unaware of its existence. Probably the most attention-grabbing aspect along Apliu Street is the open air market. Almost anything one cares to imagine, and a few items that are probably best *not* thought about too much, can be found on offer here. As a place to stock up on towels and bedding, cheap but durable household goods, and comfortable, 'around the house' clothing items, Apliu Street Market is probably the best place in Kowloon to shop.

Not all the bits and pieces on offer are, at least these days, as prosaic as one might think. True to the name of the street, a few shops around here still periodically sell live chicks and ducklings. At first thought it seems unlikely that anyone living in Kowloon's densely crowded urban areas would bother to rear them these days, or indeed have the space to do so.

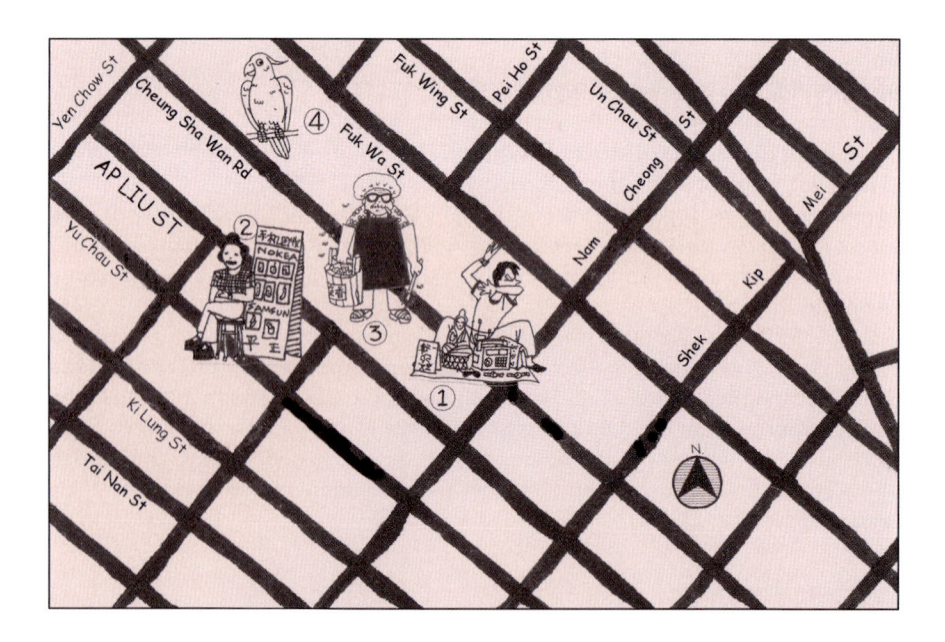

❶ Apliu Street 'Thieves' Market' ❸ Public washrooms
❷ Mobile phone stalls ❹ Poultry and bird food shop

STREETS

Apliu Street

Raising poultry in coops on the verandah was a far-from-uncommon practice in many households less than a generation ago. In the postwar years many entrenched rural habits and practices were transported straight into Hong Kong's rapidly developing high-rise world, without much anxiety — or awareness — about wider public health concerns. In spite of repeated avian flu outbreaks in recent years and official bans, home poultry rearing still occurs in the older parts of Kowloon. Where do those day-old chicks and ducklings end up otherwise?

1 Apliu Street 'Thieves' Market'

Apliu Street's local reputation as Kowloon's pre-eminent 'Thieves' Market' is a little overstated these days, but nevertheless there is always plenty to see and do around here. At first glance, there would seem to be very little market for second-hand items in a society with Hong Kong's conspicuous consumption levels and constant craze for the new, or at least novel. The widespread general poverty of many Sham Shui Po residents, in particular the large numbers of *sun yee mun* (new immigrants from China) who have made their homes in the district in recent years, all combine to make this perennially thronged street market an exception.

At any time of the day and well into the night, the interested browser can find all manner of second-hand goods on offer. While most items have been legitimately sold for resale, more than a few bits and pieces, it is alleged, 'fell off the back of a truck' somewhere en route to Apliu Street, and look too suspiciously new for 'second-hand' goods. Most are electronic items such as stereos, televisions, videos, VCD and DVD players, and some electric fans and rice cookers.

Apliu Street

The general Hong Kong desire to jettison items from the past in favour of the present does have some unexpected benefits. The 'junk' stalls along Apliu Street often provide a remarkable variety of old vinyl records, as well as some early, hard-to-find compact discs; these places are always worth a browse.

② Mobile phone stalls

Apliu Street sells a surprisingly large quantity of pre-loved mobile phones. In manically status-conscious Hong Kong, a three-month-old mobile phone is practically an antique to some and simply too *outré* to be seen with. Not all of these handsets, however, end up in a landfill.

As well as large quantities of the second-hand product, numerous booths along Apliu Street sell brand new mobile phones. The main customers are visitors from China, or so it would appear by the amount of Mandarin and heavily accented Cantonese spoken around these stalls. The sheer volume of counterfeit production in China — and the convincingly high quality of many fakes — means that scores of Mainlanders come to Hong Kong specifically to buy the genuine article.

Whether this item is a handbag, quality cosmetics and pharmaceuticals or something as prosaic as a reliable mobile phone, Hong Kong has a solid reputation elsewhere in China for authenticity and reliability. The amusing irony, of course, is that droves of Hong Kong people head northwards every weekend to stock up on China-made pirated versions of everything from DVD players and computer software to 'Louis Vuitton' luggage and 'Chanel' handbags.

Apliu Street

③ *Public washrooms*

Public washrooms such as this one are a grim reminder of the widespread, and apparently growing, urban poverty in Sham Shui Po and the surrounding areas. Known as one of the territory's most deprived areas, Sham Shui Po is where Hong Kong's steadily expanding income gap — internationally acknowledged as one of the widest in the 'developed' world — is immediately apparent to even the most casual observer.

In Sham Shui Po it is not uncommon for a family of five to live in a cubicle the size of a small bedroom in a subdivided old tenement building, with shared kitchen facilities and no private interior sanitation. Many of those with little choice but to live in such conditions are unskilled recent immigrants from China, who somehow manage as best as they can on arrival in Hong Kong. The continuing presence of public bathing facilities, such as this one in older urban areas, make clear and obvious this largely unseen, officially downplayed situation.

While the relevant government departments do their best to keep public bathing facilities such as this one at Apliu Street as hygienic as possible, the large numbers of people who use them mean that they are far from pleasant at any time. Public bathhouses are also considered unsafe, especially at night, and many women report being molested in such places. As a result, many residents in surrounding buildings make do as best they can after dark. Unsurprisingly, perhaps, the many small household goods shops in business around Apliu Street all stock plastic and enamel wash tubs and chamber pots. 'Asia's World City', with its sleek images of affluence and modernity, appears a fatuous and hollow designation when contrasted with the realities of Sham Shui Po life.

Apliu Street

(4) Poultry and bird food shop

Located just around the corner on Kweilin Street, this long-established shop sells numerous varieties of flower and vegetable seeds, gardening chemicals and insecticides, plastic and terracotta flower pots and planters, as well as orchid pots and hanging baskets. They also stock various types and grades of poultry food, all in quantities suitable for home-raising of fowls. Bird seeds and other avian requisites are always in stock. Limited selections of plants, such as cacti, some orchids and common, easy-to-grow house plants are occasionally on offer.

Small shops like this one can be found all over Kowloon's older urban areas, a clear indicator that in spite of often impossibly overcrowded domestic conditions, a great many Hong Kong people have an evident enjoyment of plants and other living things, and try to encourage them wherever possible.

How To Get There

By Bus:	No. 2 and No. 6 from Tsim Sha Tsui 'Star' Ferry.
By MTR:	Sham Shui Po Station.
By Taxi:	深水埗鴨寮街 (*Sum Soy Poh, Ngap Liu Gaai*).

Yen Chow Street
欽州街

The area around Yen Chow Street was reclaimed in the early 1920s. The original plan for Sham Shui Po, as put forward by the then colonial secretary Sir Claud Severn, was to provide an additional residential area from which people working in southern Kowloon or the city of Victoria could commute easily, the intention was to relieve serious overcrowding in what were then Hong Kong's urban areas.

A direct ferry service between Central and Sham Shui Po was inaugurated in January 1919. Tramlines linking Sham Shui Po and Tsim Sha Tsui were proposed, although they were unfortunately never built. Severn saw the extended 'New Kowloon' area as the future home of a large number of factories, as it was later to become between the 1930s and the 1950s. Workshops that established themselves around 'New Kowloon' were initially small-scale operations, which manufactured, amongst other items, thermos flasks, enamelware, flashlights, plimsolls, clothing items and gumboots.

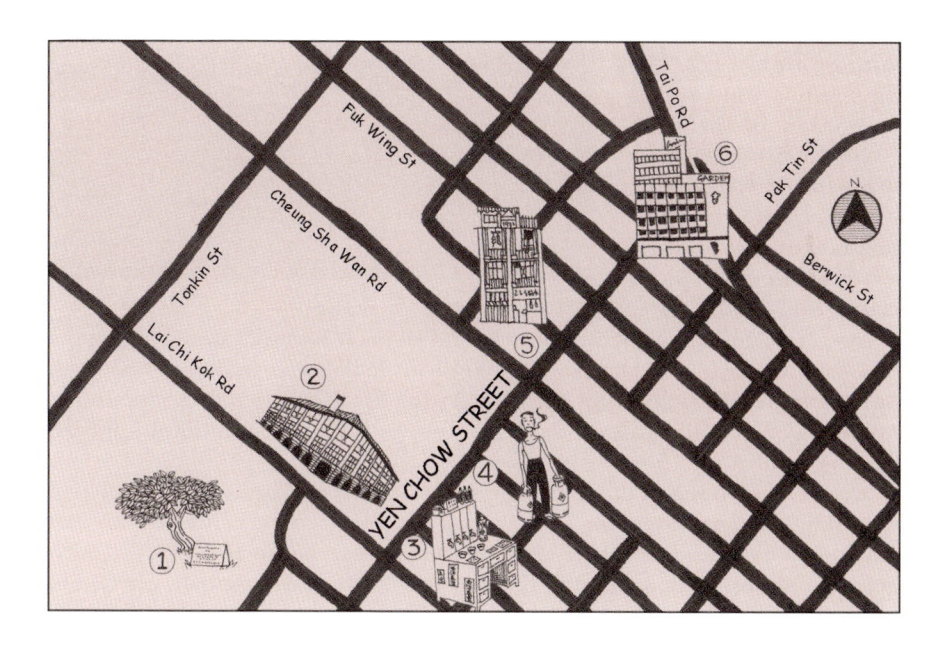

❶ Sham Shui Po Camp Prisoner-of-War Memorial Plaques
❷ Sham Shui Po Police Station
❸ Hing Cheong Hong
❹ Tai Yau Hong
❺ Old buildings along Yen Chow Street
❻ Garden Bakery

New Kowloon

STREETS

Yen Chow Street

A large open area at the harbour end of Yen Chow Street was originally intended to house a police station, post office, other government offices, open spaces for recreation and a school. Only Sham Shui Po Police Station was eventually built, however, as the military requisitioned the entire area in 1927 and a sizable British Army camp was built on the site.

① Sham Shui Po Camp Prisoner-of-War Memorial Plaques

Now the site of a peaceful park and a popular, well-patronized public swimming pool, Sham Shui Po Park was once part of a large British Army camp that stood on this location from 1927. The then waterfront site was reclaimed in the mid-1920s to provide more space for light industrial expansion in New Kowloon. Part of this land was given over for military use in 1927, and a series of barracks, known as Nanking Barracks and Hankow Barracks, were built on the site. A substantial block of flats on the waterfront, later known as Jubilee Buildings, was subsequently acquired by the military for use as married quarters. It had originally been built as a speculative venture by the prominent local Eurasian Hotung family.

Largely as a result of the camp's presence Sham Shui Po, along with much of Kowloon, had a considerable Army flavour to it for decades. Echoes of this past time still remain in some corners, in the form of numerous small businesses, such as tailor's shops, cafés, bars and provision shops, which all originally opened to cater to the military trade, and have since stayed in business with a different clientele.

After the British surrender of Hong Kong to the Japanese in 1941, Sham Shui Po Camp was used as an Allied prisoner-of-war camp until the colony was liberated in 1945. Waterfront access enabled a number of prisoners-of-war to successfully escape into Free China in the first few months of internment. After the war, the camp remained on the defence estate until the early 1970s when it was returned to the Hong Kong government.

Yen Chow Street

Like Argyle Street Camp in Mong Kok, Sham Shui Po was used for a time in the 1970s and 1980s to accommodate Vietnamese boat people. Jubilee Buildings and the remaining camp buildings were demolished in the late 1980s, and no vestige of the Army camp now remains, other than a series of memorial plaques dedicated to prisoners-of-war, which were erected in the early 1990s.

② *Sham Shui Po Police Station*

This attractive old two-storied building was opened on 15 June 1925. It replaced the first permanent police station at Sham Shui Po which was built in 1903, five years after the New Territories, which included Sham Shui Po, was leased to Great Britain. An adequate police presence in the area was important as by the early 1890s, the 'New Kowloon' areas adjacent to British territory had become hotbeds of illicit gambling dens and opium divans.

The original Sham Shui Po Police Station building, located somewhat further inland than the contemporary station complex, was also used as the Harbour Master's office for 'New Kowloon'. The old police station was almost completely destroyed by the disastrous typhoon in September 1906 that claimed thousands of lives elsewhere in Hong Kong. The police station was rebuilt and finally vacated in 1925 when the present building was completed.

One of the very few buildings of any real historical interest still left in Sham Shui Po, the police station is inadequately protected by existing heritage legislation.

Yen Chow Street

③ Hing Cheong Hong

This interesting little shop on the corner of Yen Chow Street and Lai Chi Kok Road stocks all sorts of weird, not-so-weird and frankly wonderful Chinese wines, which range from foully medicinal to potently intoxicating. Probably the best-known 'wine' is Kweichow Maotai, ever-popular at Chinese wedding banquets and opulent businessmen's parties. A smallish mouthful of the stuff is guaranteed to almost blow most people's heads off; approach with caution!

Kwangtung Miju (Guangdong rice wine) comes in various grades and bottle sizes ranging from small enough to fit into a back pocket — only a few dollars and very popular with Sham Shui Po's less discriminating tipplers — to four-litre flagons bound up with raffia and string. Sam Sei Chiu is made with the bile of three different snakes, and is meant to be a 'potent restorative'. The stuff tastes as violently bitter as the proverbial gall — perhaps this fact proves its authenticity. Worth trying once.

④ Tai Yau Hong

These little neighbourhood gas merchants are found all over Hong Kong, especially in rundown areas such as Sham Shui Po where mains gas supply to old buildings has not yet been installed. A large bottle of Liquefied Petroleum Gas will last the average family a month to six weeks, with delivery to the door.

Tai Yau Hong also sells LPG-fired gas cookers, in various sizes, shapes and price ranges. Self-starting one-burner gas stoves, popular due to the small and

Yen Chow Street

often makeshift kitchens in old tenement blocks nearby, go for several hundred dollars. Fairly basic cast iron gas rings that need to be lit with matches can be bought for very little — and they last for years.

The shop also sells glass bottles of *for shui* (kerosene). More than a few households in Sham Shui Po and other older areas of Kowloon still use kerosene stoves. For the most part the main consumers are older, single people, as *for shui* is even cheaper to use than gas. Perhaps more importantly for many customers, this fuel avoids the periodic major cash outlay incurred for a bottle of gas. Kerosene can be bought in small quantities for modest sums as and when needed. This is an important consideration for many Sham Shui Po residents, where total household incomes for single retirees and new immigrants from China is often only a few thousand dollars a month.

⑤ Old buildings along Yen Chow Street

These decaying old terrace shop-houses at 53 Yen Chow Street date from 1932. In the interwar period most of Sham Shui Po's streets were lined with buildings like these. These sole survivors have recently been the focus of preservation efforts — well-intentioned but rather sad when one considers the really wonderful buildings elsewhere in Hong Kong and Kowloon that have been lost to private greed and public apathy over the years.

Yen Chow Street

The black-painted metal grilles are especially decorative, unlike the stark bars and gold-and-chromium grilles so widely found today. These buildings, along with others of the type, were advertised as a 'rat-proof design' when built. How that minor miracle was rendered possible anywhere in Hong Kong was not made clear — perhaps by means of sturdy iron mesh grilles fitted over the drains and gutters.

6 Garden Bakery

Garden Bakery is one of the most popular bakeries in Hong Kong; it supplies a large proportion of the *fong bao* ('square' or Western-style fresh bread) consumed locally. Most comes from here at Sham Shui Po and another factory further along Castle Peak Road at Sham Tseng. Given that this is Hong Kong, after all, where commercial descriptions need not be precise or even accurate, there is not a garden in sight anywhere close to the premises, not so much as a wilted shrub or grime-encrusted bush anywhere, but no matter. Their sandwich breads are high-quality, reasonably priced and generally keep very well.

One of the Garden Company's most popular product lines is Honey-and-Egg Bread, more like a sweet, fluffy cake than the sort of bread one would find anywhere outside Asia. They also make various kinds of biscuits and crackers. These have become so popular in China that — inevitably — a rip-off Garden Bakery look-alike brand and logo has appeared there.

How To Get There

By Bus:	No. 2, 6, 6A from Tsim Sha Tsui 'Star' Ferry.
By MTR:	Sham Shui Po Station.
By Taxi:	深水埗欽州街 (*'Sum Soy Poh, Yum Chow Gaai'*).

STREETS

Tai Po Road
大埔道

Tai Po Road, as the name would suggest, extends from Kowloon to the northern New Territories town of the same name. Until the Lion Rock Tunnel opened to road traffic in 1967, it provided the main route from Kowloon to Sha Tin and areas in the New Territories. Tai Po Road starts at Sham Shui Po and has a number of areas of interest clustered around the lower end.

The division between older, more established parts of Kowloon and the resettlement estate areas that evolved in the 1950s is very apparent around here. Cross the road in some corners and the differences are immediately apparent. Waterfall-fronted, walk-up *tong lau* ('Chinese buildings') several stories high stand

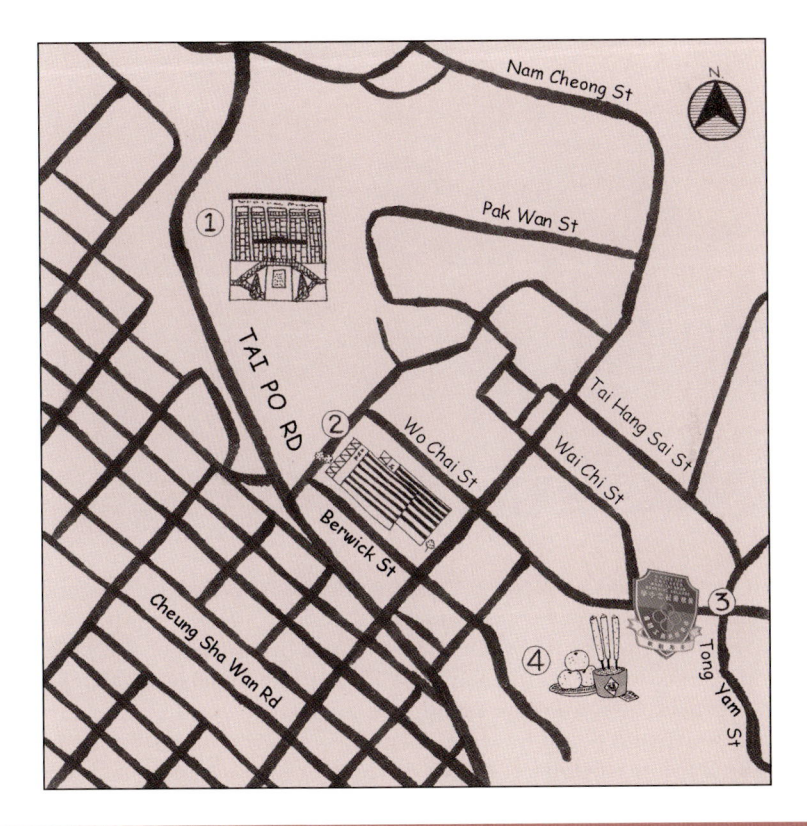

① North Kowloon Magistracy building
② Shek Kip Mei Estate
③ The Hong Kong Sze Yap Commercial and Industrial Association Primary and Secondary Schools
④ Fook Tak Kwu Miu ('Happiness and Virtue Ancient Temple')

Tai Po Road

just across from block after block of Hong Kong's oldest surviving public housing estates, surrounded by open verandah corridors and heavily grilled windows and doors. Very few visitors to Kowloon ever seem to stray into these areas — a great pity as there is much of interest to see, smell, taste and explore.

1 North Kowloon Magistracy building

Solid and granite-faced, the North Kowloon Magistracy is designed to reflect the sober dignity of the law. When it was built in the early 1950s, the Magistracy building was one of the more impressive public structures in this part of Kowloon, then largely an area of squatter settlements and the earliest, most basic public housing estates. It remained a prominent landmark for many years afterwards. In these years, the North and South Kowloon Magistracies were responsible for hearing cases from the entire mainland section of Hong Kong south of the Kowloon hills — a substantial jurisdiction.

The future of the North Kowloon Magistracy building is somewhat uncertain. Possible future roles for the building such as a centre for the elderly or a library for the Film Services Office, have all been discussed, but no firm decision has been made.

Tai Po Road

② *Shek Kip Mei Estate*

Shek Kip Mei is Hong Kong's original government public housing estate. A number of buildings here date from the mid-1950s. Effort has been made to ensure that at least one block is retained at Shek Kip Mei for future generations to see what life was like for so many people in Hong Kong in the postwar era.

These early H-blocks, so-called because of their shape, provided homes and shelter for thousands. Apartments were one room only, which were partitioned as individual needs dictated. There were no kitchens, and residents generally cooked on a kerosene burner on a bench outside the door, on the verandah. Communal toilets and washing facilities were located in the cross-section of the H. These were generally unsanitary and reports of late-night robberies and molestations were commonplace.

Grim as all this may appear to a modern observer, life in the H-blocks was infinitely better than the ramshackle squatter huts that preceded them, where those who had no choice but to live in them were in constant danger of flooding, landslides and fires. The most devastating squatter area fire occurred on Christmas Day 1953, when tens of thousands were made homeless in the course of a few hours.

These early-generation public housing blocks were gradually replaced by better quality estates with more sophisticated facilities, and slowly the memory of life in places like Shek Kip Mei Estate has begun to recede. In an attempt to document something of the vanishing life in these blocks, a privately funded 'people's museum' was established in one of the blocks. This very worthwhile initiative proved extremely popular with local visitors keen to see for themselves — often for the first time — the type of accommodation that was once part of the common experience for many thousands of new arrivals to Hong Kong in the 1950s. Similar exhibits can also be seen at the Heritage Museum at Sha Tin.

Tai Po Road

(3) The Hong Kong Sze Yap Commercial and Industrial Association Primary and Secondary Schools

The continued persistence of *tung heung wui* ('same native place' associations) in contemporary Hong Kong and Kowloon, and the various support services they offer, is one of the enduring surprises to urban life.

As well as sub-dialect familiarity and a social and business network, 'same native place' associations, both in Hong Kong and elsewhere in the Overseas Chinese world, also provided schools and other educational and welfare facilities for members and their families. Originally, admission to these schools was dependent on some family or clan affiliation with the *tung heung wui*; present-day students are drawn from widely diverse backgrounds.

The Sze Yap ('Four Districts') are Toi San, Sun Wui, Hoi Ping and Yan Ping. All are located in the West River region, not far from Macao. The Sze Yap area was a major supplier of migrants to both Macao and Hong Kong; many prospered greatly in their new locations. One of the most well-known was the early twentieth-century opium trader and property magnate Lee Hysan, who in the 1920s named the streets in his East Point Hill development at Causeway Bay after the 'Four Districts'.

Tai Po Road

④ Fook Tak Kwu Miu ('Happiness and Virtue Ancient Temple')

This small, rather ramshackle hillside temple is located down a side alley and is almost invisible until the pedestrian has stumbled past it. Once inside the gates, though, its role is unmistakeable; the vivid cinnabar reds and incense smoke provide an immediate answer. A great many Fook Tak Chi ('Happiness and Virtue Shrines') can be found in many parts of Kowloon and Hong Kong, and they are also prevalent in the backstreets of Macao.

On the upper level, hundreds of images and idols are arranged under deity-specific shelters. Found right across Hong Kong, Fook Tak Chi are minor temples where discarded, unwanted or otherwise supernumerary household gods are placed. It is considered very inauspicious to simply throw away an unwanted idol, as the deity may then seek its revenge on you

Tai Po Road

in some dire, unforeseen manner. If an unwanted god or goddess is placed at a Fook Tak Chi, others will worship it, however inadvertently, and harmony and peace — as well as personal safety — will prevail.

From the deities distributed here, one can infer that Kwun Yum (the Goddess of Mercy), Kwan Tai (the God of Loyalty and Bravery) and Sau Sing Kung (the God of Longevity) are among the most popular gods in the Hong Kong Chinese pantheon. From time to time other idols and images from different religious traditions can be found in places such as this one, even, occasionally, a Virgin Mary, St Anthony, Vishnu or Ganesha.

How To Get There

By Bus: No. 2, 6, and 6A from Tsim Sha Tsui 'Star' Ferry.
By Taxi: 石硤尾大埔道 ('Sek Kip Mei, Dai Poh Doh').

Cheung Sha Wan Road
長沙灣道

Cheung Sha Wan means 'Long Sandy Bay'. Hong Kong has at least one other Cheung Sha Wan, on the south coast of Lantau. For now anyway, Lantau's still enjoys a series of magnificent open beaches that seldom get really crowded even on weekends. Not so here, where only the name remains unchanged.

By the early 1920s the beaches and coastline at Cheung Sha Wan had, for the most part, given way to shipyards, boat-building yards and light industrial overflow from Sham Shui Po. Modern Cheung Sha Wan can seem a bit bleak at first, but has a surprising number of historical relics, most notably a well-preserved Han Dynasty tomb.

The main attraction for the area though, is that Cheung Sha Wan is a vital chunk of that most elusive of places, the 'real' Hong Kong — a vital world far removed from the tourist clichés and misleading advertising hyperbole.

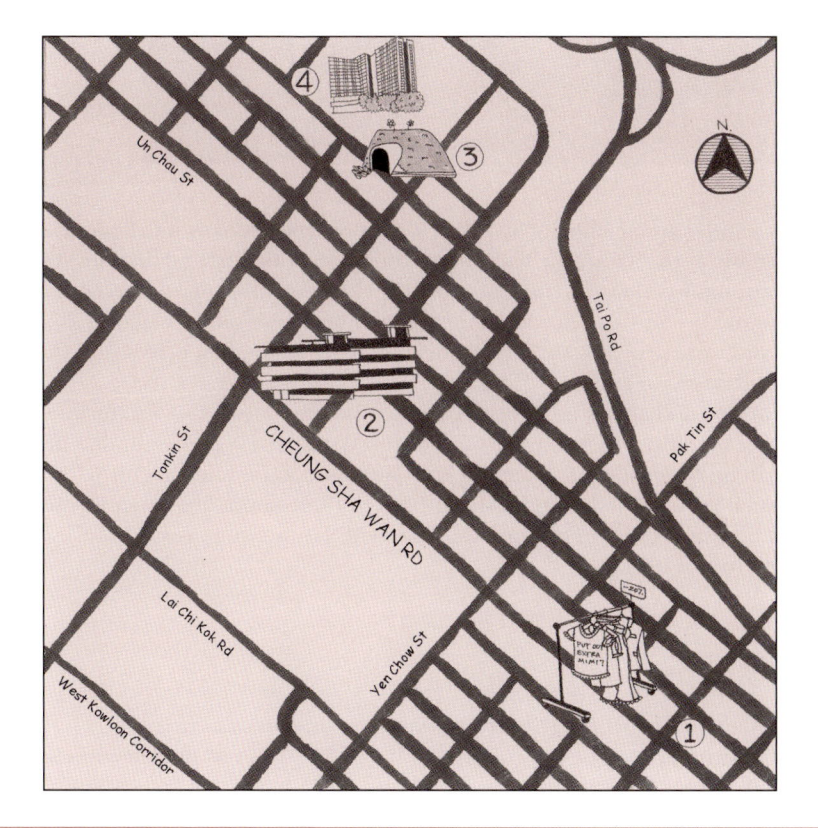

① Fashion wholesale and fabric shops
② Factory flats
③ Lei Cheng Uk Han Tomb
④ Lei Cheng Uk Estate

Cheung Sha Wan Road

1) Fashion wholesale and fabric shops

A brief wander along Cheung Sha Wan Road does make one wonder why so much fuss is made about Tsim Sha Tsui's numerous export outlets and Stanley Market's internationally renowned 'factory seconds' garment shops. *Everything* that those places stock — and a great deal more — can be found along Cheung Sha Wan Road, and were probably sourced from along here in the first place! And they are almost all *much* cheaper!

Clothing and accessory items on offer at these outlets are — for the most part — only really suited to Asian sizes and tastes. With persistence a number of good deals can be made all along Cheung Sha Wan Road, especially on cheap, everyday items such as shirts, jeans and T-shirts. Staff in these shops are generally helpful, though as this is deep in the heart of 'the real' Hong Kong, very little English is spoken around here.

2) Factory flats

Back in the days when the Hong Kong economy was heavily reliant on manufacturing, much of the colony's industrial output was produced in factory blocks like these. Workshops were contained within individual factory flats. These places produced just about everything imaginable. A small plastic-moulding factory that made doll's heads could be right alongside another enterprise knitting sweaters or weaving towels, while further along the corridor other workshops assembled electric fans, enamelled cooking ware or Thermos flasks.

STREETS

Cheung Sha Wan Road

Most large-scale industrial production, of textiles in particular, shifted from Hong Kong to China throughout the 1980s. By the mid-1990s virtually no full assembly manufacturing operations were still in existence in Hong Kong. A few businesses still somehow carry on in these factory flats, but a great many units either stand empty or have been given over to storage — very often of goods manufactured elsewhere in China but exported through Hong Kong.

The international textile quota system within the General Agreement on Tariff and Trade (GATT) helped prop up a pseudo-textile-and-garment industry in Hong Kong for more than twenty years after the industry had moved over the border. This has now been abolished, and it remains to be seen how many small 'finishing' outlets will continue to operate around Cheung Sha Wan, as well as other decaying industrial areas elsewhere in Hong Kong, such as Kwun Tong, San Po Kong or Wong Chuk Hang, in the coming years.

③ *Lei Cheng Uk Han Tomb*

Uncovered in 1955, the Han Tomb at Lei Cheng Uk is one of the most significant physical reminders of Hong Kong's early Chinese era. Discovered during site formation work for the building of Lei Cheng Uk resettlement estate, the tomb was one of the most intact Han burial sites discovered in southern China. Numerous others have since been uncovered elsewhere in the region, including a magnificent funereal complex right within the urban area of Guangzhou. The tomb at Lei Cheng Uk takes the form of a brick-lined vaulted chamber, which has been covered with a concrete structure to prevent damage from exposure to the elements.

Cheung Sha Wan Road

When opened, the Lei Cheng Uk Tomb was found to contain some fifty-eight pottery and bronze objects. It was built during the Eastern Han period (AD 25–220). Migration of Han Chinese from northern China into the Hong Kong region only occurred on any significant scale from the time of the Tang Dynasty (AD 618–907) and accelerated during the collapse of the Southern Song Dynasty (AD 1127–1279), the Mongol invasion of China and subsequent establishment of the Yuan Dynasty (AD 1279–1368).

Like Hong Kong's other archaeological sites, such as the Neolithic carvings at various places on Hong Kong Island, the Lei Cheng Uk Tomb is principally of localized significance, but clearly indicates that there was some Han Chinese settlement in the Hong Kong region two thousand years ago. The overwhelming majority of human inhabitants in the region then, however, were Yao, Miao and Yue peoples. Now regarded as 'minorities', two millennia ago these groups were the majority population in this part of China.

4) Lei Cheng Uk Estate

Resettlement estates were one of Hong Kong's major postwar success stories, and in the last half century they have provided homes, or at least shelter and the eventual hope of something better, for millions of people. Reliable, affordable, fireproof housing helped many recent arrivals to Hong Kong get onto the first rungs of relative stability, and in due course achieve a measure of prosperity. These estates were not built — as is popularly supposed — to provide desperately needed housing in the postwar years, but rather to free up land occupied by squatters for development.

Lei Cheng Uk was one of the earliest resettlements estates and has one dubious claim to local fame; this was where the so-called 'Double Tenth' riots broke out in October 1956. Nationalist agents and Triad-affiliated hoodlums fomented trouble among the refugees from China who lived at Lei Cheng Uk, and the flashpoint came when a Nationalist flag was torn down.

Cheung Sha Wan Road

Rioting quickly spread from Lei Cheng Uk to other parts of Kowloon. The army was called out to deal with rioters in Tsuen Wan, and a number of people were killed and seriously injured there. During one incident, the car in which the wife of the Swiss consul was travelling was set upon, and the car was burnt — with the passengers still inside it. She subsequently died.

In a related case another taxi with European passengers was attacked, overturned and set on fire. The driver, trapped by his arm under the vehicle, was roasted to death. The rioters responsible for these specific outrages were convicted of murder and later hanged.

Modern Lei Cheng Uk Estate is a very different place from the grim, tense mid-1950s resettlement complex, and differs little in most respects from dozens of other public housing estates elsewhere in Kowloon, Hong Kong and the New Territories.

How To Get There

By Bus:	No. 2, 6, and 6A.
By MTR:	Cheung Sha Wan Station.
By Taxi:	長沙灣長沙灣道 (*'Cheung Saa Wan, Cheung Saa Wan Doh'*).

Lai Chi Kok Road
荔枝角道

Lai Chi Kok ('Lychee Point') has very little to suggest its rural origins. Overwhelmingly urbanized, Lai Chi Kok still has a few fragmented villages strung around the hillsides, and some of these do, indeed, have a few straggly lychee trees scattered here and there among the ramshackle huts, open sewers, scrap yards and rubbish heaps.

For decades, one of Lai Chi Kok's most famous attractions was a well-patronized amusement park. Like much else in Hong Kong in the 1990s, Lai Yuen (Lai Chi Kok Amusement Park) fell victim to rapidly changing local tastes and expectations, and spiralling property prices, and closed down in the late 1990s. The site has been redeveloped, and no trace remains.

Lai Chi Kok Road sprawls northwards for a long distance from Sham Shui Po, and a thorough exploration will take some time — and considerable energy.

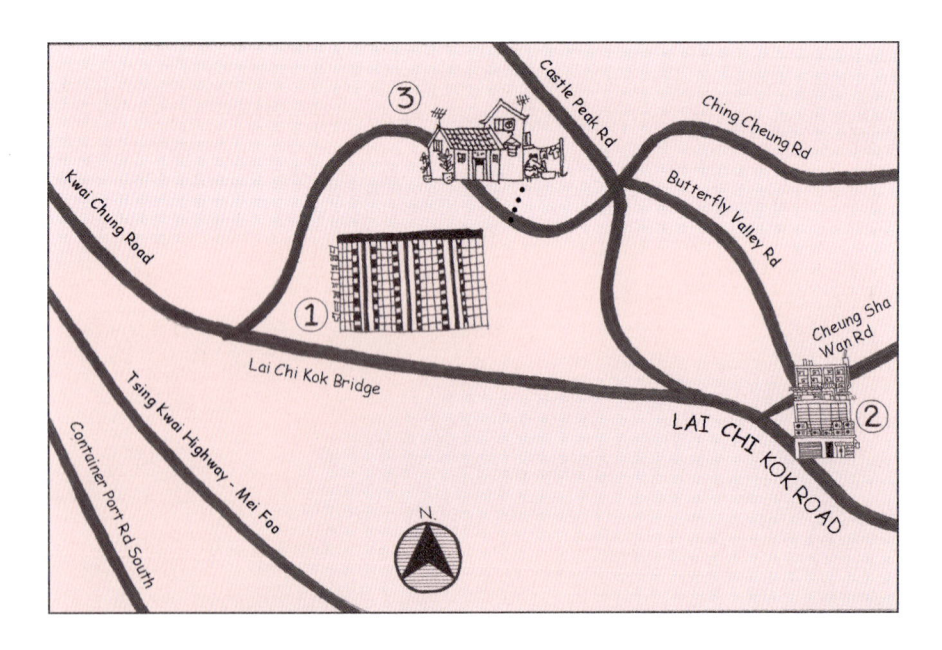

❶ Mei Foo Sun Chuen
❷ Factories
❸ Kau Wa Keng Village

STREETS

Lai Chi Kok Road

1) Mei Foo Sun Chuen

Mei Foo Sun Chuen, one of Hong Kong's first 'middle-class' residential estates was built at Lai Chi Kok in the late 1960s on the site of the large Standard Vacuum Oil storage facilities. The Chinese name for the American-owned Standard Vacuum Oil Company was Mei Foo; for more than three decades the firm traded kerosene into the interior under the slogan 'Oil for the Lamps of China'.

The estate takes its name from the company's own label of kerosene lamp. Very popular throughout China, the lamp was branded, with the Chinese love for euphonious names, as Mei Foo — 'Beautiful Companion'.

By the 1960s Lai Chi Kok was considered too close to Kowloon's rapidly expanding urban districts for the safe storage of petroleum, and these facilities were relocated further north to Tsing Yi where they still remain.

Mei Foo Sun Chuen remains one of Kowloon's more popular older private estates, as the balconied apartments are well-built and comfortable with a reasonable amount of open space around them. Recent construction of the West Rail railway link through Mei Foo to the northwest New Territories has also greatly increased the area's desirability due to greatly expanded commuter convenience.

New Kowloon

STREETS

Lai Chi Kok Road

② *Factories*

Industrial production has been very much in decline in Hong Kong since the late 1980s. Formerly thriving factory areas in various parts of Kowloon, such as around Lai Chi Kok, have been largely abandoned. These days, most 'Made in Hong Kong' garments are completely assembled in China, but are finished in some minor way — in some cases by little more than the addition of a 'Made in Hong Kong' label. This is yet another well-known instance where the letter of the law in Hong Kong is strictly adhered to, while its spirit is either routinely flouted or else imaginatively circumvented. Hong Kong life certainly brings out the entrepreneurialism in its residents.

③ *Kau Wa Keng Village*

One of the last original villages in this part of Kowloon, contemporary Kau Wa Keng is a combination of well-built old village houses and ramshackle squatter settlement. Modern Hong Kong has several thousand houses located in villages within various parts of the urban areas, such as Pok Fu Lam village on Hong Kong Island that are just like this one. Dogs and cats run free, festoons of washing are strung out over the village paths and skeins of dodgy-looking electrical work can be seen everywhere. But the worst is surely to be found in between the houses.

Kau Wa Keng, along with other similar 'villages', is completely without anything remotely resembling adequate modern sanitation, and in consequence homes

Lai Chi Kok Road

here are a serious disease risk. Mosquito problems are endemic; Hong Kong's periodic dengue fever outbreaks are often traced to places such as this one. Most houses have open kitchens built over the village's central drainage nullah. Home-made sewerage pipes disgorge gobbets of urine-sodden toilet paper and fresh human faeces only a few feet away from plates of fresh food, kitchen utensils, drying plates and open windows — another enduring, post-SARS image from 'Asia's Third World City'!

The continued existence of places such as Kau Wa Keng and other similar village slums well into the twenty-first century clearly indicates how ineffective the Hong Kong government's hygiene and public education campaigns have been over the years. The obvious continued indifference of a great number of people to dangerous levels of filth right in their immediate vicinity clearly proves the point.

Shocking sanitary conditions aside, Kau Wa Keng is attractively situated among a wooded hillside, and with a concerted effort could be made a much more pleasant place than it is. Many residents here, as in other such places, are avid plant lovers, and numerous potted plants and well-tended shrubs are clearly in evidence throughout the village and its surroundings.

How To Get There

By Bus:	No. 2, 6, 6A from Tsim Sha Tsui 'Star' Ferry.
By MTR:	Lai Chi Kok Station.
By Taxi:	九龍荔枝角道 (*'Gau Loong, Laai Jee Gok Doh'*).

Tsuen Wan and Beyond

Perceived by many as little more than the northernmost terminus of the MTR Tsuen Wan Line, the sprawling modern conurbation of Tsuen Wan offers much more than the impressions first created by the district's dozens of public housing estates, grimy factory buildings and densely crowded streets. There are even a few historic sites of note.

Wong Kwu ('Emperor's Aunt') Grave at Tsuen Wan commemorates an interesting local legend which dates from the time of the Mongol invasion of China. During the flight of the Southern Song dynasty court, the aunt of the emperor sought refuge with the Tang clan, who lived in the area but did not disclose her identity. She subsequently married into the family and lived the quiet, hardworking, virtuous life of an ordinary village woman.

The emperor's aunt's identity was discovered years later, but she refused to leave and insisted on staying in the village where she had been made welcome. A magnificent tomb was subsequently erected to her by the Tang clan. It is still maintained well today, and can be seen near the old District Office compound off Castle Peak Road, at the northern end of Tsuen Wan.

The original village area at Tsuen Wan was located at Hoi Pa, which means 'Embankment by the Sea'. At the time of the New Territories lease in 1898, a number of lime kilns operated at Tsuen Wan; the product was used for building purposes and as fertilizer. There were also a couple of small boatyards and rope works. But other than those enterprises, few other commercial activities were to be found there, a far cry from today.

A few old village buildings at Hoi Pa were spared when the area was redeveloped in the 1970s and these have been incorporated into modern Tak Wah Park. Located not far from the Yan Chai Hospital complex, this well-laid-out garden is one of backstreet Tsuen Wan's most pleasant, unexpected open spaces.

As with other areas within a reasonable distance to Hong Kong Island, market gardening was a major and profitable early enterprise. Villagers at Tsuen Wan had supplied markets on Hong Kong Island with fresh vegetables and other agricultural produce since at least the mid-nineteenth century. This business was obviously profitable because in 1857, during the Second Anglo-Chinese War, Chinese troops were dispatched to Tsuen Wan to stop the villagers from selling their produce to the British colony. This prohibition on trade led to serious localized clashes with the district's farmers, who were naturally very unwilling to lose this lucrative source of income.

Fresh pineapples were also a major export item from the district into Hong Kong Island; the sandy soil around Tsuen Wan and Kwai Chung was especially suitable to pineapple cultivation. The *Hong Kong Guide 1893* mentions that 'a good deal of this pleasing district is taken up with pineapple cultivation'. All the pineapples grown at Tsuen Wan and Kwai Chung were consumed fresh in Hong Kong and Kowloon; no commercial canning or preservation of locally produced pineapple, other than some small-scale drying, was ever undertaken.

STREETS

- Tsuen Wan Market Street
- Castle Peak Road
- Sai Lau Kok Road
- Route TWISK
- Shing Mun Road

Incense mills were also well-known features in the Tsuen Wan area. These mills were driven by waterwheels, which powered stone hammers that crushed the sandalwood into fine powder. The sandalwood powder was then brought down to Hong Kong Island for manufacture into incense sticks and spirals. The distinctive fragrance borne on the breeze was obvious from some distance out to sea from Tsuen Wan. In 1905 there were no fewer than twenty-four incense mills operating around Tsuen Wan. Most were in the Muk Min Ha area, now completely built over with densely populated resettlement estates.

Soybean processing works were also well established in Tsuen Wan. One bean curd works was described in an 1898 Government Report as having operated at Tsuen Wan 'for at least fifty years'. One of the reasons why these industries developed around Tsuen Wan was the proximity of secure and growing markets in Hong Kong Island and Kowloon, with relatively easy access to them either by boat or on foot. Another was the district's relative isolation from urban areas; soybean processing in particular is a notoriously foul smelling occupation, and was best conducted as far away from urban areas as possible to minimize the stench nuisance.

Malaria and dengue fever were endemic in the Tsuen Wan area for decades. Villagers and government officials stationed in the district routinely came down with these diseases, and fatalities were common. In due course successful eradication measures were introduced, and the incidence of malaria and other mosquito-borne illnesses dramatically declined. Some resurgence of dengue has occurred in recent years, mainly caused by poor environmental hygiene standards, and, it must be admitted, an ongoing general public indifference to basic civic cleanliness.

A Chinese Maritime Customs Station was built on the island of Ma Wan before the New Territories were leased, and smuggling from Tsuen Wan into China was never a very easy undertaking. While the risk was great, so too were the profits,

Tsuen Wan and Beyond

and attempts were regularly made. Smuggler's Ridge, above Tsuen Wan, takes its name from an old smuggling path which wound over the hills to Tai Po, and from there on into the interior of China.

One of the main contraband items smuggled into the Mainland was common salt; the Chinese government maintained a stringently enforced monopoly on the manufacture and sale of this commodity, and penalties for offenders were high. Modern Ma Wan is now little more than an extra pylon for the massive Tsing Ma (Tsing Yi–Ma Wan) Bridge to the airport, and a luxury housing development stands next to the straggling old village.

Small-scale commercial fishing was another local industry based at Tsuen Wan; this has dramatically declined since the 1960s. These days no one but the very foolish or desperately hungry would eat anything caught from the grossly polluted, foul smelling waters of Rambler's Channel, but numerous recreational anglers nevertheless still throw in their lines all along the foreshores between Tsuen Wan and Castle Peak.

Between 1949 and 1958, more than a million people voluntarily left behind their homes and families in the 'socialist workers' paradise', then being created on the Mainland, for a new life in the British colony. For most new arrivals the alternative to life in China were long hours and little pay in Hong Kong's burgeoning factory areas such as Kwai Chung, Tsuen Wan and eastern Kowloon. Industrial conditions were extremely grim, but in those years there was no shortage of refugee workers from China willing to endure long hours and low wages in Hong Kong in return for some respite from constant political campaigns, internal upheavals and class conflict.

In the 1950s, numerous spinning, weaving and dyeing factories developed in Tsuen Wan, mostly financed with émigré Shanghainese capital. These new factories were as notorious for appalling industrial safety and hygiene conditions as had been the case years earlier in Shanghai. Practically all development was undertaken without recourse to long-term urban planning. The prevailing business ethos in

Tsuen Wan and Beyond

Hong Kong during that uncertain era was one of 'make-it-quick-and-then-get-out', and it clearly shows in the built legacy from those years.

Modern Tsuen Wan is an integral part of Hong Kong's 'Housing Estate Heartland' and the sprawling New Town is home to over a million people. For those searching for a glimpse of the 'real' Hong Kong, a visit to Tsuen Wan provides numerous insights into what everyday life in Hong Kong is really like for the overwhelming majority of the Hong Kong Chinese population. All these aspects can be found just at the end of the MTR line, only half an hour or so from Central.

STREETS

Tsuen Wan Market Street
荃灣街市街

Have you ever wondered what daily life looks, sounds and smells like in the 'Housing Estate Heartland', that place populated by millions of 'real' Hong Kong people? Quite a distance in every respect from the 'international, cosmopolitan' parts of the city, Tsuen Wan Market Street is a fascinating window into ordinary, everyday Hong Kong life.

Gum mo (blond haired), dragon-tattooed *laan jai* (literally 'rotten kids', or Triad-affiliated hoodlums) in muscle-boy T-shirts amble along the street, their stick-thin, pouting girlfriends clinging to their arm, middle-aged *see lai* (housewives) in floral blouses and baggy black trousers head off to the market with a plastic shopping bag tucked under their arm, garrulous old men sit out in the park and play cards, chat with their cronies or just while away the time on a bench. And perhaps inevitably, a fume-belching procession of minibuses, light-goods vehicles and taxis endlessly passes by all day long and most of the night as well.

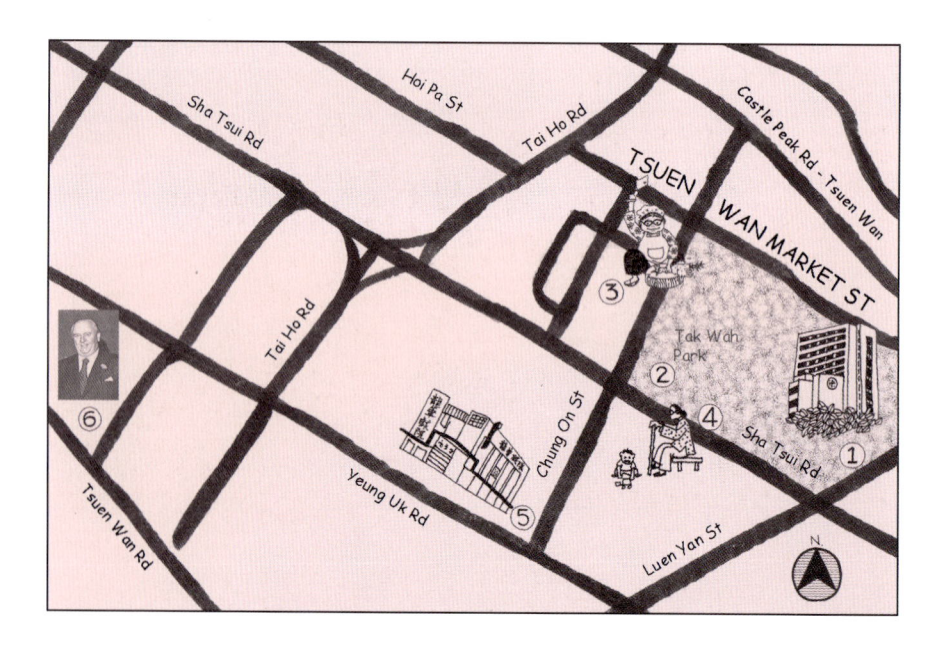

❶ Yan Chai Hospital
❷ Hoi Pa Village and Tak Wah Park
❸ Tsuen Wan Market
❹ 'Sitting-out' area
❺ Lung Wah Theatre
❻ Clague Gardens Estate

Tsuen Wan Market Street

The bustling scenes one can observe along Tsuen Wan Market Street have fundamentally the same characteristics, whether it is in Tsuen Wan, Kwun Tong, Chai Wan, Ap Lei Chau, Tuen Mun or any large housing estate area anywhere else in Hong Kong. Streets are full of ordinary people going about their daily lives in their own resolutely southern Chinese way; in every respect a whole world removed from the glitz and hype so often associated with 'Asia's World City', and a much more authentic slice of life than Hong Kong's 'international' zones.

1 Yan Chai Hospital

Construction of Tsuen Wan's major hospital, Yan Chai Hospital, was first proposed in 1961 due to the massive increase in population during the previous decade. The foundation stone was laid in 1963, but due to rising costs and other associated problems construction was halted. Work on the hospital recommenced after a $750,000 Hong Kong government subsidy, and the Yan Chai Hospital finally opened in August 1973. It has been further extended since that time.

Yan Chai Hospital, like many other hospitals elsewhere in Hong Kong, has numerous fund-raising activities such as film shows, fairs and Chinese opera performances, all organized by bands of volunteers that are well supported by the local Tsuen Wan community. Flag days are held a few times a year, and dozens of schoolchildren and retirees collect what must surely be very large sums of money from the legions of commuters passing through Tsuen Wan MTR Station.

STREETS

Tsuen Wan Market Street

② Hoi Pa Village and Tak Wah Park

One of Tsuen Wan's original villages, Hoi Pa ('Embankment by the Sea') was originally on the coast, but such remnants as still survive are now several hundred metres inland. A few old village houses have been saved and incorporated into Tak Wah Park, which is one of the hidden pleasures of the area. As in many such locations, the trees and greenery around Tsuen Wan take some searching out but are still there among the unremitting mouldy concrete and urban ugliness that makes up so much of modern urban Hong Kong and Kowloon.

Old men walk their birds and sit chatting or play draughts with their friends. Loud-voiced grannies clad in quietly patterned *saam foo* ('blouse and trousers', or pyjama suits) mind their grandchildren. And from time to time amateur singing groups are set up under the trees to practise, and they either provide onlookers with a free concert, or depending on the musical and vocal standards on offer that day, a very compelling reason to get up and walk away!

Tucked away behind high walls, Tak Wah Park is relatively quiet compared to the busy street outside, and full of attractive trees and shrubs, as well as numerous examples of *gwai shek* ('strange rocks'). The crag-like miniature mountains popular in Suzhou's classical Chinese gardens are meant to look like rugged rocky regions elsewhere in China, such as Guilin or the Yellow Mountains.

Tsuen Wan Market Street

③ *Tsuen Wan Market*

Depending on how you view them, *gai see* (wet markets) like this one in Tsuen Wan are one of Hong Kong's enduring delights, or a chamber of horrors to be avoided at all costs. Just about everything in the way of fresh produce is available in them, from freshly picked vegetables dripping with water and peevishly nipping crabs, to wide-eyed reef fish and various kinds of live poultry squawking their last. In recent decades local wet markets have been partially superseded by ever-larger chain supermarkets, but most Hong Kong housewives still regard wet market produce as synonymous with freshness and good value, and a trip to the *gai see* is a daily occurrence for many householders.

Wet markets like this one always contain a few *jaap foh poh* ('mixed goods shop'), which stock just about everything that can be dried, salted and preserved, along with soybean sauces and other Chinese condiments, pickled vegetables, canned goods, and fresh, salted and preserved eggs. There are also flower and fruit stalls, with prices that are as competitive — at least for now — as those charged by the major supermarket chains.

④ *'Sitting-out' area*

Tiny 'sitting-out areas' like this one are found all over Hong Kong's urban areas. Positioned on tiny scraps of space, which is too small for any purpose other than a bench or two, 'sitting-out areas' nevertheless provide at least a little respite for nearby residents living in tiny, grossly overcrowded apartments.

STREETS

Tsuen Wan Market Street

While many 'sitting-out areas' across Hong Kong and Kowloon have been improved and beautified in recent years, most are grubby and uninviting, and frequently lack shade or anything more appealing beyond a bench to perch one's weary legs upon. Perhaps unsurprisingly, many such spots appear to be seldom, if ever, used. A sharply appropriate Cantonese term for these places, *saam kok see hang* ('three-cornered shit pit'), pithily sums them up. In other words, a patch of waste ground fit for nothing else.

⑤ Lung Wah Theatre

Tsuen Wan Market Street

Now abandoned, the Lung Wah Theatre was once Tsuen Wan's principal movie hall and was also used for other theatrical performances. Like many other theatres of its kind elsewhere in Hong Kong, this one gradually fell victim to advancing technology and changing consumer tastes. The steady advance of television and video in the 1970s and 1980s meant that few people bothered to go to the cinema any more.

Many such cinemas eventually resorted to showing *haam peen* (soft porn movies) on weekday afternoons to stay in business; most of the customers were elderly *haam sup lo* (dirty old men). Gradually even this clientele, it would appear, moved on to cheaply pirated VDC and DVD films, and the older-style cinemas finally closed.

The Lung Wah Theatre now has a couple of hardware shops and religious goods dealers on its ground floor and the rest of the building is boarded up. Three decades ago, the Lung Wah Theatre was thronged with people and a Saturday night there would have been a popular excursion for Tsuen Wan people — sadly no longer.

6 Clague Gardens Estate

Thousands of people live in the Hong Kong Housing Society's Kei Tak Chuen Sun Chuen, as Clague Gardens Estate is named in Cantonese, but very few remember whom it was named after. The distinctive complex was named after Hutchison International *tai pan* Sir Douglas Clague, who was also the longest-serving chairman of the Hong Kong Housing Society. The estate was completed and named after Clague in 1991, a decade after his death.

A Manxman who first came to Hong Kong in 1940 as a young Royal Artillery officer, Clague was best known to the Chinese as 祈德尊 (Kei Tak Chuen). A highly decorated war hero, Clague was a senior member of the wartime resistance organization British Army Aid Group (BAAG) in China and subsequently took the Japanese surrender in Bangkok at the end of the

Tsuen Wan Market Street

Pacific War. He returned to Hong Kong in 1947, established a very successful commercial career as chairman of the Hutchison International group of companies, and became heavily involved in community affairs. Clague was eventually knighted for his services to Hong Kong in 1971, and died in 1981.

A number of other Hong Kong Housing Society estates were named after individuals. One of the very first ever built, in Shau Kei Wan at the eastern end of Hong Kong Island, was named after R. O. Hall, M.C., the long-serving Anglican bishop of Hong Kong. Lai Tak Tsuen, above North Point, was named for Lai Tak (Michael Wright), the long-serving director of public works and first Hong Kong government commissioner to London. Cronin Garden in Sham Shui Po was named after Fr. Fergus Cronin, S.J., and Sir Cho-yiu Kwan was honoured with Cho Yiu Chuen in Kwai Chung.

How To Get There

By MTR: Tsuen Wan MTR Station, Exit A.
By Taxi: 荃灣荃灣街市街 (*'Tsuen Wan, Tsuen Wan Gaai See Gaai'*).

Sai Lau Kok Road
西樓角路

The name of this busy thoroughfare means Western Building Point and is derived from the large, old foreign-style house that stood for decades nearby on Castle Peak Road. This was home to the Yip family, wealthy and prominent in Tsuen Wan affairs in the years before the Pacific War. Old photographs of Tsuen Wan show a completely different place from today's high-rise district, with village houses overlooking fields of pineapples, clean sandy beaches, and the rugged, mountainous island of Tsing Yi beyond.

Industrial development on a large scale only started in the area after the Pacific War, when a great number of refugees came down from the Mainland to escape the civil war. Unlike previous migrant influxes into Hong Kong, these new arrivals showed no sign of returning when more settled times came. China's involvement in the Korean War led to a United States-led United Nations trade embargo in 1951 that strangled the colony's traditional entrepôt trade, and Hong Kong rapidly industrialized to meet changing circumstances and survive.

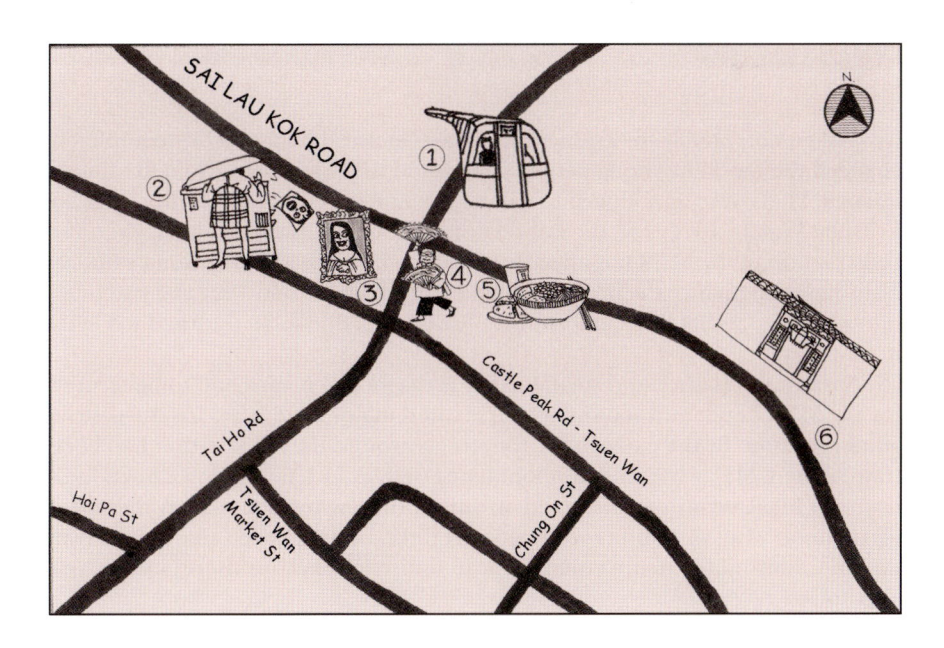

1. Tsuen Wan MTR Station and crowds
2. Photocopying shops
3. Shing Tai Framing Shop
4. Sai Lau Kok Garden
5. Wai Yut Meen Gar (Shanghai noodle shop)
6. Sam Tung Uk

STREETS

Sai Lau Kok Road

① Tsuen Wan MTR Station and crowds

Now taken completely for granted, the Mass Transit Railway (MTR) completely changed the way Hong Kong people get around the urban areas from the time it opened. Plans were announced to extend the line into the New Territories as far as Tsuen Wan in 1977, and the last section was opened two years later. Even the construction of the MTR was an early vote of confidence in Hong Kong's future; loans raised to finance the project all had expiry dates beyond 1997 and extended into what was, at that time, an extensive leased area due to be returned to China in that year.

Sprawling squatter and small-factory areas in Tsuen Wan had to be cleared for the MTR depot and station, which created major headaches for the district administration. By the early 1980s, the streets around the MTR station had been transformed. Major housing developments, such as Luk Yeung Sun Chuen built over the MTR terminus, attracted an influx of new residents from the older urban areas who, with improved transport links, no longer felt that Tsuen Wan was an undesirable, inconveniently located district 'way out there' in the New Territories.

Sai Lau Kok Road

② *Photocopying shops*

Fed up with paying up to a dollar a flash for photocopies at some rip-off stationery shop, or waiting in line for ages at a public library every time bureaucracy requires a copy of your HKID card? If so, this little place near Tsuen Wan MTR Station and others like it across Hong Kong are the places to come for super-cheap photocopying. Prices charged vary depending on the quantity and speed required, but if you are prepared to wait a day and have a couple of hundred copies to make, prices here can be as low as seven cents per page.

Only Australian-made copy paper 'manufactured from renewable resources' is used, according to the boxes stacked outside, so you need not fear that the last of Brazil or Borneo's tropical jungles are disappearing whenever you make a few photocopies. Staff are amiable and helpful, and they will even do copies of textbooks for you.

Back in the days before the Intellectual Property Department really got their act together and cracked down hard on rip-offs, the nearby three-storied Tsuen Fung Centre shopping arcade was *the* place in Tsuen Wan to come for pirate computer software, CD-ROMS, VCDs and DVDs. With computer programmes identical in quality and function to the original selling for a tiny fraction of the hundreds or even thousands of dollars asked for the genuine item, it is hardly surprising that the place was so popular. And — SSSHHH!!! — if you know where to ask, it is *all* still available in Tsuen Wan.

Low-end fashion shops selling gold and silver lamé tops, slinky T-shirts and clunky sandals, as well as a few real estate agents offices, are found on the upper level, while on the lower levels there are some quite good electronics stores and legitimate computer supply shops with very reasonable prices for printer cartridges and other everyday items.

Sai Lau Kok Road

③ Shing Tai Framing Shop

Have you ever wanted a large framed picture on your living room wall of vivid red and white *koi* fish, swimming by the dozen in a whirlpool-like circle? Or perhaps a painting of massed pink, red, yellow and white peonies, on a cream coloured background? Or maybe a Chinese ink rendering of the famed Yellow Mountain peaks of Anhui Province, wreathed in trailing clouds with the occasional dark green longevity pine clinging to a rocky crag. Or perhaps a white-robed sage in a faraway pavilion, surrounded by mist and lost in contemplation of the infinite, meets the needs of your new home décor?

If pictures like these sound like what you are looking for, then Shing Tai Framing Shop is the place to come. Those brightly coloured *koi* fish paintings start at several hundred dollars or so, and go up to over a thousand. The quality of the artworks and framing is high, if this type of home decoration is to your taste, and the man who runs the shop is very friendly and obliging.

Sai Lau Kok Road

(4) Sai Lau Kok Garden

This 'garden' (with the Regional Council lettering scratched out over the entrance but still legible) is, along with many other such places, one of Hong Kong's enduring enigmas. The original intention for building these places was to provide pleasant areas for residents living in nearby, often hopelessly overcrowded estates to go for some open space. Unfortunately, something seems to have got lost along the way in terms of the design.

Scorching hot and frankly uninviting, the 'garden' is completely paved over except for a few wan-looking palm trees and other sad, diesel-blackened shrubs growing in carefully marked out squares in the concrete. No one seems to ever 'sit out' here, as Sai Lau Kok Garden is surrounded on three sides with very busy roads and a flyover.

Even on a mid-afternoon summer day during the school holidays, Sai Lau Kok Garden is almost completely deserted. There were no children playing, no old men with their caged birds and draughts sets, not even a sleeping drunk. The only other person there was an old woman who sat down briefly to rearrange her shopping bag, then got up and walked quickly away.

Sai Lau Kok Road

(5) Wai Yut Meen Gar (Shanghai noodle shop)

This unprepossessing small shop, whose name grandly but very accurately means 'The One and Only', sells what must be some of the best Shanghai noodles, *haam beng* ('pastry with filling'), filled with *gau choy* (Chinese chives) and minced pork, and *woh tip* ('pot-stickers' or pan-fried dumplings) in all of Hong Kong. Wai Yut Meen Gar also serves some of the freshest *dau cheung* (soybean milk) around; like everything else on offer in the shop, the soybean milk is homemade.

Staff are very friendly. Most are Shanghainese *sun yee mun* ('new immigrants') which guarantees the authenticity of the fare on offer. The best of all is that Wai Yut Meen Gar stays open reasonably late. You can eat very well here for very little, and at peak times there is always a queue — a good sign in Hong Kong.

(6) Sam Tung Uk

This old whitewashed Chinese village dwelling was first built in 1786. It originally comprised three small lanes and gradually extended to its present size. Sam Tung Uk was established by members of the Chan clan, Hakka villagers who moved down from Guangdong to settle near the coast at Tsuen Wan. It eventually became one of many small village settlements scattered around the Tsuen Wan area.

By the 1960s, the village structure had become somewhat dilapidated and unhygienic, and was closely surrounded by the numerous weaving, spinning and dyeing mills where so many newcomers to Tsuen Wan worked. Sam Tung Uk's

Sai Lau Kok Road

own residents moved out of the complex in 1980, and the structure was formally declared a monument the following year. Following extensive restoration and refurbishment in 1986–87, the complex was opened as a folk and ethnographic museum.

Right next to the MTR depot and dwarfed by dozens of tower blocks, Sam Tung Uk now seems very incongruous, and its rural origins are surprisingly difficult to visualize. Like folk museums elsewhere in Hong Kong, Sam Tung Uk feels strangely dead within, and this is no adverse comment on either the museum staff's efforts, or the overall fabric of the buildings. When real people no longer live in something as basic as a village environment, the whole place somehow loses part of its essence, and that feeling is very evident here.

At Sam Tung Uk, there are no children playing, no old people sitting around and, most implausibly for a New Territories village, no festering piles of *laap saap* (rubbish) cheerfully strewn about, no loud mah-jong games or barking dogs, no appetizing cooking aromas, or foul drainpipe smells. It is simply a well-preserved cluster of old, village-type buildings, where daily life has long since packed up and gone elsewhere.

Possibly the most vital aspect of Sam Tung Uk is the To Tei Miu (Earth God Shrine) located not far from the entrance. This is still well tended by elderly ex-residents of Sam Tung Uk, who now live in the housing estates nearby, and come down daily to light incense. A generation or so later, this Earth God Shrine will possibly become a museum piece as well.

How To Get There

By MTR:	Tsuen Wan MTR Station.
By Taxi:	荃灣西樓角路 (*'Tsuen Wan, Sai Lau Gok Loh'*).

Route Twisk
荃錦公路

Like many other roads in Hong Kong, Route TWISK, the scenic mountain road over Tai Mo Shan ('Big Hat Mountain'), was originally built in the late 1940s as a tank access road for military use. The acronym 'TWISK' stands for 'Tsuen Wan Into Sek Kong'.

For most of its length Route TWISK passes through areas of considerable natural beauty. For a few days every winter, a cavalcade of vehicles from the urban areas come up to the top of Tai Mo Shan to see the 'snow' — hoarfrost left after a particularly cold night on the top of Hong Kong's highest mountain. Traffic can be backed up almost into Tsuen Wan on these occasions. For most of the year the road is very quiet, except on weekend nights when dozens of 'boy racers' hurtle round the numerous hairpin bends on motorbikes, or behind the wheels of souped-up Japanese cars.

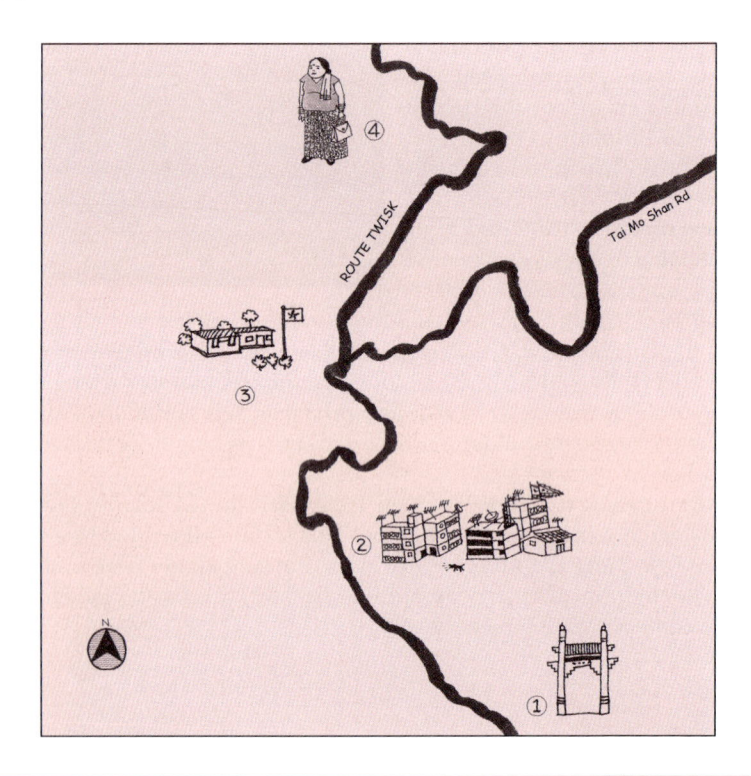

❶ Shek Pik Resettlement Village
❷ Chuen Lung Village and tea pavilions
❸ Country Parks Management Office, Tai Mo Shan
❹ Sek Kong Village

STREETS

Route TWISK

1. Shek Pik Resettlement Village

Hong Kong's perennial water shortages became critical in the postwar years, and led to the construction of a number of reservoirs in the 1950s and 1960s. All involved the resettlement of long-established villages to new locations. One of the most significant early postwar reservoir projects was at Shek Pik, on the southern coast of Lantau.

Shek Pik's villagers shrewdly decided that they preferred to be resettled in the rapidly evolving Tsuen Wan urban area, where there was a possibility of work in factories and a higher standard of living, rather than resettlement in another rural location on Lantau where they could continue to farm. Lengthy negotiations ensued between government and villagers, and finally in 1960, the villagers moved to their new location above Tsuen Wan and brought their ancestral tablets and temple images with them. Family temples were very carefully sited to ensure the best possible geomantic aspect. Had this not been guaranteed, the villagers would have flatly refused to move, and Shek Pik reservoirs construction work endlessly delayed.

Even after almost half a century at Tsuen Wan, these ex-Lantau villages still maintain a strong original identity. They are completely different in layout to other resettlement estates elsewhere in Tsuen Wan, the majority of which were established to accommodate the inhabitants of cleared squatter settlements from elsewhere in the district.

Route TWISK

② Chuen Lung Village and tea pavilions

Very popular for its high quality tea brewed with fresh mountain spring water, Chuen Lung village gets a lot of visitors on weekends, but nevertheless remains quiet on weekdays. As far back as 1688, extensive tea plantations on Tai Mo Shan were recorded in Chinese gazetteers. In the 1860s tea was cultivated on the slopes of Tai Mo Shan beyond Chuen Lung, and over the ridge into the Lam Tsuen valley. Distinctive herringbone-shaped stone terraces can still be seen in some locations, particularly after a hill fire has cleared away long grass. A number of other scattered villages once existed on the slopes of Tai Mo Shan; all of these, except Chuen Lung, have long since been abandoned.

Grantham's Camellia (*Camellia granthamiana*) was discovered on the slopes of Tai Mo Shan in 1955 and named after Sir Alexander Grantham, the then governor of Hong Kong. This variety is apparently the largest camellia in the world, and is still very rare in the wild; specimens have so far only been found in Hong Kong. Commercially grown tea bushes cultivated in other parts of the world are a type of camellia, and there has been some speculation that Grantham's Camellia was a natural evolution from one of these varieties.

Tai Mo Shan is renowned for wild tea, known as *wun mo cha* ('cloud and mist tea'), which is collected on the hillsides in the springtime. Tea is brewed from mountain spring water, and numerous cafés around this village serve basic *dim sum*. The environment is rustic and unsophisticated, but from the number of car-borne visitors that make the journey up the mountain a great many people from the urban areas seem to enjoy this ambience.

Route TWISK

③ Country Parks Management Office, Tai Mo Shan

Tai Mo Shan and the surrounding countryside provide a large number of very enjoyable hiking opportunities within close and easy reach of Tsuen Wan. Most are on catchment paths or well-maintained trails, with clearly defined start and finish points. The Country Parks Management Office at Tai Mo Shan has full details of these paths, fire risk warning indicators and taps to fill up your water bottles before setting out. From here one can enjoy easy, if rather time-consuming, walks on to Shing Mun, Tsing Lung Tau, or Yuen Long, or back down to Tsuen Wan.

④ Sek Kong Village

Route TWISK

A visit to Sek Kong Village these days feels dreadfully like ghosts come-a-haunting to those who knew it even a decade ago. Since the handover, Sek Kong Village has not so much changed functions but entirely lost its reason for existence. The People's Liberation Army, unlike the British Army in previous times, only come to Hong Kong for short periods and are not permitted to bring their families with them. Consequently, the dozens of empty married quarters and the school, hall and supermarket that serviced them are completely redundant — and they look it!

The NAAFI (Navy, Army, Air Force Institute) supermarket, with a swimming pool next door and 'Lion and Rickshaw' club bar upstairs, was effectively the 'village centre' of Sek Kong, popular and always full of people. The staircase leading up to the bar had a large — and hilariously politically incorrect — painted mural of an enormous British lion waving the Union Jack, seated in a rickshaw and being pulled along by a scrawny, grinning Chinese coolie. No one who saw this 'artwork' could ever quite forget it.

These days, instead of sun-reddened soldiers' wives toiling up the hillside in the summer heat, burdened down with shopping bags and cranky toddlers, a solitary PLA soldier stands guard outside the recently renovated and extensively rebuilt NAAFI, now known locally as the 'Great Hall of the People'.

Five kilometres away in the valley below is the reason Sek Kong Village was built in the first place — the military airfield and extensive barracks at Borneo Lines (now prosaically renamed 250 Kam Tin Road) and TDBG (Training Depot Brigade of Gurkhas) at Malaya Lines (which has now reverted to Sek Kong South Camp, its original name in the 1950s). These camps remain Hong Kong's largest military installations; an airfield control tower dominates the centre of the valley, and helicopters on training flights constantly circle around for most of every day.

This stunningly scenic route over to Tsuen Wan has once more become what it was thirty years ago: a slow, seldom frequented rural service only used by villagers higher up the mountain on the Tsuen Wan side, hikers getting to or from a trail, and the occasional nostalgic sightseer returning to Hong Kong from the other side of the world.

How To Get There

By Bus:	No. 51 from Tsuen Wan MTR Station (on Tai Ho Road flyover above the station).
By Taxi:	新界石崗村 ('Sun Gaai, Sek Gong Tsuen').

STREETS

Shing Mun Road
城門道

A winding, semi-rural road just above Kwai Chung, Shing Mun Road leads up to some of the Kowloon hills lesser-known delights. For many visitors, the main point of interest is the scenic Shing Mun Reservoir with its numerous picnic spots and hiking trails.

Others with an interest in Hong Kong history come to explore the crumbling remains of the Inner Line. Often referred to as the Gin Drinker's Line, this is an interconnecting chain of tunnels, bunkers, gun positions and a bullet-scarred redoubt — Hong Kong's answer to the Maginot Line. It was briefly fought over during the Japanese invasion of the colony in December 1941.

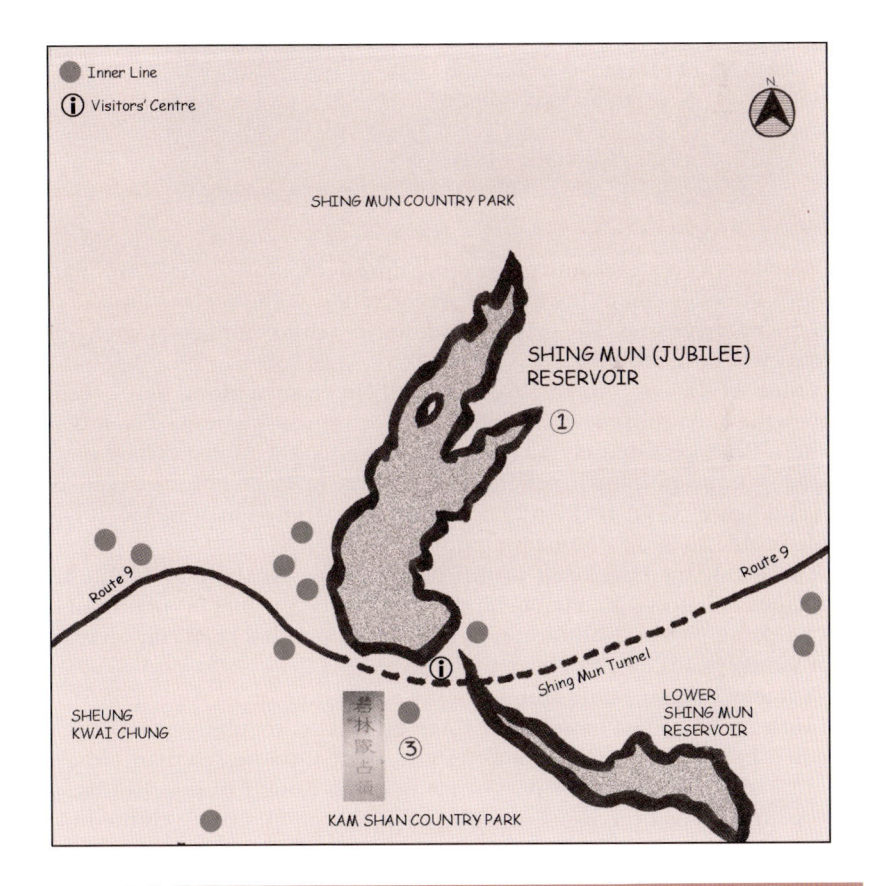

❶ Shing Mun Reservoir
❷ Inner Line (Gin Drinker's Line)
❸ Wakabayashi Inscription

Shing Mun Road

A well-kept visitor's centre, providing information on Shing Mun's natural history and details about the area's wartime relics can be reached up the stairs from the mini-bus stop. The centre is well worth a visit before going on to either the reservoir or the tunnels.

Tribes of Rhesus monkeys can generally been seen along here, crashing through the undergrowth on the sides of the road and all just immediately beyond northern Kowloon's densely packed urban conurbation. Monkeys have reached almost plague proportions in certain sections of the Kowloon hills, especially Shing Mun and nearby Golden Hill which, due to their large-scale presence, is known locally as Ma Lau Shan ('Monkey Mountain').

These simians have bred prolifically in recent years, largely due to an abundance of leftover food left behind around barbeque sites by urban residents after weekend picnics. Contraception in various forms has been considered, but so far monkey culls have not been undertaken.

A note of caution: Shing Mun's monkey population can be really quite vicious. And with the mindless harassment some picnickers regularly give them, why wouldn't they be? Poking at them with sticks, stone throwing, constant shrieking, shouting and waving on the part of many Hong Kong Chinese visitors, is — distressingly — just the usual reaction whenever monkeys are sighted in the Kowloon hills.

Shing Mun Road

1 Shing Mun Reservoir

This scenic reservoir and the interwar negotiations that led to its construction are an interesting and little known aspect of Hong Kong's later 1997 story. The colony's freshwater supply situation had become acute in the 1920s and a new reservoir was desperately needed. Both the Colonial Office in London and the Hong Kong government were reluctant to sanction the finance of major capital works in what, after all, was leased territory due to be returned to Chinese administration in less than seventy years.

Sir Cecil Clementi, then the governor of Hong Kong, proposed a possible solution that would have solved once and for all the eventual 'New Territories question' long before it ever arose, as well as ensure that the reservoir scheme could proceed without undue delay. Clementi suggested that the New Territories be ceded outright to Great Britain on the same terms as Hong Kong Island and Kowloon, in exchange for the early retrocession of Weihaiwei (now Weihai) to China. This small territory, on the northern coast of Shandong Province, was leased to Great Britain in 1898 under very similar conditions to Hong Kong's New Territories.

Nothing came of Clementi's farsighted proposals, which were rejected mainly because of Foreign Office fears of Chinese protest about other concessions and treaty ports in China.

In due course Hong Kong's chronic water shortages forced the issue and construction started on the Shing Mun Reservoir project in 1930. At that time the scheme was the largest water project in the British Empire, which involved the removal of entire villages from the valley. The inhabitants were resettled in Kam Tin in the northwest New Territories.

Tsuen Wan and Beyond

STREETS

Shing Mun Road

The upper and lower Shing Mun reservoirs were declared open in 1935, which was also the year of King George the Fifth's Silver Jubilee; the reservoirs were thus officially named the Jubilee Reservoirs. By the late 1930s the Jubilee Reservoirs supplied freshwater to most areas in Kowloon, and were linked by a submarine pipeline under Victoria Harbour to Hong Kong Island.

(2) *Inner Line (Gin Drinker's Line)*

The defensive installations above Kwai Chung are usually referred to as the Gin Drinker's Line, after the (now completely reclaimed) Gin Drinker's Bay below to the southwest. The Inner Line was built in 1938, largely abandoned in 1940 and then revived as a defence plan in late 1941. It was anticipated that the Inner Line, with the aid of heavy reinforcements from outside Hong Kong, could hold out for at least three months. The entire complex eventually fell to the Japanese after less than four days.

Tunnels within the complex were named after well-known London thoroughfares such as Shaftesbury Avenue, Oxford Street, Charing Cross and Regent Street. These names were given by the 1st Battalion the Middlesex Regiment, the resident British battalion who initially trained on them. This was done for strategic purposes; the tunnel names follow the same pattern as the London streets, and the Middlesex soldiers (Londoners almost to a man) knew their way around them automatically. Due to later changes in defence strategy, the Middlesex Regiment were deployed on Hong Kong Island at the time the Japanese invaded.

Shing Mun Road

The Inner Line is one of the most extensive extant historical structures found anywhere in Hong Kong. It is also an extreme example of what *not* to do with built heritage. In spite of intermittent proposals by enthusiasts, the complex lacks adequate legislative protection, or even some basic interpretative signage.

③ *Wakabayashi Inscription*

The Japanese characters roughly inscribed here read: 'Captured by Wakabayashi Unit'. Completely uncommemorated by any plaque or marker and totally unprotected by any existing heritage legislation, these words were chipped in by men of the Japanese 228th Regiment shortly after their capture of the Shing Mun Redoubt in December 1941.

The abandoned state of this genuine historic inscription mutely indicates the woeful state of heritage protection in Hong Kong. An abundance of resources have been found for urban marker plaques to commemorate marginal events that took place in buildings demolished decades earlier, yet this rare authentic example from a dark period in Hong Kong's history simply stands here, abandoned and slowly decaying, at risk of defacement or destruction from any passing vandal.

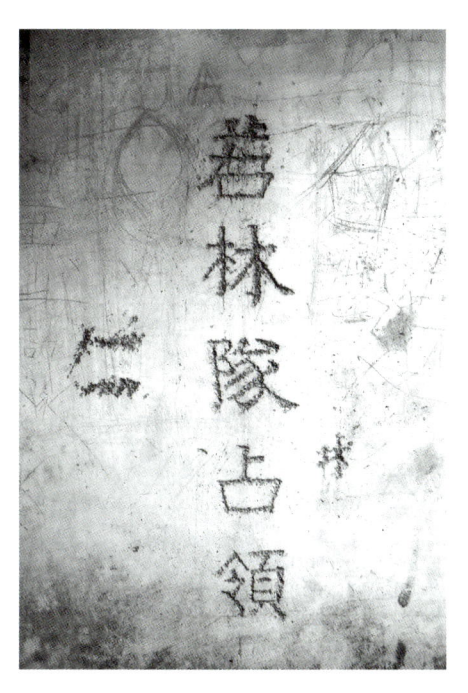

How To Get There

By Minibus:	Green Minibus No. 82, from Shiu Wo Street, Tsuen Wan (close to Tsuen Wan MTR Station).
By Taxi:	新界城門水塘 (*'Sun Gaai, Sing Moon Sui Tong'*).

Castle Peak Road
青山道

Castle Peak Road was the first arterial road built in the New Territories, and linked the urban area of Kowloon with Castle Peak, Yuen Long and Fanling. Built from 1916 to 1917, part of the road was constructed along the scenic, rocky stretch of beach-fringed coastline that lay beyond the then small village of Tsuen Wan. This helped to open up the area to holiday trippers. Castle Peak Road was described in one travel account as 'Hong Kong's La Corniche', and the drive along here was, until recent years, one of Hong Kong's most scenic.

The Castle Peak area eventually became very popular with urban residents, many of whom maintained bathing sheds for weekends and holiday use along the

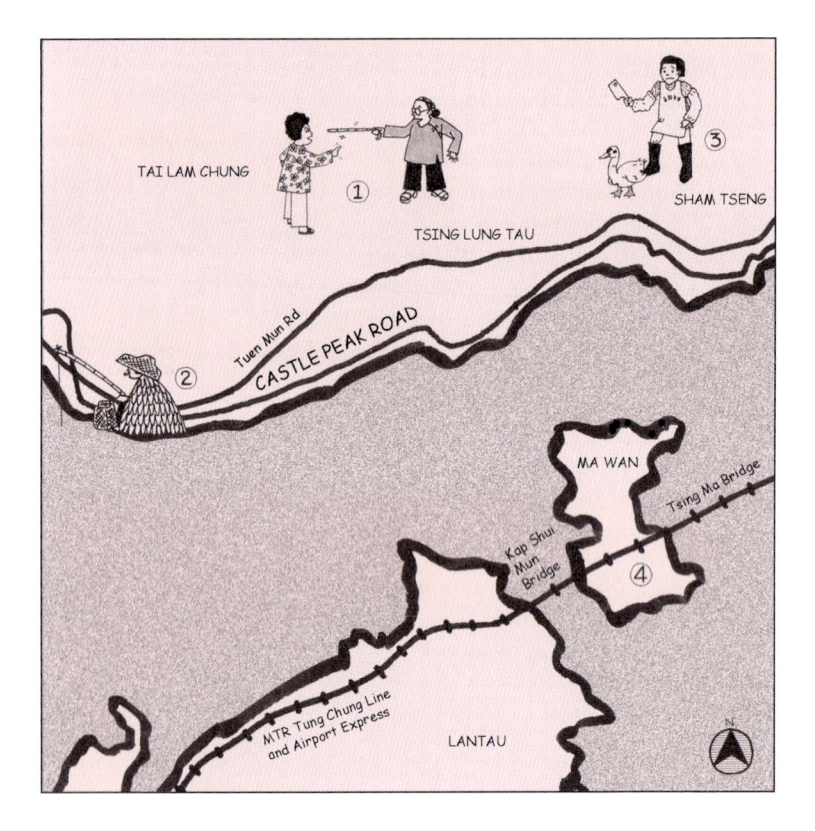

❶ Village life
❷ Fishing tackle and bait shops
❸ Roast goose restaurants
❹ Lantau bridges

STREETS

Castle Peak Road

then remote beaches. By the 1940s and 1950s, many wealthy city-dwellers had built spacious out-of-town homes along here. Many of these residences still exist, hidden away behind high walls and surrounded by huge old trees, mostly with breathtaking views of mountains, islands and sea.

Construction of the Tuen Mun Highway in the early 1980s relieved traffic issues and made this stretch of Castle Peak Road even quieter and more remote. Tsing Lung Tau and Sham Tseng somehow still appear relatively cut-off from the city today, even with the massive bridges and highways built for the new airport visible in every direction.

This stretch of Castle Peak Road could be, and should be, one of Hong Kong's most scenic routes, yet few tourists venture up here and the stretch of coast is neither promoted nor protected. Road-widening works on the lower levels in recent years have greatly degraded the area's appeal, but the Castle Peak beaches remain very pleasant in places.

Sham Tseng, Tsing Lung Tau and beyond have several attractive sandy beaches (unfortunately strewn with rubbish for most of the year), but sadly the same cannot be said for the water quality. Most of the Castle Peak beaches have been closed to bathers for many years now, a tragic irony when one remembers that, until the 1960s, Hong Kong was regionally renowned for its pristine bathing beaches and this stretch of coast was among the most popular.

Numerous prominently located signposts bear ominous looking 'skull-and-crossbones' motifs — graphic indications that bathers should avoid swimming around here altogether. Water quality at the beaches along Castle Peak is consistently rated poor; by Hong Kong's lax standards this means that a quick dip here would be like swimming in an unflushed toilet bowl; a dreadful analogy to make but, alas, only too true.

① Village life

The coastal strip between Tsuen Wan and Castle Peak was always relatively sparsely settled, due to the rocky coastline, shallow sandy soil and open exposure to the sea. Villages at Sham Tseng, Ting Kau, Tsing Lung Tau and other isolated hamlets on the road towards Tuen Mun only supported a few hundred people. In recent years these have grown into substantial dormitory areas for Tsuen Wan; ocean and island views are a major attraction for many residents.

Quite a few village houses still stand along this stretch of coastline, and some rather patchy vegetable cultivation still occurs in the sandy fields close to the water's edge. Papayas, pomelos, *wu tau* (taro root) and other plants eke out a precarious existence, and a few remaining inshore fishing boats still go out from time to time.

Castle Peak Road

② Fishing tackle and bait shops

Massive overfishing in Hong Kong waters in recent years has decimated inshore fish stocks. Yet recreational angling from piers, rocky promontories and off beaches is still a popular pastime. Nothing more substantial than a few herring-sized tiddlers still swim beneath the waves, but this doesn't deter fishing enthusiasts.

Numerous anglers' shops at Tsing Lung Tau and nearby Castle Peak beach areas sell bait, fishing lines, rods and reels, hooks and tackle. A reel of nylon line, a fishhook, lead sinker and a few pieces of bait cost a few dollars, which makes fishing a popular recreation for many. Of course, it is also possible to pay hundreds of dollars for lightweight, high-tensile tackle, and there are no shortage of anglers who want to own nothing but the very best, or the most expensive.

Incredibly, many anglers in Hong Kong do actually eat their catch — at least a few of them say that they do — in spite of the fact that the waters in which the fish were caught are officially considered polluted enough to be permanently closed to swimmers, and the beaches nearby are dotted with skull-and-crossbones signs.

③ Roast goose restaurants

Famous throughout Hong Kong and beyond, the 'greasy goose' restaurants at Sham Tseng have been popular for many years. Birds destined for the table along Castle Peak Road are bred in their thousands near Shantou further up the coast and imported live into Hong Kong.

The famous Sham Tseng 'greasy goose' is specially air-dried for some hours after initial basting with honey, oil and spices. This process, apparently, helps to crisp the skin and makes the flesh moist and tender. Sham Tseng *siu ngor* ('roast goose') is renowned all over Hong Kong, and there is even a branch at the airport to take overseas.

STREETS

Castle Peak Road

Tsuen Wan and Beyond

Weekend evenings are especially popular times to visit Sham Tseng, and the goose restaurants are one of those perennial local favourites that too many visitors to Hong Kong never see or experience. Well worth trying!

4 Lantau bridges

One of the more impressive view points towards Lantau and the airport bridges is located at Ting Kau. This was built on the site of the former official residence of the District Officer South, known as 'Dunrose'. According to one former occupant, the house was originally built by a retired China missionary couple named Duncan and his wife Rose; the building's name was an amalgam of the two. 'Dunrose' has long since been demolished, and the name largely forgotten.

On a clear day the popular view point affords a spectacular prospect over Ma Wan and Kap Shui Mun, and south to the Rambler's Channel, Tsing Yi and the Tsuen Wan — Kwai Chung conurbation. For much of the year, however, the outlook is obscured by the thick yellowish smog which comes down every day from China.

Two main bridges span the narrow Kap Shui Mun Strait. The massive Tsing Ma Bridge links Tsing Yi and Lantau via the small island of Ma Wan. Now a combined village settlement and luxury housing area, Ma Wan was the location of a Chinese Maritime Customs Station prior to the British lease on the New Territories.

Ting Kau Bridge, which links Tsing Yi with Ting Kau on the New Territories mainland, connects to the highway which leads on to Hong Kong's border with Shenzhen.

How To Get There

By Bus:	No. 53 from Tsuen Wan Castle Peak Road towards Yuen Long. Alight at Tsing Lung Tau Pier.
By Minibus:	For Yuen Long/Tuen Mun from Saigon Street (just off Temple Street in Yau Ma Tei). Alight at Tsing Lung Tau Pier.
By Taxi:	新界青龍頭碼頭 (*'Sun Gaai, Ching Loong Tau Ma Tau'*).

STREETS

Kowloon Tong

Glowered over by Lion Rock, one of Kowloon's best-known natural landmarks, Kowloon Tong was laid out in the 1920s as a pleasant, leafy garden suburb. As the Chinese name suggests, Kowloon Tong takes its name from a freshwater pond, or *tong*. Like most of urban Kowloon's original natural features, this has long since vanished. The interior of Kowloon Tong's MTR Station is tiled a light blue, apparently to give the impression of clear summer skies reflected on clean pond water.

The Kowloon-Canton Railway Station at Kowloon Tong is one of Hong Kong's busiest; thousand of daily commuters from the New Territories pile onto the MTR interchange there during peak hours. This — in itself — is also one of those 'authentic Hong Kong' sights that many visitors never experience.

Kowloon Tong, Paul Theroux's forgettable novel brought out to coincide with the pre-handover flurry of interest in Hong Kong, conveys the impression — to those who know no better — that Kowloon Tong is a gritty industrial district. The truth is that the area has always been one of Kowloon's most sought-after residential areas, and never had any industrial development; all that was found further to the east, part Kowloon City, or northwest beyond Sham Shui Po.

Despite considerable transformation and change in recent decades, Kowloon Tong somehow still maintains something of its earlier suburban flavour, pleasingly demonstrating that there is much more to Kowloon's urban districts than the unremitting concrete jungle would first suggest. Kowloon Tong's quiet backstreets offer a nostalgic glimpse of what much of the rest of Kowloon looked like before the high-rise construction frenzy of recent decades radically and permanently altered the way the peninsula looks, feels, sounds and smells.

Traffic-choked, noisy Waterloo Road has been Kowloon Tong's main thoroughfare since the area was first developed from farmland in the 1920s. Surrounding side streets were named after the more picturesque English counties, such as Durham, York, Kent, Sussex, Hereford, Cumberland and Rutland. Many older apartment buildings found around here are three or four stories high, shaded by mature trees and surrounded by large verandahs — a pleasant reminder of earlier, more spacious decades.

Kowloon Tong has numerous attractive old churches, such as the Roman Catholic St Teresa's Church and Anglican Christ Church. These buildings are an attractive reminder of the area's solidly bourgeois beginnings, and provide a valuable sense of continuity with the past. A number of prestigious, long-established local schools are also found in Kowloon Tong, such as La Salle College, originally an offshoot of St Joseph's College on Hong Kong Island, and the Maryknoll Convent School, one of Kowloon's best girls' schools.

One of Kowloon Tong's better known local landmarks is the multi-generational compound residence of the Harilela clan on Waterloo Road. Prominent members of Hong Kong's Sindhi community, the Harilelas got their start as provision contractors for the British forces in the pre-war years, and as a result of a number

- La Salle Road
- Cumberland Road
- Waterloo Road
- Broadcast Drive

of astute investments in the mid-1940s branched out into property development and, subsequently, a chain of highly successful hotels. The now deceased Harilela matriarch insisted that her sons and their families all lived together under one roof. To accommodate this sizeable extended family, a large compound house was built. The Harilela clan remain probably the most well-known local Indian family in Hong Kong; their photographs are very frequently seen in the local society pages.

For several decades, Kowloon Tong's close proximity to Kai Tak Airport did much to preserve the area's distinctive low-rise character. The incredible, thrilling sight and sound of inbound jet aircraft passing only a few hundred feet overhead remains one of those formerly common Kowloon experiences that with Kai Tak Airport's closure, have now been completely relegated to memory.

La Salle Road
喇沙利道

La Salle Road is a pleasant, low-key area of mostly medium-rise apartment blocks, one of Kowloon's more popular residential areas with good schools and little commercial activity. There are a few pockets of interest and the area is an agreeable place to stroll away from downtown Kowloon's teeming streets.

A good reason to come along here is to notice the sharp contrast within relatively short distances, the serried ranks of public housing blocks start several hundred metres away just behind Kowloon City, and Mong Kok's ceaselessly crowded tenements are only a few streets to the south. But in Kowloon Tong there are mature trees along the roadside, window-boxes full of plants, a sense of relative quiet, and an overall ambience of bourgeois comfort and security.

Much of the earlier residential character of Kowloon Tong, even if not many of the original buildings, still survives. Relaxation of building height regulations due to Kai Tak Airport's closure in 1998 means that the area's pleasantly suburban character — so strikingly at variance with much of the rest of Kowloon — has still been maintained.

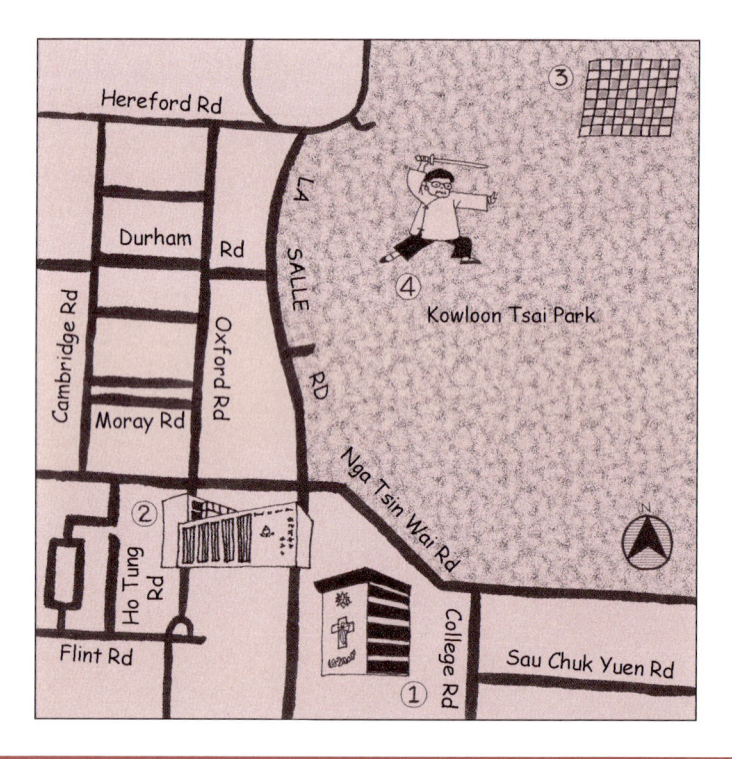

❶ La Salle College
❷ Bishop Hall Jubilee School
❸ 'Checkerboard' hillside
❹ Kowloon Tsai Park

La Salle Road

1) La Salle College

One of Kowloon's prestigious boys' schools, the Roman Catholic-run La Salle College occupies a large site on La Salle Road. The college grew out of an earlier Kowloon branch of St Joseph's College on Hong Kong Island, and was established on Chatham Road in Tsim Sha Tsui in 1915. Many early students here, as at its predecessor institution, were local Portuguese. As more members of this then sizeable local community settled in Tsim Sha Tsui in the interwar years, the school gradually expanded, and when student numbers became too large for its Tsim Sha Tsui premises, a new site was obtained in Kowloon Tong.

The original La Salle College was built here in 1934; its distinctive white dome was a well-known local landmark for decades. After the outbreak of the Second World War in Europe in 1939, the La Salle College buildings and grounds were used to intern German and Italian nationals resident in Hong Kong. While freedom of movement was obviously restricted, conditions at the college were comfortable, personal possessions were permitted and both medical and food supplies were plentiful. All German and Italian internees were released two years later, following the Japanese capture of Hong Kong.

Run by the De La Salle Order, quite a few of Hong Kong's 'movers and shakers' have attended La Salle College over the years and continue to fill the ranks of government and business to this day. These include figures such as prominent local Portuguese businessman A. de O. Sales, who served for many years as the chairman of the now defunct Urban Council, and West Indies-born Urban Councillor Hilton Cheong-leen.

La Salle College produced at least one internationally famous Old Boy, the *kung fu* actor Bruce Lee. Of Eurasian heritage, Lee attended the college for several years in the 1950s before moving to the United States. Then as now, La Salle College was one of Hong Kong's elite local schools, and the tough, 'Kowloon street-kid' mythology that subsequently grew up around Bruce Lee was mostly that — sheer myth. Really poor children simply did not get the chance to attend this school in those years.

La Salle Road

The old school buildings were torn down in 1979 to make way for the present fairly anonymous premises. The late 1970s were a black period for heritage conservation and historical awareness in Hong Kong, and such a decision would — just possibly — not be taken today.

② Bishop Hall Jubilee School

This substantial local secondary school was named after R. O. Hall, the popular Anglican bishop of Hong Kong who served the local community with great dedication from 1932 until his retirement in 1966. Better known by the Chinese as 'Ho Ming-wah', Bishop Hall was a vocal early champion of wider Chinese participation in public life in Hong Kong.

Hall was greatly ahead of his time in many other social attitudes; in 1944 he ordained Florence Lee, the first ever woman to serve as a priest in the Anglican Church, to assist the Anglican community in Macao. Though not occupied, Macao was isolated due to the Japanese occupation of neighbouring Hong Kong and in the absence of a male clergyman, Hall took the initiative and ordained her. Lee's appointment was revoked on higher authority after the war. Nevertheless she blazed the trail for others, and female clergy are now commonplace in the Anglican Church, and in many other Christian denominations.

La Salle Road

R. O. Hall was unkindly known by more than a few critics in Hong Kong as the 'Pink Bishop' due to his firmly expressed humanitarian views. During the 1950s his open admiration for the many early achievements of the Communist regime, especially in the eradication of vice, drug addiction and official corruption, led to him being labelled a Communist dupe by some observers. 'R. O.' was also a driving force behind the establishment of the Hong Kong Housing Society and the Family Welfare Society, as well as numerous orphanages, juvenile aid societies, schools and charitable organizations in Hong Kong.

This well-regarded school in Kowloon Tong bears Bishop Hall's name, in tribute to his life's work and was opened in 1957, the year of R. O. Hall's Silver Jubilee as Bishop of Hong Kong. A resource centre for Chinese migrants to Great Britain, based at London's historic church of St Martin's-in-the-Fields, is also named after this remarkable man.

③ 'Checkerboard' hillside

Other than the disused runway itself, this black-and-white painted 'checkerboard' on the hillside overlooking Osborn Barracks is one of the few, rapidly fading relics of the old Kai Tak Airport — even the old terminal buildings have been demolished. This otherwise unremarkable little spot marks the point where flights coming in over Kowloon made a sharp right-hand turn — only five hundred metres or so overhead — before finally coming down on the runway. Passengers themselves could see the checkerboard pattern quite clearly as they flew over — they were *that* close to the ground by then!

A radar post was also installed here to assist with the visual reference provided by the checkerboard and flashing light, and while the hillside was officially a restricted area, access to the slope immediately below the aircraft turning point was very easy in pre-terrorist years. For decades the hillside was a very popular place for Hong Kong's plane-spotters, especially during early evenings, and many local people simply came up to sit and watch the aircraft roar overhead.

STREETS

La Salle Road

Since 1998, Kai Tak Airport and its world-famous, dramatic final approach low over the Kowloon rooftops has been relegated to photographs and memory, and very few people bother to come to sit here any more; with no planes coming in, the excitement has vanished. The hillside lookout is a very quiet place these days, abandoned, like the fading paint on its checkerboard, to changing times.

4. Kowloon Tsai Park

Very popular with early morning joggers, Kowloon Tsai ('Little Kowloon') Park is one of the largest open public spaces in north Kowloon. Like most of the larger parks elsewhere in Hong Kong's urban area, this one has a pleasant combination of well-equipped playgrounds, quiet sitting areas and well-tended mature trees and shrubs.

During early morning hours, often as early as 3 a.m., the paths and open spaces in Kowloon Tsai Park are patrolled by numerous, mostly elderly, early morning walkers. Even in the winter months the place can seem quite crowded by 5 a.m. or so. Several impromptu *tai chi*, sword dance and fan dance sessions are in progress at any one time, as well as badminton games and aerobic practice.

Participants in these activities are generally older people, mostly retirees who live in the many large public housing estates around Wong Tai Sin and Kowloon City. By 7 a.m. or so most of these people have either gone home, or headed off for breakfast with their friends in one of the enormous, permanently thronged *dim sum* palaces in the neighbouring districts.

How To Get There

By Bus:	No. 208 from Tsim Sha Tsui East via 'Star' Ferry.
By Taxi:	九龍塘喇沙利道 (*'Gau Loong Tong, Lah Sah Lei Doh'*).

Cumberland Road
金巴倫道

Generally fairly quiet — and for that reason very popular with learner drivers on Sunday mornings — tree-shaded Cumberland Road still gives a flavour of what most of Kowloon Tong looked like until relatively recent years. And like other parts of the district, there is a suburban sameness here that disappears with closer acquaintance.

Numerous old family homes, generally dating from the 1920s and 1930s, have been mostly converted into 'motels' or high-priced kindergartens. At certain times of day Kowloon Tong's backstreets — like this one — are thronged with dozens of tiny Chinese tots and South East Asian domestic helpers carrying their charge's schoolbags. For some reason, though, one seldom sees an obviously recognizable 'Mummy' personally come to collect her child around here.

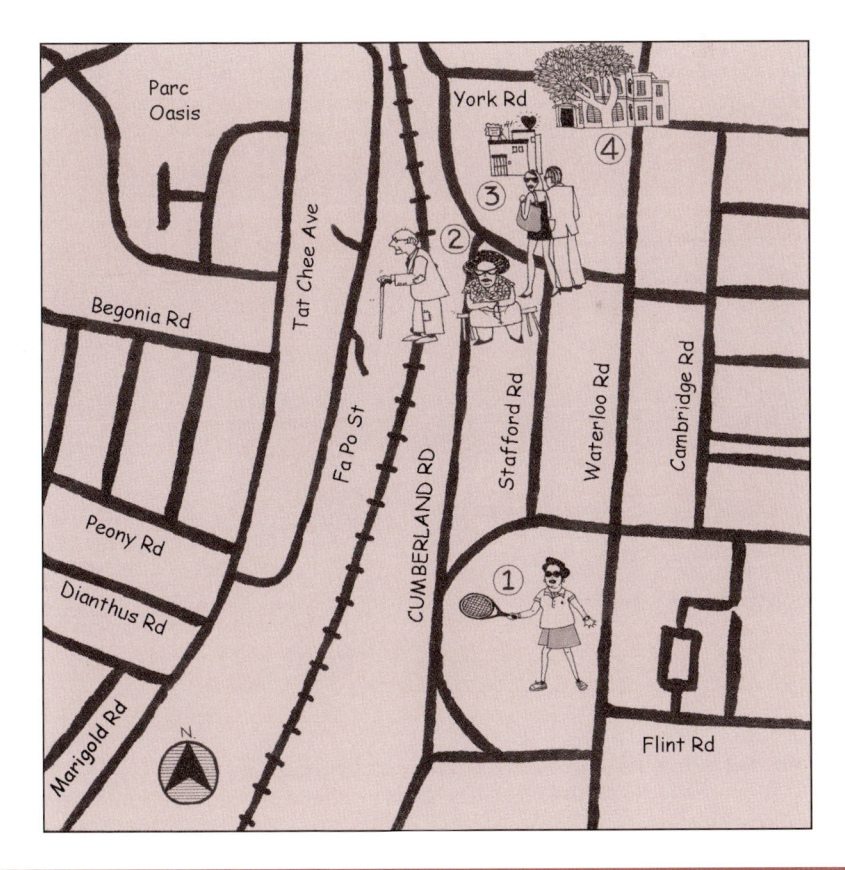

❶ Kowloon Tong Club
❷ China Coast Community
❸ 'Love motels'
❹ House at York Road

Cumberland Road

Such private houses that still remain along here and elsewhere in Kowloon Tong are mostly set within garden compounds surrounded by high walls and forbidding-looking gates. Some even have security cameras, and many fences are topped with that time-honoured Far Eastern combination of barbed wire, rusty nails and broken glass. These grim deterrent features combine to give some places a forbidding, fortress-like, 'us-against-everyone-else' outlook when seen from the street.

Given that Hong Kong is generally a very safe society, with one of the world's lowest levels of random violence and almost no gun crime, one sometimes cannot but wonder whether *all* these security precautions are really that necessary? Quite a few residents around here obviously think that they are. Given the spate of high-profile kidnappings in Hong Kong during the 1990s, when a number of superwealthy Hong Kong Chinese tycoons — some of whom live around here — were spirited away and held to ransom in remote corners of the New Territories for enormous sums of money, perhaps these draconian looking safety measures are not quite so paranoid and unnecessary as they seem.

① Kowloon Tong Club

Surrounded by extensive grounds and playing fields, the Kowloon Tong Club was established on the site in 1931 and has been a popular social point for this part of Kowloon ever since. Initial membership of the club was only one hundred — all were residents from the surrounding area — but now number several hundred.

Most club members originally lived in the immediate Kowloon Tong area, although today they are drawn from all over Hong Kong. As with other clubs in the interwar years, there were substantial numbers of Eurasian and local Portuguese

Cumberland Road

members in its early days, a pattern repeated during those years in other social and sporting clubs elsewhere on the Kowloon side, such as the Club de Recreio and the Kowloon Cricket Club.

Like most other social and sporting clubs in Hong Kong nowadays, well over 90 percent of the Kowloon Tong Club's members are Hong Kong Chinese. The remainder are mainly Japanese and Europeans of various nationalities. Club facilities include tennis courts, a swimming pool, bowling alley, card rooms and two floors of restaurants serving various types of food. When asked, club officials admitted that they did not know exactly when the present building was constructed, but judging by the architectural style it must have been put up sometime during the 1970s.

2 China Coast Community

Located at 63 Cumberland Road, the China Coast Community is the only English-speaking old people's home in Hong Kong. It was established in the 1970s to accommodate the English-speaking elderly who either had no desire to return to their country of origin on retirement, or who had never known any other home than Hong Kong or the former Treaty Port cities in pre-Communist-era China, such as Shanghai and Tientsin (Tianjin).

While there are still quite a number of Europeans at the home, many residents these days are Eurasians, local Portuguese or highly anglicized Chinese. All have fascinating stories to tell of life on the China Coast in decades past, of good times as well as dangers and dislocations during the various wars, invasions and political upheavals that have taken place on the Mainland; their number includes at least one ex-*tai pan*.

Cumberland Road

Generously subvented by the Community Chest and periodically assisted by private donations, the China Coast Community is housed in attractive old buildings with well-maintained grounds, and fills a vital and often overlooked social need. For more mobile residents, the China Coast Community is conveniently located near public transport links. As a result, many elderly residents still maintain full and active lives outside the home — in contrast to many elderly care facilities elsewhere in Hong Kong, which sometimes seem like a combination of prison hospital and mortuary waiting room.

(3) 'Love motels'

Numerous popular 'love motels' lurk in Kowloon Tong's backstreets, and are one of the most noted features of the area to outsiders. Most are located in once gracious old bungalows that were sold by their former occupants in the 1960s and 1970s, and eventually converted to other uses.

In the days before the Cross-Harbour Tunnel was built, the journey across to Kowloon from Hong Kong Island was time-consuming and could perhaps involve an overnight stay in typhoon weather. Private cars came into more widespread general use in those years, with a corresponding increase in various clandestine romantic possibilities.

Most people in Hong Kong still live with their families well into adulthood, which provides little opportunity for some romance with the partner of their choice. The newly opened motels fitted the bill perfectly and were carefully designed to create the desired atmosphere, with mirrored ceilings, jacuzzi baths and other such fittings.

In all these establishments the management policy is strictly 'bring-your-own' companion. Curtains or screens are discreetly drawn in front of the carports as soon as a patron and partner drives in, although one cannot really tell whether

Cumberland Road

this is to stave off the ever present Hong Kong paparazzi or to keep private detectives and jealous spouses at bay. As with many similar, long-established elements of Hong Kong life, employees in these places seldom ask — or answer — too many questions.

Over the years these 'love motels' have been very widely featured in numerous export-orientated films made in Hong Kong wherever Cantonese-language movies are shown. This somewhat sleazy cinematic image all helped make the term 'Kowloon Tong' synonymous with a short-time fling in a shady motel. In any small upcountry Malaysian town or public housing estate in Singapore virtually *everyone* has heard of Kowloon Tong in this context, even if they have never been to Hong Kong in their entire lives.

(4) House at York Road

This attractive two-storied house, plastered in rough cast stucco, with small ornamental balconies is one of the few remaining in Kowloon Tong that have not been extensively rebuilt or converted to other uses. Until recent years it was still owned by the same local Portuguese family who built it in the late 1920s, lived in it right through the Japanese occupation, and used it as their family home for over seventy years.

Most of the neighbouring houses here and elsewhere in Kowloon Tong have long since been converted into the kindergartens, 'love motels' or chintzy, utterly over-the-top bridal salons for which the area is now best known. With extensive, well-maintained gardens and a small orchard with venerable avocado trees, this well-preserved, gracious home provides a now rare reminder of what Kowloon Tong once looked like when the area really was a 'garden suburb'.

How To Get There

By Bus:	No. 7 from Tsim Sha Tsui 'Star' Ferry.
By MTR:	Kowloon Tong Station.
By Taxi:	九龍塘金巴倫道 (*'Gau Loong Tong, Gum Bar Lun Doh'*).

Waterloo Road
窩打老道

Modern Waterloo Road must be one of Kowloon's busiest as well as longest continuous thoroughfares, thronged with cars, buses and trucks at all hours. Within living memory, however, Waterloo Road was a quiet road through a garden suburb, which led to vegetable fields and small farms, before eventually petering out at the lower slopes of the Kowloon hills.

Waterloo Road began at the Yau Ma Tei Typhoon Shelter. After passing through Yau Ma Tei's densely packed tenement streets, it gradually entered more open country towards Kowloon Tong and extended as far as the lower slopes of Lion Rock. A large, uncovered, periodically odoriferous nullah once ran up the middle of Waterloo Road, but it has long since been covered over. Fascinating corners can be encountered all along Waterloo Road, and the area's character and usage changes, often substantially, every few hundred metres or so.

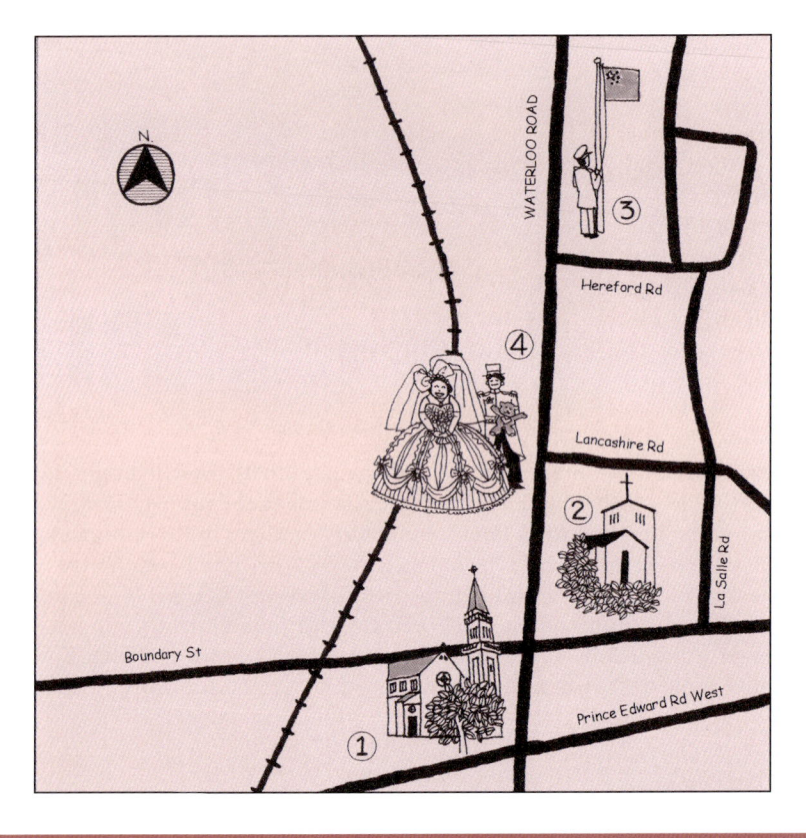

❶ St Teresa's Church
❷ Christ Church
❸ Barracks
❹ Wedding boutiques

STREETS

Waterloo Road

1) St Teresa's Church

Now surrounded by much higher buildings, this attractive Italian Renaissance-style building at 99A Waterloo Road was once one of the most prominent built landmarks in northern Kowloon. Seen from a distance, the exterior walls almost look like dressed stone. Although built of reinforced concrete — like so many other contemporary buildings in Hong Kong — the combination of age, sporadic maintenance and the effects of a humid climate have gradually given St Teresa's a dignified, ecclesiastical ambience, and the gracious patina of years.

The foundation stone for St Teresa's Church was laid in on 23 April 1932, by the Roman Catholic bishop of Hong Kong, Enrico Valtorta, P.I.M.E. St Teresa's Church formed part of a considerable expansion of Roman Catholic buildings undertaken in the 1930s. The Italianate design was approved by Bishop Valtorta who, perhaps unsurprisingly, was himself an Italian.

St Teresa's distinctive national style can be seen, in some respects, as a reflection of how Hong Kong's Roman Catholic diocese was an Italian preserve for well over a century until the late 1960s; all of Hong Kong's Roman Catholic bishops were from Italy. Benito Mussolini, the Fascist dictator of Italy, was also a major donor to this church, and Il Duce's generosity is recorded on a plaque just inside the doors, along with numerous once prominent local Portuguese names. Many of St Teresa's early parishioners were local Portuguese, living in either Kowloon Tong or Ho Man Tin nearby.

St Teresa's was constructed by the Franco-Belgian firm Credit Foncierre d'Extreme Orient along with scores of other ecclesiastical buildings built elsewhere in Hong Kong in those years, such as the Carmelite convent in Stanley and the Little Sisters of the Poor in Ngau Chi Wan, as well as a number of neighbouring housing developments in northern Kowloon.

Now overshadowed by the busy flyover running next to it (which, incidentally, was the first one ever built in Kowloon), St Teresa's impressive dome and campanile are dwarfed by surrounding buildings and almost permanently shrouded in diesel fumes. Somehow the interior of the church remains remarkably quiet, even with the constant traffic roaring past the windows.

Waterloo Road

② *Christ Church*

With its white stucco walls and clean, plain lines, Christ Church looks like a Spanish mission church somewhere in California, Arizona or New Mexico. Located up a flight of stone steps off busy Waterloo Road and surrounded by mature trees, Christ Church is surprisingly quiet and not as hemmed in as one might otherwise expect. A colourful mosaic set into the ground near the entrance depicts the Lamb of God, bearing the Flag of St George, an allegorical representation of the Church of England. Like most of the other churches in Kowloon Tong, Christ Church also dates from the 1930s; the foundation stone was laid on 31 March 1936 by the then governor, Sir Andrew Caldecott.

At Christ Church's inaugural service some months later, R. O. Hall, the Anglican bishop of Hong Kong, irately lambasted the assembled congregation for donating a collection of expensive and — he felt — completely unnecessary altar decorations to the new church. Bishop Hall decried this donation as 'sheer wickedness' when thousands of poverty-stricken refugees who had decamped from China to Hong Kong had 'neither roof nor bowl of rice in a city where Christian people could spend hundreds of dollars in unnecessary ornaments in their churches'.

Despite such periodic outbursts, Bishop Hall was very popular within the wider community and numerous successful social welfare initiatives owe their beginnings to his unstinting commitment to the colony's poor and underprivileged. This church also has a memorial plaque for members of its congregation, many of them local Eurasians, who died during the Pacific War.

③ *Barracks*

Osborn Barracks on Waterloo Road was renamed in the 1970s after Company Sergeant-Major John Osborn, a Norfolk-born migrant to Canada who served with the Canadian forces in Hong Kong during the Japanese invasion in December 1941. Osborn was killed in action near Jardine's Lookout when he threw himself

Waterloo Road

on a Japanese grenade to protect the men surrounding him. He was posthumously honoured with the Victoria Cross, the only such award made for the Hong Kong campaign.

Osborn Barracks provide an extensive, low-profile Kowloon base for the People's Liberation Army, and has been officially renamed Kowloon East Barracks. The spacious, valuable married quarters on Waterloo Road now stand completely empty, decayed and unused. Since the handover to China in 1997 the same crumbling fate has befallen military married quarters in other prime locations, such as Stanley Fort at the southern tip of Hong Kong Island and Sek Kong Village in the New Territories.

4 *Wedding boutiques*

Waterloo Road

Need to plan for 'that special day' and don't know where to get all you need — or think you may need? Along with a few well-known corners of Mong Kok such as Sai Yee Street, Waterloo Road has numerous bridal boutiques offering complete wedding packages that include virtually everything except the prospective bride and groom.

'Western-style' weddings have gradually become *de rigueur* over the last two decades in Hong Kong. Like a great many other 'Western-style' confections found locally, weddings accoutrements found here are unlike *anything* found in the West — with the possible exception of Las Vegas. Heavily derived from the Japanese and Taiwanese notion of 'Western' wedding styles, from the outside these boutiques give a fairly clear indication of what is offered within; a gimcrack fantasy of Parisian-style glamour, filtered to Hong Kong via Hollywood, Tokyo and Taipei.

White tulle and lace-embroidered wedding gowns tend to predominate in the boutiques along here — somehow the frothier and more implausible the better. Men's outfits are almost as unlikely; highly coloured, Japanese-influenced pastiches of a traditional English-style morning suit being the usual choice. Overwhelmingly, these fanciful garments are for rental purposes only — very few people, after all, would *ever* wear the same unfeasible outfit again in any other context.

As a fascinating window on an integral aspect of modern Hong Kong Chinese popular culture, a glimpse into one of Kowloon's larger wedding boutiques are certainly in a league of their own and not to be missed.

How To Get There

By Bus:	No. 7 from Tsim Sha Tsui 'Star' Ferry.
By Taxi:	九龍塘窩打老道 (*'Gau Loong Tong, Wor Dah Loh Doh'*).

Broadcast Drive
廣播道

This winding, mixed residential area lies beneath the very shadow of Lion Rock. It takes its name from the radio and television stations found along various sections. Kowloon Tong slopes towards the Kowloon hills here, and not far behind Broadcast Drive the urban area gives way towards more open country. Other roads in the vicinity are related to the development of broadcasting. Fessenden Road is named for Reginald Fessenden, the Canadian pioneer who sent the world's first successful radio message in 1900. Marconi Road recalls the much more well-known Italian inventor Guglielmo Marconi who, in 1901, broadcast the first message across the Atlantic, from Cornwall to Newfoundland.

    Broadcast Drive and its environs are one of the more desirable residential areas in Kowloon. High enough to enjoy a view and for the most part south-facing, and therefore cool and breezy in the Hong Kong summer, apartments around here have long been sought after. Unlike much of Kowloon, Broadcast Drive is also fairly quiet, with most major roads located some distance away. Most blocks of flats around here were built in the 1960s and 1970s, and are much more spacious and well-designed than those constructed in recent decades.

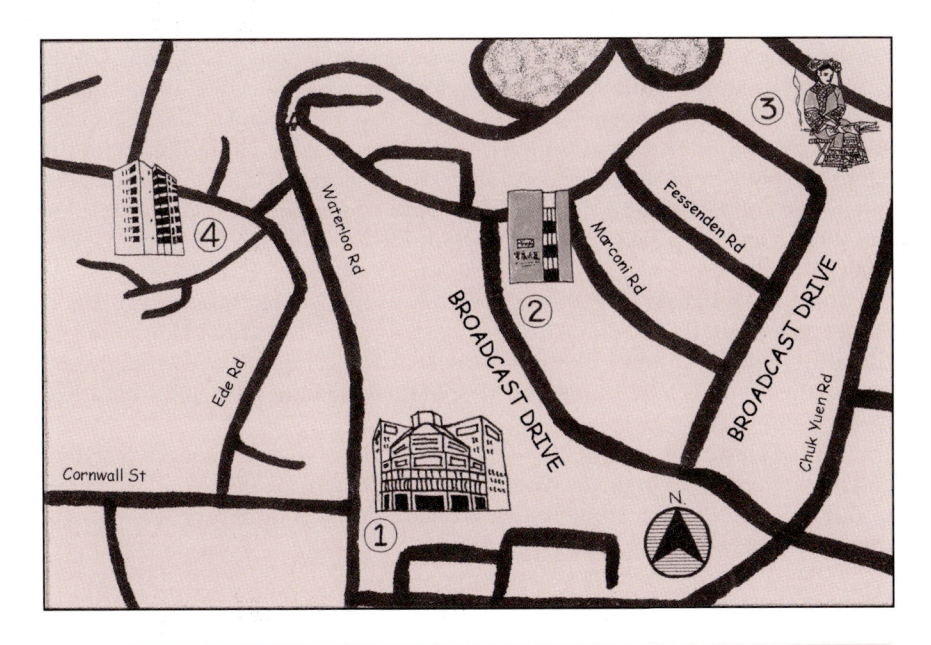

Kowloon Tong

❶ Hong Kong Baptist University
❷ Radio Television Hong Kong (RTHK)
❸ Asia Television (ATV)
❹ Luso Apartments

STREETS

Broadcast Drive

1) Hong Kong Baptist University

One of eight degree-issuing institutions in modern Hong Kong, Hong Kong Baptist University grew out of the earlier Baptist College, which was first established in Hong Kong in 1956. This line of descent makes Baptist University the third oldest tertiary institution in Hong Kong, after the University of Hong Kong and the Chinese University of Hong Kong. Another contemporary tertiary institution grew out of a grouping of colleges; the Chinese University of Hong Kong developed in the 1960s from New Asia College (1949), Chung Chi College (1951) and United College (1956).

Hong Kong Baptist University is government-funded, but firmly maintains its earlier American, Baptist emphasis. Popularly known throughout Hong Kong as 'Baptist U', the institution has three closely linked campuses clustered around the northern end of Waterloo Road. Most of these buildings date from the 1960s to the 1990s.

Baptist University was the first tertiary institution to have modern teaching and research facilities in the field of Traditional Chinese Medicine (TCM). Other institutions elsewhere in Hong Kong have since developed study programmes in this increasingly popular field.

Broadcast Drive

② *Radio Television Hong Kong (RTHK)*

Radio Television Hong Kong (RTHK) evolved out of an earlier Hong Kong government wireless communication entity, the pre-war radio station ZBW, which operated out of studios in Gloucester Buildings in Central. ZBW became known as Radio Hong Kong (RHK) in the postwar era. A 'Public Affairs Television Unit' within RHK was established in 1970. The unit commenced educational television broadcasts in 1971 and in 1973 established its own newsroom. Radio Hong Kong changed its name to Radio Television Hong Kong in 1976.

For decades, RTHK consistently maintained an admirably independent editorial position and has held fast to this principle since 1997. In this respect the station remains very similar to that of the BBC, on which it was closely modelled.

RTHK's public service function has meant that numerous 'educational' advertisements are aired in the course of ordinary broadcasting. These somewhat nannying, questionably useful segments exhort the general public not to light hill fires, to clear away water from mosquito-breeding spots, to wash their hands after using the lavatory and not litter and spit on the streets. In short, all the things that responsible, intelligent residents of any advanced society would surely do automatically, and *certainly* without the need to be repeatedly told.

③ *Asia Television (ATV)*

Asia Television (ATV) is one of Hong Kong's two commercial terrestrial television stations, along with Television Broadcasts Limited (TVB).

In the 1950s the Hong Kong government explored the possibility of cable broadcast services. Rediffusion Hong Kong, initially owned by Rediffusion UK, commenced operations as a cable service in 1957. It subsequently shifted to wireless broadcasts in 1973.

Broadcast Drive

An Australian consortium bought a majority stake in the company in 1981 and sold half of these the next year to a Chinese-owned concern. Later in 1982 Rediffusion Hong Kong changed its name to Asia Television Limited (ATV) and the Chinese interests bought out the Australians in 1984. Both ATV and TVB companies maintain Chinese-language and English-language services as part of their licensing arrangements.

Hong Kong is one of the world's most television-focused societies, and the latest twist and turn of a soap opera provide the city with an endless source of 'safe' office conversations, as well as a constant supply of marketing opportunities for the shrewd and entrepreneurial. Popular magazines chronicle the doings — and undoings — of the latest television starlet, and given the worldwide dispersal of Hong Kong–Cantonese culture in recent decades, all these local celebrity developments are as avidly followed in some suburbs of Vancouver, Toronto, San Francisco, Los Angeles, Melbourne and Sydney as they are in Hong Kong.

Not *all* viewers over the years have been enamoured of the standard of broadcasting provided by either commercial station or RTHK, their Hong Kong government-funded rival. Travel writer Jan Morris once acerbically described Hong Kong's television services as 'on the whole the worst I have ever watched', and there are a great many long-term local residents who would wholeheartedly agree with her assessment.

In particular, Hong Kong's English-language programme services come in for widespread criticism. Insensitive editing, crass, inappropriately timed advertisements and a consistently low standard of editorial content are the most frequent and valid complaints. The principal money-spinners for local commercial stations are the Chinese-language channels. As most proceedings conducted in English are increasingly seen by the wider Hong Kong public as — at best — a semi-relevant nuisance, little serious attention is ever paid to complaints about either programme content or editorial standards.

STREETS

Broadcast Drive

④ Luso Apartments

These spacious pleasant flats were originally built for the local Portuguese employees of the Hongkong and Shanghai Banking Corporation, and as a result were known for years as the 'Bank flats'. 'Luso' is a clear indication of the origins of the principal occupants.

Two successive Chief Managers of the Hongkong Bank, Sir Arthur Morse (1943–53) and Sir Michael Turner (1953–62), were responsible for the construction. Both men had been greatly impressed by the loyalty to the British cause displayed by the local Portuguese community during the Japanese occupation of Hong Kong (Turner had been a civilian internee in Stanley during these years), and wished to do something tangible to reward their employees' steadfastness during that period. Luso Apartments was the eventual result, and ownership of a property here helped many local Portuguese enter the Hong Kong property market for the first, and in some cases only, time in their lives.

Political upheaval in China, combined with riots in Hong Kong during 1956, 1966 and 1967, caused many local Portuguese to reconsider their family's long-term futures in the colony, and many decided to leave. Eventual sale of their homes in the 'Bank flats' provided many families with the capital to emigrate to the United States, Australia, Canada and elsewhere in the 1960s and 1970s.

In spite of the community's widespread numerical decline in recent decades, there are still quite a number of local Portuguese who live on in Luso Apartments. This makes the enclave one of the more tangible lingering remnants of this once sizable, now largely vanished local community. Like many formerly distinct aspects of Hong Kong life, the local Portuguese community seems set to decline further with the passage of time and Hong Kong's 'steadily' increased Cantonese-influenced cultural homogeneity.

How To Get There

By Bus:	No. 208 from Tsim Sha Tsui East via Tsim Sha Tsui 'Star' Ferry.
By MTR:	Kowloon Tong Station.
By Taxi:	九龍塘廣播道 (*'Gau Loong Tong, Kwong Boh Doh'*).

STREETS

九龍 Kowloon City

Few areas in Kowloon have changed as much over the last decade as Kowloon City. During the 1990s two major landmarks that helped to define the district in the popular imagination for most of its existence passed into history: seedy, mysterious, perennially fascinating Kowloon Walled City, the squalid lair of Triad fraternities and associated criminal elements, and Kai Tak Airport, for almost half a century the main international gateway to Hong Kong and one of the world's most exciting airport approaches.

Gau Loong Sing ('Kowloon City') was the base of a Qing dynasty magistrate from the early nineteenth century onwards. A small fortified *yamen* (magistrate's compound) was built near the Kowloon Bay waterfront in the 1810s. Around the same time various other fortifications were built elsewhere in the Hong Kong region, such as Tung Chung and Fan Lau forts on Lantau, one on Kowloon Point (where the Marine Police Station later stood) and, much more extensively, further up the Pearl River at the Bocca Tigris (present-day Humen), on the southern approaches to the city of Canton.

When what became the New Territories were leased to Great Britain in 1898, the walled section around Kowloon City was specifically excluded. Mainly for defence considerations, the Kowloon Walled City mandarin and his staff were subsequently expelled from Hong Kong in 1899 and the area incorporated, more or less, into the surrounding district.

After the Qing dynasty collapsed in 1912, a group of Manchu loyalists decamped from China and settled within Kowloon Walled City. These émigrés regarded the walled city as an integral part of Imperial China and maintained, as far as possible, the traditional customs that the Republican period saw abolished, such as the wearing of queues. A group of these diehards lived in Kowloon City until the 1920s, and were locally regarded as quaint, anachronistic, somewhat harmless figures. Films and documentaries have been made about them.

The ambiguous constitutional status of Kowloon City led to various diplomatic problems between China and Great Britain in the postwar era. The Communist authorities on the Mainland periodically used the Kowloon Walled City issue to show 'who was *really* the boss' in Hong Kong, with, in general, very limited success. Hong Kong Police incursions into Kowloon Walled City, however necessary, were always loudly protested by Beijing (and periodically Taipei as well), and in due course the various Triad societies became the real locus of power and authority in the area.

Prostitution and pornography rackets, backyard abortionists, sex toy manufacturers, wholesale and retail narcotic trading and other illicit drug manufacture were all commonplace within the walled city, along with fish-ball and *dim sum* processing works. Hong Kong's unsavoury, thoroughly well-deserved reputation as a centre for the international narcotics trade in the 1950s and 1960s was not helped by Kowloon City's immediate proximity to Kai Tak Airport — from there the Walled City's worst products went out into the wider world.

- Hung Hom Road
- Ma Tau Wai Road
- Sung Wong Toi Road
- Nga Tsin Wai Road
- Tak Ku Ling Road
- Tung Tau Tsuen Road

As well as Kowloon City's darker, more sinister reputation, this small area was justly renowned as one of the best places in Hong Kong to go for inexpensive dental treatment. Dozens of (more or less) competent Mainland-trained dentists, who were unable to legally practise as their qualifications were unrecognized in Hong Kong, set themselves up in business in Kowloon Walled City. Charging far lower prices than Hong Kong or overseas-qualified dentists, two generations of Hong Kong's poorer residents made an expedition to Kowloon City whenever they needed to get their teeth fixed.

With the signing of the Joint Declaration between the United Kingdom and China in 1984, the lingering political questions over Kowloon City were gradually removed. It was obviously in the long-term interests of the Mainland authorities to clean up the festering Kowloon Walled City before 1997, and the once constant political interference over the area quietly ceased.

Ambitious redevelopment plans for the area were implemented, and the dreadful, jerry-built slum dwellings found within Kowloon Walled City were gradually demolished and finally completely cleared in 1994. What was once one of Hong Kong's most fearful, unsanitary areas is now an expansive, well-landscaped public park, and the old Qing dynasty *yamen* buildings (which almost miraculously survived intact during the slum years) have been beautifully restored and opened to the public.

Hung Hom Road
紅磡道

A number of distinct village entities existed in this part of pre-British Kowloon. These were Hung Hom, Hok Un, Tai Wan, Kwo Lo Wan, Shek Shan and Lo Lung Hang. All have long since been subsumed into the wider Kowloon area, but some localized place names, such as Tai Wan and Hok Un, as well as Hung Hom itself, are still in use.

Modern Hung Hom ('Red Cliff') retains very little from the past that suggests the area — not so very long ago — was a major heavy and light industrial complex. The main area of activity was focused around the Hong Kong and Whampoa Dock Company yards, better known to four generations of Hong Kong people as the Kowloon Docks, or simply 'The Dock Company'.

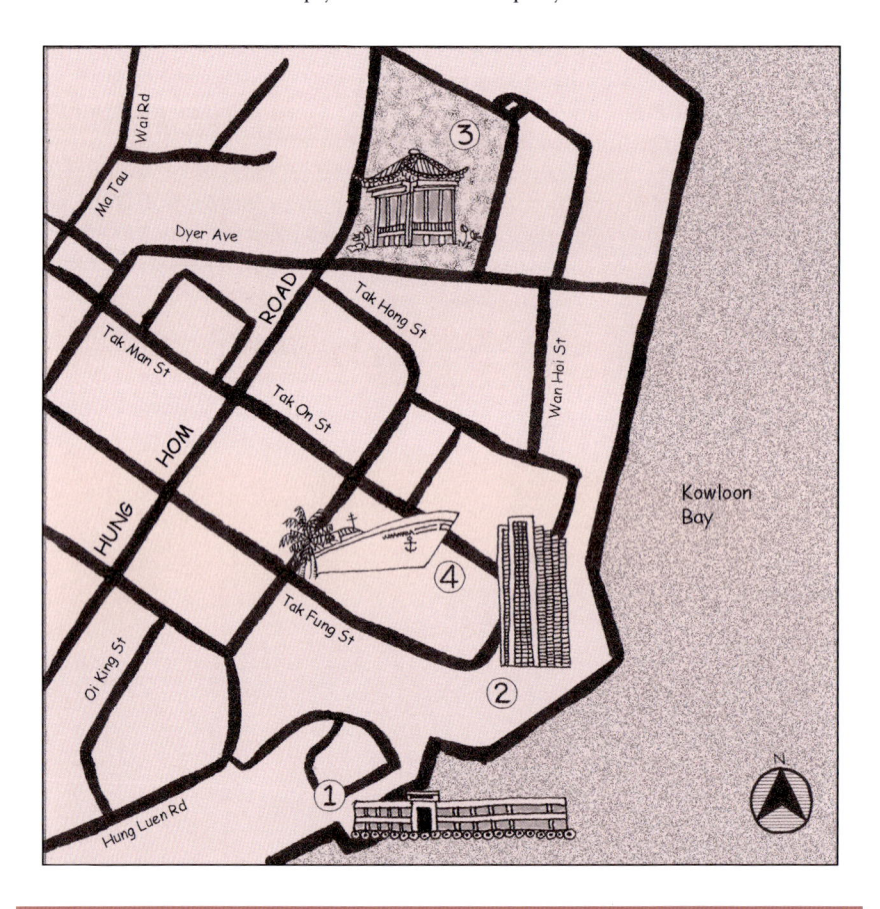

❶ Hung Hom Ferry Pier	❸ Hutchison Park
❷ Harbour Plaza Hotel	❹ Marooned 'ship' at Whampoa Gardens

STREETS

Hung Hom Road

Ship-building and ship-repairing was a major local industry in this part of Kowloon from the late nineteenth century until the late 1960s. Hung Hom-built vessels were used as far away as Papua New Guinea, the Solomon Islands and Fiji. For decades a massive hammerhead crane reared over the dry dock at Tai Wan, on the Hung Hom waterfront. One of the most immediate built landmarks along the Kowloon waterfront in the past, the crane has long vanished both from the skyline and most people's memories.

Hung Hom has experienced some gentrification in recent years, which moves the area even further away from its working-class, ship-building origins. Massive new luxury housing developments along the waterfront that look across towards North Point and a number of large-scale hotel and office complexes indicate significant changes in the coming years.

① *Hung Hom Ferry Pier*

The 'Star' Ferry crossing from Tsim Sha Tsui to Central provides the usual tourist view of Victoria Harbour, with breathtaking vistas of Hong Kong Island's combination of gleaming tower blocks and heavily forested mountainsides — at least when both can be seen through the smog.

There are, however, a number of other 'Star' Ferry routes across the harbour, including one from Tsim Sha Tsui to Wan Chai. All these routes provide a different visual perspective to Hong Kong Island, as it crosses to Central in front of Causeway Bay and Wan Chai. Probably the most un-touristed of all these possibilities is the Hung Hom Ferry.

Hung Hom Road

Unlike the others, the Hung Hom crossing is a true local passenger ferry, and one of the last operating in the main Victoria Harbour area. Like a wander around Hung Hom, a ferry ride across the water from here provides a glimpse of genuine urban Hong Kong life — far away in every respect — from the overhyped tourist areas nearby.

② *Harbour Plaza Hotel*

Cheung Kong Holdings' magnificent Harbour Plaza Hotel on the Hung Hom waterfront briefly hit the international media spotlight during Hong Kong's handover ceremonies in 1997, when then President of China Jiang Zemin and other Chinese dignitaries stayed there. The hotel has numerous excellent restaurants and the Harbour Grill is particularly good. While the restaurant may be expensive, it is worth a visit now and again for a treat, and the superb views to Hong Kong Island and beyond on rare smog-free days are definitely a reason to come here.

Like many other newer buildings around Victoria Harbour, the Harbour Plaza complex was built in complete contravention of Metroplan town planning guidelines. First codified in the early 1990s, these specified that future high-rise developments should not break the ridgeline of either Hong Kong Island or the Kowloon hills when seen from the harbour itself. As a 'guideline', rather than binding legislation, developers were not obliged to pay much attention to Metroplan's dictates, and they have been widely ignored, most notably with the IFC development in Central.

Hung Hom Road

The Harbour Plaza Hotel's massive marble atrium, unabashedly designed to impress, is all that one would expect in a five-star Hong Kong hotel like this one. There are also Harbour Plaza Hotels in Chongqing and Nanjing — never mind that both cities are riverine ports hundreds of miles inland from the sea.

③ *Hutchison Park*

The land that forms Hutchison Park was part of Hutchison International *tai pan* Sir Douglas Clague's visionary expansion of his group of companies in the late 1960s. The extensive redevelopment of the former dockyard site marked a movement away from the Hong Kong that had evolved in the immediate postwar era, one whose economy actually *made* things — whether they be plastic flowers, garments or ocean-going passenger-cargo ships — to one whose prosperity revolved more and more around the financial services industry, rollercoaster-ride stock market investments and boom-bust property bubble cycles.

Clague astutely recognized that by the late 1960s Hong Kong had already started to develop what would, in time, become a sizeable Chinese middle class, and saw that eventually this group would want private home ownership in quality residential estates. By this time the rapid growth and transformation of international shipping, and the rise of containerization, meant that relatively small vessels, such as those built and serviced at the Kowloon Docks, would soon be obsolete.

Hutchison International bought into the expansive Hung Hom dockyard site in 1969 and over the next decade transformed a large section of it into a housing

Hung Hom Road

estate. The redundant dockyard's sizeable land bank provided the long-term answer, and the process of development at the Hung Hom waterfront began in the late 1970s, after Clague's time at Hutchison International had ended. It has continued ever since.

(4) Marooned 'ship' at Whampoa Gardens

This completely fake concrete ship, moored out of time and context in the middle of a sprawling residential area, is virtually the only reminder of Hung Hom's former dockyard complex. The realistic-looking 'ship' accommodates numerous shops and a popular cinema complex.

Most Kowloon residents nowadays have no memory of why a 'ship on the shore' would seem appropriate at Whampoa Gardens. The changes over the last thirty years, after all, have been so rapid and comprehensive as to almost completely obliterate the past. Like many other aspects of the local past, Hong Kong's oldest and for a long time most important industry seems destined, sadly, to be forgotten. Kitsch reminders like this marooned replica, however, only serve a memorial purpose if enough people still know what they are meant to be reminded of when they look at it.

How To Get There

By Bus:	No. 5C from Tsim Sha Tsui 'Star' Ferry.
By KCR:	Hung Hom KCR Station.
By Taxi:	黃埔花園紅磡道 (*'Wong Bo Fa Yuen, Hung Hom Doh'*).

STREETS

Ma Tau Wai Road
馬頭圍道

Ma Tau Wai ('Horse Head Walled Village') is one of Kowloon's more unexplored corners to outsiders, despite being very busy at all hours. On the surface, it is easy to think that Ma Tau Wai Road is just another traffic-clogged road that criss-crosses around northern Kowloon. Only a few years ago most local residents would have passed through here many times without bothering to look around them; Ma Tau Wai was simply somewhere to pass through on the way to and from Kai Tak Airport.

After the airport was relocated to Chek Lap Kok in 1998, there has been no real reason for most non-residents to come to the area, except that it is a very interesting authentic place to wander about. Ma Tau Wai bears witness to no dazed-looking tourists with slung cameras and sunburnt faces, no sly whispers of 'copy watch' and no slick modern malls crammed full of 'designer' consumer items. Yet, Ma Tai Wai is within walking distance, almost, of Tsim Sha Tsui.

During the Japanese occupation, two internment camps in the area housed Indian troops taken prisoner when the colony fell. One was located at nearby Ma Tau Chung, while the other was at Ma Tau Wai, near Kai Tak Airport. British officers in the Indian Army battalions were kept separate from their men, and living conditions at Ma Tau Chung and Ma Tau Wai were as grim and uncomfortable as in other Japanese prison camps elsewhere in Kowloon.

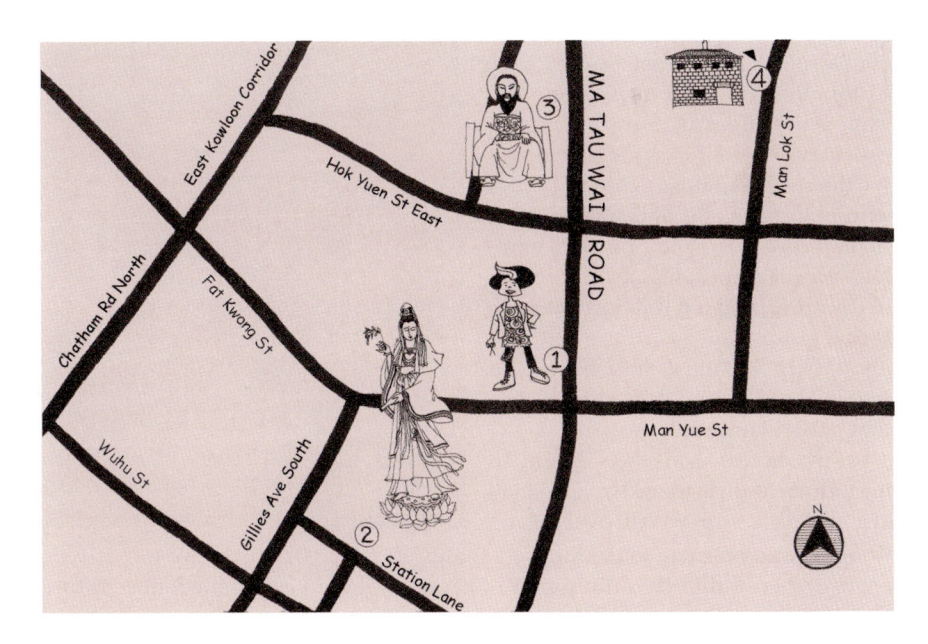

| ❶ | Local hairdressing salons | ❸ | Pak Ti Temple |
| ❷ | Kwun Yam Temple | ❹ | Cattle Depot |

STREETS

Ma Tau Wai Road

Ma Tau Wai and surrounding areas developed considerable amounts of light industrial development in the 1950s and 1960s. Sweeping urban renewal plans for the area mean that this rundown district will experience major changes and redevelopment in coming years.

Be forewarned: this part of Kowloon is a gritty, yet very vital area of less-than-lovely streetscapes, thousands of pedestrians and the ever-present warning sound of a full-throated gob on the pavement behind you. Ma Tau Wai is a slice of the 'real' Hong Kong and one the local tourism board would be in *no* hurry whatsoever to promote, either locally or overseas. There is much of interest around here and Ma Tau Wai is worth the effort — for an undiluted glimpse into authentic local Kowloon life.

1. Local hairdressing salons

Hairdressing salons provide a fascinating window into popular culture in Hong Kong. Everyone, it seems, goes to them at least every few weeks, and virtually every Kowloon backstreet has at least one or two. Competition for clients is keen and while some salons are fairly basic, each provides a tremendous creative outlet for the skills and imagination of those who own, manage and work within them. Local people are possibly more hairstyle-conscious than anywhere else in the world, and it is very rare that one sees a Hong Kong Chinese out and about with unkempt hair unless, of course, that happens to be the 'in' style that particular month or week.

The latest haircuts seen in magazines or on screens big and small are slavishly copied all over Hong Kong. If one popular television personality sports a particular dye job or style change, then within days thousands of people will want *exactly* the same coiffure done for themselves. All this fevered imitation adds up to a very successful local hairdressing industry. Hong Kong hairstyles are also widely copied in overseas Chinese communities; modified versions of what was once fashionable in Hong Kong are proudly displayed in small towns across Malaysia or Taiwan several months later.

Ma Tau Wai Road

For the most part, local stylists such as these along Ma Tau Wai Road are very reasonably priced and, generally speaking, very friendly and accommodating. In recent years local salon prices have dropped considerably, mainly due to increased competition from Shenzhen. Salons there these days offer much the same styles and standards as in Hong Kong, but at much lower prices.

2) Kwun Yam Temple

This pleasant small temple was built by a group of Hung Hom residents in 1873, the twelfth year of the Tongzhi reign. These initial subscribers banded together to fund the construction of the building and later became its first management committee. In 1896, the temple committee applied for and was granted a Crown Lease for the temple's present site.

Kwun Yam, the Goddess of Mercy, was, according to popular legend, a princess who later attained Buddha status. She is recognized as the embodiment of all the traditional womanly virtues: beauty, gentleness, mercy, wisdom and filial piety. The busiest times of the year for the temple are during the four Kwun Yam Jit (Kwun Yam Festivals), which are held on the nineteenth day of the Second, Sixth, Ninth and Eleventh Moons of the Lunar calendar. The main Kwun Yam image found in this temple is dressed in the Empress robes of Tin Hau, the popular sea goddess; unsurprising, given the temple's immediate proximity to the harbour front before reclamation work.

A word of caution: beware of the numerous predatory pests that lurk outside this temple. As at other religious locations elsewhere in Kowloon, such as the Wong Tai Sin Temple, these persistent nuisances will stuff 'lucky' talismans into your hands and then *demand* that you pay for them. They refuse to take back the object once you have touched it and by doing so absorbed its *hei* ('vital energy'), and threaten you with all manner of dire curses into the bargain. Clench your fists, tell them to get lost in whatever language you prefer, threaten them with the police (this usually has some effect!), and walk straight past them into the temple.

Ma Tau Wai Road

Temple touts, whether out to exploit the religious devotee or the merely curious visitor, are an ongoing problem at the more popular Chinese temples all over Hong Kong, one which the relevant authorities seem prepared to completely ignore. Perhaps being bothered and harassed all the way along the street just adds a little more 'local colour' to the experience.

③ Pak Ti Temple

The Pak Ti Temple at Hok Yuen has much of interest and is far enough off the tourist beat to qualify for 'authentic' Chinese temple status. Dedicated to the God of the North, this temple was built by Hung Hom residents in 1929. The present structure is a substitute for the old Pak Ti Temple built on the eastern end of the present Tsing Chau Street in 1876. This temple was later demolished to make way for further urban development and was relocated to its present site.

The oldest items in the present temple are a bell, dated 1893, which was presented by the Wo Hing Tong and a set of incense burners (dated 1901–02) which were presented by the 'whole community of Hung Hom Dockyard Village'. The residents of this now vanished settlement were principally workers employed by the nearby Hong Kong and Whampoa Dock Company.

Ma Tau Wai Road

④ *Cattle Depot*

The old Ma Tau Wai Cattle Depot, originally located close to the Kowloon Bay waterfront, was just that. Live beasts imported into Hong Kong were kept here for veterinary examination prior to slaughter. The Cattle Depot buildings mostly date from the 1920s, and are pleasingly built of red brick and roofed with Canton tiles.

These days the Ma Tau Wai Cattle Depot site houses numerous workshops for young artists, dramatists, poets, actors, painters and sculptors. Visitors are free to wander about, and the many artists-in-residence found here are, for the most part, very friendly and welcoming. At first glance, it seems hard to imagine that within a decaying light industrial district like Ma Tau Wai there should be such amounts of creative energy — but there is.

For all the loud talk about the government-sponsored development of 'cultural hubs' on the West Kowloon reclamation and in other parts of Hong Kong, and the annual expenditure of large sums on 'the arts', it seems to have escaped most planners that right in the middle of Kowloon more genuine artistic ferment happens than in many cities of comparable size elsewhere in the world.

Thriving local arts complexes, like this one, need not cost very much to run either. A similar low-budget arts complex also exists in Macao, located in a disused dairy at Mong Há in the northern part of the city. Like the Ma Tau Wai Cattle Depot, the Macao arts facility continues to thrive and provide opportunities for budding artists, both to work and display their products.

In stark contrast to this positive initiative, just across the road from the Ma Tau Wai Cattle Depot, there is a massive complex of residential-commercial blocks, all connected by a complex of private streets, which is possibly the most ill-kept

Ma Tau Wai Road

and filthy in all of Kowloon. The relevant government departments, it seems, have no authority on the streets here. But neither the owners nor their tenants seem to mind, and as it is no one's specific responsibility to keep the place clean, nobody bothers! So much for more effective Hong Kong government co-ordination in the wake of devastating outbreaks of insanitation-caused disease such as SARS!

How To Get There

| By Bus: | No. 5 from Tsim Sha Tsui 'Star' Ferry. |
| By Taxi: | 馬頭圍道 ('*Ma Tau Wai Doh*'). |

Sung Wong Toi Road
宋皇臺道

This noisy corner of Kowloon City, unremarkable at first glance and consequently easy to pass by and ignore, contains one of the last significant reminders of pre-British Kowloon: a large square-cut stone with an inscription that dates back to the Southern Song dynasty (AD 1127–1279). The Sung Wong Toi, or Song Emperor's Terrace, briefly records the escape through the Kowloon hills of Zhao Bing, the last emperor of the Southern Song dynasty.

    The young boy-ruler fled into this then remote area to escape from the Mongol hordes that invaded China and subsequently established themselves as the short-lived Yuan dynasty (AD 1279–1368). Zhao Bing was eventually captured, and unfortunately drowned some distance to the west of present-day Macao. His older brother and immediate predecessor as emperor, Zhao Shi, died of illness while staying in the Hong Kong region.

    In the nineteenth century, the shores of Kowloon Bay (and the foreshores in most other parts of the Hong Kong region) were lined with large granite boulders worn smooth by time and tide. These were gradually cut down to provide building

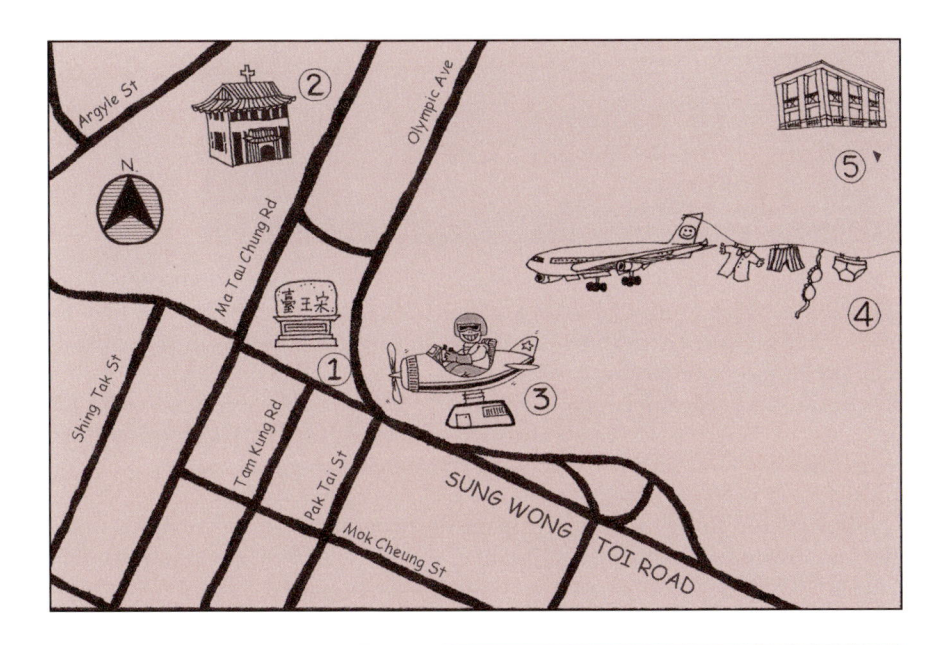

❶ Sung Wong Toi Park
❷ Holy Trinity Church
❸ Hong Kong Aviation Club
❹ Kai Tak Airport
❺ Former Officers' Mess Building, RAF Kai Tak

STREETS

Sung Wong Toi Road

stone as, after British settlement in 1841, a new city took shape on the other side of the harbour. Waterside boulders were the most readily accessible, and so were cut first. By the late nineteenth century, almost none of any size or significance still remained. All had been quarried away with the exception of the Sung Wong Toi, which was retained for historical reasons.

1 Sung Wong Toi Park

The 114-feet-high Sung Wong Toi Hill was widely regarded, before the Second World War intervened, as the most important Chinese antiquity in Hong Kong. The present inscriptions were carved in 1807; there had been a series of earlier inscriptions recorded down the centuries. In 1898 legislative councillor Sir Kai Ho Kai (also known as Ho Kai) succeeded in having the Sung Wong Toi gazetted as an historical monument — one of the very first instances of proactive historical preservation in Hong Kong.

In 1915 the Hong Kong Government Department of Works attempted to sell the land for redevelopment, but the plan was made public by a man named Li Sui-kum. Li was an example of what is probably Hong Kong's rarest species — a heritage-minded building contractor. Hong Kong University lecturer in Chinese Lai Chai-hei and vice-chancellor Sir Charles Eliot subsequently petitioned the then governor Sir Henry May for the area's retention on historical grounds, and plans to demolish the Sung Wong Toi and redevelop the site were shelved and finally abandoned.

Sung Wong Toi Road

Li Sui-kum later donated a sum of money for gardens and pavilions to be built for visitors, and by the 1920s the Sung Wong Toi was one of the more popular tourist spots in Kowloon. The site mostly appealed to Chinese visitors who were attracted by the tragic story of the last boy-emperor of the Southern Song dynasty and his doomed flight from the Mongol invaders through the Kowloon hills.

In 1943, as part of extensions to Kai Tak Airport's runway undertaken during the Japanese occupation, the greater part of Sung Wong Toi Hill was blasted away for landfill and the massive boulder was split into three parts. Fortunately, the section inscribed with the characters remained intact and was preserved.

The attractive present-day park was laid out in December 1959. The inscribed remnant stone forms a centrepiece to the gardens, while the well-maintained, generally quiet grounds provide a rare corner of relative tranquillity in the midst of Kowloon City.

(2) Holy Trinity Church

One of several eclectically styled churches in Hong Kong, Holy Trinity Church began in 1890, when a Christian convert named Koo Kai-tak and his wife began having religious meetings in their house in the nearby Fuk Lo Tsuen ('Hoklo Village').

The informal church group steadily expanded and by 1900 they formally applied to the government for permission to build permanent premises at the base of Sung Wong Toi Hill. A church with a seating capacity of over one hundred was completed in 1902, but relocated the next year. Then finally new church was completed in 1905. In due course, the church established a free dispensary, an old people's home and a Christian cemetery behind Kowloon Walled City.

As the congregation expanded the older buildings became inadequate and in 1937 the Holy Trinity Church's distinctive present building, which incorporates various Chinese architectural characteristics, was built. The church survived the war years more or less intact, and after the Japanese surrender the

Sung Wong Toi Road

buildings were used as a temporary holding area for Japanese prisoners-of-war, before their, eventual repatriation to Japan. Still in use today, Holy Trinity Church is one of the most appealing, and least recognized, older buildings still standing in Kowloon City.

③ Hong Kong Aviation Club

Hong Kong has a considerable number of keen recreational aviators, some of whom even own their own light planes. For decades the Hong Kong Aviation Club was based out of modified Nissan huts right next to the Kai Tak Airport runway. For many years, one of the old airport's most incongruous sights were small aircraft buzzing in to land, these looked much like wasps or dragonflies when compared to the ranks of massive jumbo jets parked alongside the main terminal buildings.

When Kai Tak Airport finally closed in 1998 and the international airport was relocated to Chek Lap Kok, the Hong Kong Aviation Club found itself in a quandary. They had well-equipped hangars, comfortable club buildings, and all the necessary facilities in place — everything, in fact, except an aerodrome to fly from.

This problem was fortunately solved by the good graces of the People's Liberation Army, who had taken over the military runway in Sek Kong from the Royal Air Force in 1997. While the Hong Kong Aviation Club still maintains its clubhouse and other premises in the old location adjacent to Kai Tak, all flights these days are undertaken from Sek Kong airfield in the New Territories.

Sung Wong Toi Road

(4) Kai Tak Airport

Now rather abandoned and forlorn-looking, from the 1950s until its closure in 1998, Kai Tak Airport was Hong Kong's principal gateway to the world. For decades it provided one of the world's most exciting airport approaches, and more than a few visitors to Hong Kong came to the colony especially to experience the takeoff and landing.

The earliest phase of Kai Tak Airport was built on partially reclaimed land on the edge of Kowloon Bay developed by businessmen Ho Kai (also known as Sir Kai Ho Kai) and Au Tak (also known as Au Chak-mun). The name for the project, originally known as Kai Tak Bund, was taken from their combined names, hence 'Kai Tak'.

First used for aviation purposes in 1924, for some decades afterwards the civilian airport was also home to RAF Kai Tak, the local Royal Air Force station; a few former military buildings still exist scattered around the area. Kai Tak's airport runway was expanded during the Japanese occupation of Hong Kong, mainly using prisoner-of-war labour and stone obtained from the remaining walls of Kowloon City, Nga Tsin Wai and the Sung Wong Toi, as well as several other localized sources.

In the immediate postwar era, the road which linked Kowloon City and eastern Kowloon ran right across the sporadically used airfield, much like is still the case in Gibraltar. When an aeroplane was due, a level-crossing was lowered, and the traffic stopped to allow the plane to land.

To cope with increasing passenger demand, a major new runway extension out into Kowloon Bay commenced in the mid-1950s and finally opened in 1958. Developed just as jet aircraft started to supersede sea travel, Kai Tak Airport rapidly became Hong Kong's principal international entry and exit point. For the next forty years the breathtaking landing approach directly over Kowloon's rooftops was a major tourist attraction in its own right, one which now (like many once common elements of local life) has relegated to memory and the pages of picture books that depict 'Old Hong Kong'.

(5) Former Officers' Mess Building, RAF Kai Tak

Part of the history now, along with the airport it once supported, the Royal Air Force Station at Kai Tak, better known as RAF Kai Tak, was the furthermost extent of Great Britain's Far East air defences.

The first RAF station at Kai Tak opened in 1924. On the morning of the Japanese invasion of Hong Kong, 8 December 1941, the entire RAF contingent then based in the colony — five obsolete planes — were destroyed on the ground.

Sung Wong Toi Road

The Hong Kong Garrison was greatly strengthened during disturbed conditions in China in the late 1940s, and further reinforced during the Korean War (1950–53) when Hong Kong was a major supply and reinforcement base for that conflict. Until the drawdown of British Forces in the Far East after 1969, RAF Kai Tak contained, at various times, Spitfires, Canberra bombers and Vampire fighter aircraft.

After RAF Kai Tak was closed, until the handover in 1997, the remaining Royal Air Force presence in Hong Kong was based at RAF Sek Kong in the New Territories. Almost the only aircraft used in the last decade of British rule were a number of antiquated Wessex helicopters, which were subsequently sold to Uruguay.

The former Officers' Mess Building on Kwun Tong Road is a pleasing example of pre-war institutional architecture of its kind, once commonplace in British military installations across the Far East, and one of the few surviving significant remnants of RAF Kai Tak. It has been sympathetically restored, and now houses the offices of a charity.

How To Get There

By Bus:	No. 5 from Tsim Sha Tsui 'Star' Ferry
By Taxi:	九龍城宋皇臺道 (*'Gau Loong Sing, Soong Wong Doi Doh'*).

Nga Tsin Wai Road
衙前圍道

This long thoroughfare through Kowloon City was once a quiet country road through vegetable fields, on which now stand some of Kowloon's busiest and most crowded areas. Some corners, such as Nga Tsin Wai itself, the only extant walled village south of Lion Rock, remain unique to the area.

Like other parts of Kowloon City, Nga Tsin Wai Road and nearby streets have numerous highly visible Hong Kong–Thailand connections, such as well-stocked provision shops and clusters of small, surprisingly authentic restaurants, mostly patronized by the ethnic Thai community resident in Hong Kong or locally domiciled Thai-Chinese.

① Nga Tsin Wai Tsuen (Walled Village)

The last remaining walled village in the Kowloon urban area, Nga Tsin Wai Tsuen is an interesting, if at first glance somewhat disappointing, place to wander about. Dating back over seven hundred years, it was similar in style and layout to the

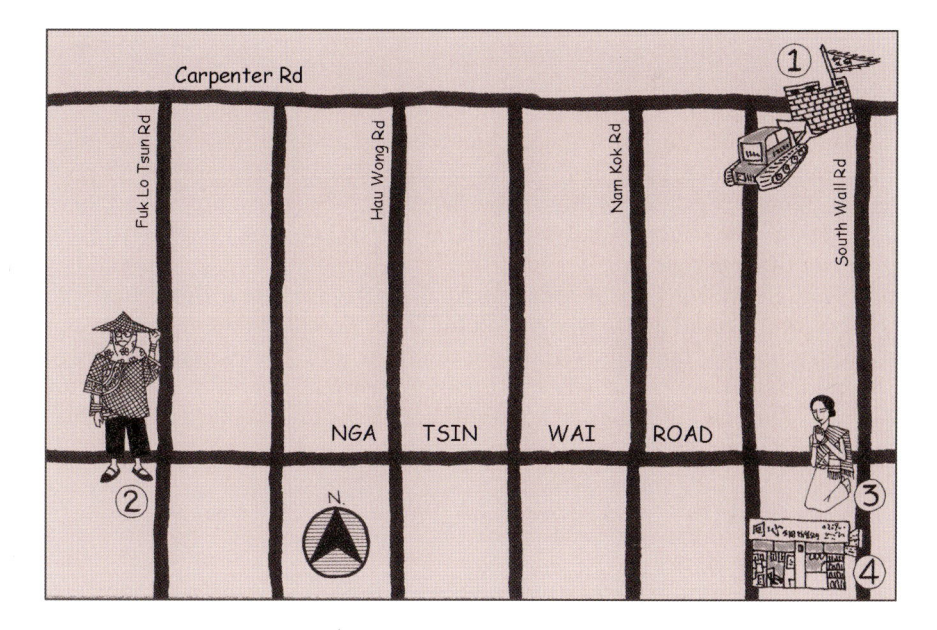

| ① Nga Tsin Wai Tsuen (Walled Village) | ③ Lanna Thai |
| ② Fuk Lo Tsun Road | ④ Ruamjai Thai Grocery Shop |

Nga Tsin Wai Road

innumerable other *wai tsuen* (walled villages) dotted around the South China countryside. Such fortified structures were once prevalent in remote, underprotected, bandit- and pirate-prone coastal areas such as Kowloon Bay. On maps of urban Kowloon as recent as 1924, Nga Tsin Wai still appeared as a distinct walled village surrounded by cultivated fields.

Plentiful examples of strongly built *wai tsuen* still survive in various parts of the New Territories, in particular around Kam Tin and Fan Ling. Most of these are fairly dilapidated, particularly in the Kam Tin area, but none is in such a poor state of general repair as the one at Nga Tsin Wai. The best examples of *wai tsuen* these days can be seen in mainland China; as ever, rural poverty has been a great preserver of these relics.

Nga Tsin Wai is one of those on-again-off-again Hong Kong heritage conservation sagas that has trudged on for years; potential developers, various statutory bodies, factions within the amateur and professional heritage communities, as well as the villagers themselves, are all unable to agree to any concrete solutions. And while all interested parties continue to bicker and dither, the remaining fabric of the village further crumbles and decays.

② Fuk Lo Tsun Road

This road takes its name from the Fuk Lo people — more commonly known as Hoklo — who lived in the area and established a *tsuen* (village) in Kowloon Bay. The Hoklo originally came from Fukien (Fujian) Province (hence the name Fuk Lo, which means, literally, 'men of Fukien').

Nga Tsin Wai Road

Hoklo people were traditionally discriminated against by land-dwelling Chinese, though not to the extent of the Tanka or Shui Sheung Yan Gaa, who were openly despised and sometimes ill-treated. For many generations the Hoklo lived on their boats in sheltered coves and inlets, scratching a bare living by localized fishing, small-scale trading and occasional, seasonal manual labour on land.

Contemporary Hong Kong's Hoklo population have been mostly rehoused on land since the 1960s, and the younger generation are largely assimilated, through the school system and popular culture, into the wider Cantonese mainstream. Like the Tanka, many younger members of the community do not advertise their Hoklo ancestry; ingrained discrimination established over many centuries take a long time to die out. The local Hoklo and Tanka communities still periodically suffer low-level animosity from other traditionally land-dwelling Chinese ethnic groups, a trend that is unseen and unreported in modern Hong Kong.

③ Lanna Thai

One of the many small Thai-owned and managed eateries in the Kowloon City area, Lanna Thai serves up reasonably priced, authentic Thai foods, including a number of street-style delicacies more usually found in Bangkok, Phuket or Chiang Mai than in Hong Kong.

Nga Tsin Wai Road

Most 'Thai' food sold in Hong Kong, even in quite upmarket, high-priced restaurants, is in fact a heavily diluted local version of the real thing designed to appeal to the chilli-shy Hong Kong Chinese palate. 'Thai' dishes served in Hong Kong are usually much sweeter and oilier than would be the case in Thailand, which shows both the heavy Cantonese influence and innate local conservatism. While Hong Kong abounds with Thai restaurants of varying standards and price ranges, authentic Thai tastes can be surprisingly difficult to find, and many enthusiasts find a culinary pilgrimage to Kowloon City every so often is well worth the journey.

Named after the ancient northern Thai kingdom centred around Chiang Mai, Lanna Thai is, unsurprisingly, mostly patronized by expatriate Thais and those Hong Kong Chinese who appreciate the authenticity on offer here. Excellent *kai yang* or *moo yang* (Thai-style grilled chicken or pork on a stick) can be purchased off the griller rack outside and munched on as you wander around the area; Lanna Thai's *kai yang*, in particular, is locally very well-known and, like a meal in the restaurant, a few pieces is worth making the journey to Kowloon City to enjoy.

4 Ruamjai Thai Grocery Shop

Ruamjai Thai Grocery is definitely the place to come to if you want to stock up on practically anything that you might need or want from Thailand. All manner of otherwise pricy or hard-to-obtain Thai herbs and vegetables are on offer here, all selling for much less than elsewhere in Hong Kong.

Nga Tsin Wai Road

Every possible variety of Thai curry paste is on offer, in packets, jars, freshly ground and packed in plastic bags. Ready packed *tom yum* herbs — lemongrass, galangal root, Kaffir lime leaves, plenty of *prik kee noo* ('mouse dung chillies') and a juicy green lime, go for a few dollars a pack, while any quantity of the separate ingredients can be purchased. Ruamjai Thai Grocery also sells an interesting variety of fresh Thai desserts, as well as freshly prepared coconut milk — just the thing for preparing that weekend curry lunch.

The shop also has a popular currency exchange booth in the rear, dealing mostly in Thai Baht and remittances to and from Thailand. In addition, it sells a wide variety of Thai cassette tapes and CDs, rents out Thai-language DVDs of popular films and soap operas, and imports a wide variety of Thai-language newspapers, periodicals and magazines, all brought in daily from Bangkok. Well worth visiting for a glimpse of 'the Land of Smiles' in the unlikely depths of Kowloon City.

How To Get There

By Bus:	No. 1, 1A, 5 and 9 from Tsim Sha Tsui 'Star' Ferry.
By Taxi:	九龍城衙前圍道 (*'Gau Loong Sing, Nga Tsin Wai Doh'*).

Tak Ku Ling Road
打 鼓 嶺 道

Just around the corner from the old Kai Tak Airport, Tak Ku Ling Road has a number of pleasantly unexpected surprises. Most immediately noticeable are the highly visible Hong Kong–Thailand connections found both along here and around the neighbouring Kowloon City streets, such as Nam Kok Road with its numerous excellent restaurants and authentic Thai massage shops.

While a couple of dozen rickety pre-war shop houses precariously survive around here, most buildings in the vicinity date from the utilitarian 1960s. The imprint of the era certainly shows in the drab design. But for now at least, Kowloon City remains much as it ever was, just without an endless succession of planes screaming down overhead any more.

Coming through these Kowloon City backstreets by bus or taxi was, for most people, their first glimpse of Hong Kong. Many never came back to the area to explore, no matter how many years they lived here; the district was just a grim-looking place to be passed through quickly on the way to and from the airport.

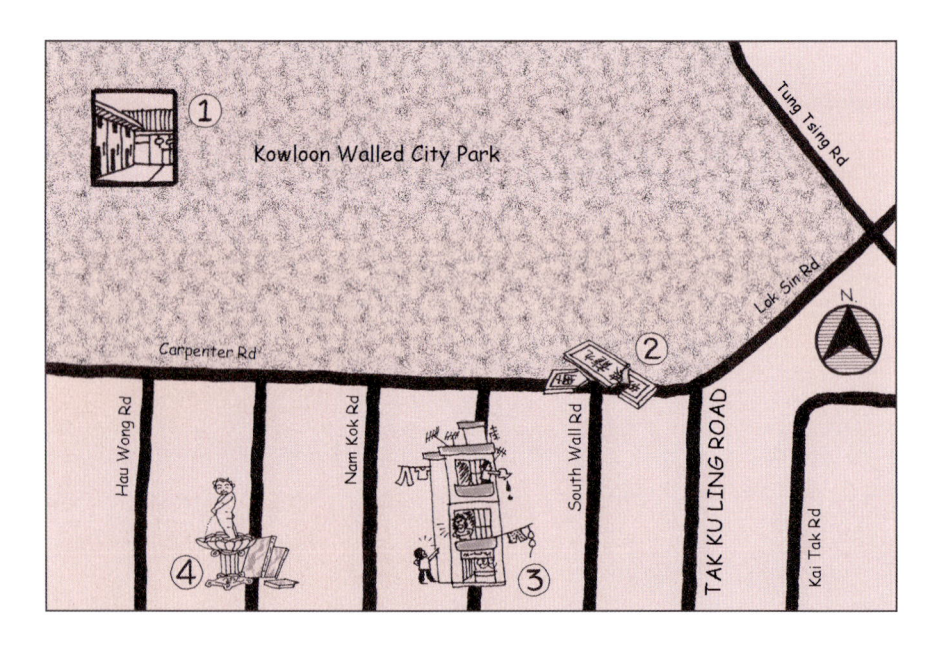

❶ Kowloon Walled City Park
❷ Remains of Kowloon Walled City's South Gate
❸ Kowloon City tenements
❹ Marble shops

Tak Ku Ling Road

1) Kowloon Walled City Park

Less than a decade ago this attractive park was one of the most festering, crime-ridden slums in Kowloon. Extensive and well-planned, Kowloon Walled City Park has numerous recreational facilities, attractive and well-thought-out garden plantings and a surprising number of quiet corners where one can sit and watch the world go by.

On any Sunday or public holiday, Kowloon Walled City Park is the gathering point of choice for Hong Kong's off-duty Thai domestic worker population, much as Statue Square attracts Filipinos and Victoria Park is a focal point for the steadily growing Indonesian migrant worker population. The Leisure and Cultural Services Department recognizes this and banners exhorting people not to litter or hawk are in Chinese, English and Thai scripts.

Many impromptu (and illegal) food stalls are set up in the park and its immediate vicinity and far more Thai than Cantonese is spoken here. Bangkok's latest pop songs and blare forth from ghetto blasters and a carnival-like, off-duty flavour prevails. By early evening on Sundays most people have packed up and gone back home, but a few revellers can still be found scattered here and there around the park till quite late at night.

2) Remains of Kowloon Walled City's South Gate

The South Gate of Kowloon Walled City was built at the order of Qing dynasty officials in 1843. Fortifications were generally strengthened shortly after the British took possession of Hong Kong Island, immediately across the harbour. The South Gate was demolished during the Japanese occupation of the colony, along with the walls, to provide materials for the Kai Tak runway extension.

During Kowloon Walled City's demolition in 1994 the South Gate's original foundations were unearthed, along with two stone plaques bearing the characters for South Gate and Kowloon Walled City. Preserved *in situ*, they can still be seen

Tak Ku Ling Road

today. The Fu Shing Pavilion, an attractive pavilion near the *yamen* (magistracy compound), can be reached by a circular moon gate, and is named after the star at the tip of the bowl of the Big Dipper. 'Fu Shing' signifies the Chinese God of Examinations.

A pair of old cannons that once guarded the Kowloon City *yamen* can still be seen close by. For several decades they lay abandoned and partially buried outside the crumbling *yamen* complex, and were finally rescued and restored when the area was cleared for redevelopment.

③ Kowloon City tenements

Tak Ku Ling Road

Until 1998 these unprepossessing tenement apartments were among the noisiest places to live in all of Hong Kong — and *that* comment alone is highly indicative! Located right under the flight path for Kai Tak Airport, residents living in Kowloon City's densely packed apartments had to endure Boeing 747s and all manner of other aircraft roaring less than five hundred feet overhead at the average rate of almost two per minute throughout the entire day, every single day of the year. All this, in addition to the usual noises, is typical to everyday Hong Kong life.

The unbelievable din went on from just before dawn when the first trans-Pacific flights came in, until shortly after midnight when the last Europe-bound planes departed, and the airport closed for a few brief hours. The next five hours or so were almost the only time Kowloon City residents could get some relatively quiet rest. Unsurprisingly, the only people who lived under the flight path were those who really did not have much choice.

④ *Marble shops*

Hong Kong has enjoyed an enduring love affair with marble since the earliest years of British settlement. From the nineteenth century onwards, restaurants, hotels and private homes have been floored (and occasionally walled and roofed) with slabs of this glistening, cold-looking, yet ever-so prestigious stone.

Sir Paul Chater, Hong Kong's pre-eminent businessman during the late nineteenth and early twentieth centuries, even named his palatial Mid-Levels home Marble Hall. Surviving photographs show an extensive use of the material

Tak Ku Ling Road

throughout. A great many other local people have emulated him, to some extent or another, down the decades to the present day.

If you feel the urge to give your home that five or six-star look, but do not know where to turn, a few shops on this Kowloon City backstreet may help to provide the answer. Various types, colours and grades of marble and polished granite can be obtained from this and other shops, at reasonable prices.

Most sales are to tradesmen, the shopkeepers say, but naturally enough they are more than happy to sell any quantity of the stuff to anyone who walks in their door. If you simply want a small piece of marble to use as a pastry board in the kitchen, they will happily oblige and cut you up a slab to whatever dimensions you might require.

How To Get There

By Bus:	No. 5 from Tsim Sha Tsui 'Star' Ferry to Choi Hung, and alight on Prince Edward Road West near old Kai Tak Airport.
By Taxi:	九龍城打鼓嶺道 (*'Gau Loong Sing, Dah Gu Leng Doh'*).

Tung Tau Tsuen Road
東頭村道

Running along the northern boundary of Kowloon City Park, Tung Tau Tsuen Road has a great many areas of interest, not least of which is the park itself, built on the site of Kowloon Walled City.

Just to the north of Tung Tau Tsuen Road, the seemingly endless serried ranks of public housing estates begin and stretch almost to the base of the Kowloon hills. Unaesthetic though many of them are, they nevertheless represent what is probably Hong Kong's least recognized postwar success stories. In the 1950s Tung Tau Tsuen was one of the most extensive squatter areas in Kowloon, periodically razed by fire and rebuilt; the estate is now home to thousands of families.

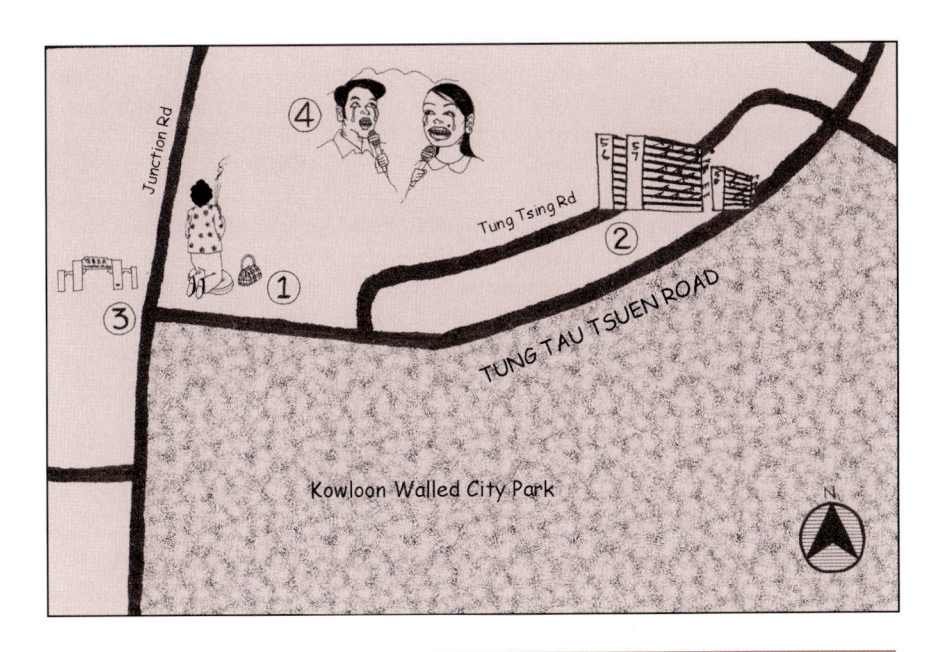

❶ Hau Wong Temple
❷ Mei Tung Estate and squatter clearance
❸ Munsang College
❹ Lion Rock

Tung Tau Tsuen Road

1) Hau Wong Temple

Surrounded by mature trees and bamboo groves, Kowloon City's green-roofed Hau Wong Temple is situated on a pleasantly landscaped low hill overlooking Munsang College. In the years before the massive, heavily touristed Wong Tai Sin Temple was established, Tung Tau Tsuen's Hau Wong Miu was one of Kowloon's most popular temples and still attracts plenty of worshippers today.

Chinese-language guidebooks to Hong Kong published in the 1950s all regarded the Hau Wong Temple as one of Kowloon's 'must-see' tourist sights; English-language works from the same period, however, completely ignore it.

One of Kowloon's oldest Chinese temples, interior inscriptions record that the building was given a major renovation in 1822 — some twenty years before Hong Kong Island was ceded to Great Britain. A smaller temple on the site predated that period, although its exact date of establishment has now been lost.

According to some sources, the Hau Wong Temple was built in 1730 to commemorate the heroism of Yang Liangji, a loyal general and attendant of Zhao Bing, the last boy-emperor of the Southern Song dynasty. The existence of the nearby Sung Wong Toi makes this both a plausible origin, as well as an attractive local legend.

At the back of the Hau Wong Temple is a stone fragment of a 'goose and crane' inscription can still be seen. This tablet was originally carved in the late 1880s; the other missing section was apparently destroyed by the Japanese in the early 1940s. Recent renovations have completely obliterated any sense of being in an old temple; all walls and features are brightly painted.

Tung Tau Tsuen Road

(2) Mei Tung Estate and squatter clearance

Washing pole-festooned public housing estates such as Kowloon City's Mei Tung Estate represent one of the greatest and most under-recognized success stories of postwar Hong Kong. These estates provide adequate subsidized housing for its people, most of whom initially came to the colony in the postwar era as uninvited migrants from China. Subsidized provision of that most basic of human needs — safe shelter — helped provide a level of social stability that, in turn, assisted to lay the foundations for further prosperity and wealth creation for many Hong Kong families.

Thousands of refugees from the Mainland flooded into Hong Kong during the Civil War in the late 1940s, as they had done in the late 1930s during the Sino-Japanese War and in the wake of other periodic revolts and political disturbances for decades before. Once in the colony the newcomers established themselves first in sprawling squatter settlements, with little or nothing in the way of sanitation or reliable water supplies.

These ramshackle shantytowns, known locally as *mook uk kui* (literally 'wooden hut areas'), were constantly prone to accidental fires and often blown away by typhoons. Hong Kong government policy at this time was to provide as little as possible in the hope of discouraging more people coming from the Mainland. Gradually through the 1950s and 1960s policy changed; squatter areas were cleared for redevelopment and their inhabitants rehoused as the first phases of public housing were initiated.

The older resettlement estates in northern and eastern Kowloon have been redeveloped and the urban renewal process still goes on. Remnant squatter areas remained around Tung Tau Tsuen and in other parts of northern Kowloon until relatively recently, and there are still a few abandoned huts here and there awaiting demolition, lingering shabby reminders of much less prosperous times.

Tung Tau Tsuen Road

3) Munsang College

One of Kowloon's more prestigious Chinese-medium schools, Munsang College has been in operation in Kowloon City since 1924 and enjoys a high academic reputation across Hong Kong.

In 1916 legislative councillor Dr Ts'o Seen-wan suggested setting up a quality Chinese-medium school in Kowloon City to help cater to the needs of the steadily growing population on that side of the harbour. The project steadily gained momentum and was greatly assisted by offers of support from prominent individuals within the Chinese community. In 1920 businessman Au Chak-mun (one of the partners, with Ho Kai, in the Kai Tak reclamation scheme at Kowloon Bay) donated $10,000 to the school building fund. In the same year Mok Kon-sang, the compradore of Butterfield and Swire, also donated $10,000 towards the school building fund. At one time Mok Kon-sang also headed both the Po Leung Kuk and the Tung Wah Hospital Committee.

In 1924 a three-storied house at 2 Kai Tak Praya was rented as school premises, along with a large field to the east of the building. The new school was named Munsang College in honour of Au Chak-mun and Mok Kon-sang, the two principal donors. Classes started in March 1926 and in 1934 the college became a special grant school.

In July 1937 Munsang College bought a plot of land at the end of Grampian Road and in September 1939 the new school buildings was completed. The school premises were occupied by the Japanese during their occupation of Hong Kong and classes were stopped.

Munsang College reopened after the war and has steadily expanded since then. The student population were overwhelmingly Hong Kong Chinese, but a

Tung Tau Tsuen Road

few local Eurasians also attended. The college is very well regarded for its Chinese-language standards. Rayson Huang, former vice-chancellor of the University of Hong Kong, is one of Munsang College's distinguished alumni; his father Rufus Huang was the school's founding principal.

4 Lion Rock

Crouched across one of the ridges of the Kowloon hills, the rocky granite outcrop of Tsz Jee Shan ('Lion Mountain') is one of Hong Kong's best-known natural features. It is also surprisingly easy to get to. Like many other aspects of Kowloon, Lion Rock looks rather more impressive when seen from a distance. Close to the top, the paths around Lion Rock are feathery with bamboos, and on a rare pollution-free day one can enjoy sweeping views across Kowloon towards Lyemun and Clearwater Bay.

Life was very hard for most people in Kowloon in the postwar era. The community spirit of the people who lived and worked in difficult conditions was successfully captured — some would suggest idealized — in *Below Lion Rock*, a popular Cantonese song used as the theme music for a very long-running Cantonese television drama series (1974–94). Written by the late songwriter James Wong, the lyrics have become something of a Hong Kong anthem in times of adversity.

How To Get There	
By Bus:	No. 1 or 1A from Tsim Sha Tsui 'Star' Ferry, alight on Tung Tau Tsuen Road.
By Taxi:	九龍城東頭村道 (*'Gau Loong Sing, Dung Tau Tsuen Doh'*).

STREETS

East Kowloon

Eastern Kowloon is a fascinating, earthy, densely clotted place to explore, and yet most locations here are seldom explored except by their own local inhabitants — and often not even by them!

To many urban dwellers, especially on Hong Kong Island, eastern Kowloon place names such as Ngau Tau Kok, Kwun Tong, Choi Hung and Sau Mau Ping automatically bring forth images of busy flyovers, dingy godowns and partially abandoned factory flats. These images closely juxtapose with densely packed streets and seemingly endless public housing estates, each with hundreds of poles of washing flapping anonymously in the breeze. Like many such initial impressions formed elsewhere in Hong Kong, the reality here is somewhat different.

Building stone quarried from the hills and shoreline of eastern Kowloon was a major export in the nineteenth century. Attractively flecked with black mica, high-quality Kowloon *fa gong shek* ('flowery granite') was keenly sought after in other parts of the Pearl River Delta. The Roman Catholic Cathedral in Canton (modern-day Guangzhou), popularly known within that city as the Shek Lau (Stone Building), was built entirely of Hong Kong-quarried granite, cut in the eastern hills of Kowloon by tough Hakka stonemasons and transported up the river by boat.

At first, the many large waterside boulders found around the harbour's shore were the main source of this high-quality stone, while inferior material was cut from the hillsides behind.

A lingering reminder of one of Hong Kong's earliest export industries, the partially overgrown, abandoned quarries are still clearly visible on the hillsides behind Lei Yue Mun and Cha Kwo Ling, while the ramps originally built to transport cut stone down to the shoreline can still be seen today on the beach at Lei Yue Mun.

Before the early nineteenth century, eastern Kowloon was a remote area of scattered small villages and more isolated hamlets. The largest of these settlements, Ngau Tau Kok, Cha Kwo Ling, Lei Yue Mun and Sai Cho Wan, were known in various imperial Chinese Gazetteers (local histories) as the 'Four Hills'. The Four Hills were originally settled in the late eighteenth century by Hakka migrants from eastern Guangdong Province.

As early as 1810, stonecutters living at Ngau Tau Kok were persuaded by the Tang clan from Kam Tin to cut stone for use in a fort at Kowloon. This fort, constructed where the former Marine Police Station in Tsim Sha Tsui now stands, was built by Qing dynasty officials as an anti-piracy measure. Several other fortified structures were built elsewhere in the Hong Kong region at around the same time, including Fan Lau and Tung Chung on Lantau.

The terms 'Four Hills' is still used by a few elderly indigenous villagers today, even though two of the four original villages — Ngau Tau Kok and Sai Cho Wan — as well as the very hills around which these settlements were situated, have been completely obliterated by urban expansion in recent decades. Until fairly

- Wong Tai Sin Road
- Clear Water Bay Road
- Cha Kwo Ling Road
- Lei Yue Mun Road

recent years indigenous Ngau Tau Kok villagers still regathered for temple festivals in the Ngau Tau Kok new town, an interesting persistence of a long-established custom which lingered long after the village itself had disappeared.

Throughout the 1850s increased numbers of migrants were attracted to the Hong Kong region from elsewhere in Guangdong Province. Most were drawn to the economic opportunities presented by the rapidly developing British colony. Many settled just across the harbour in eastern Kowloon and found work in the quarries.

Over the last half century, the Kowloon Bay coastline from Kai Tak Airport to Lei Yue Mun has been almost completely transformed by large-scale reclamation and rapid industrial development. Virtually nothing remains to remind us of the relatively recent village past in most locations in eastern Kowloon.

During the 1950s and 1960s, hundreds of small factories were established right across eastern Kowloon, each typically employing less than two dozen people. Some of these early enterprises, and the buildings that housed them, still survive, but most have long since been closed and the sites cleared for redevelopment. The majority vanished during the almost wholesale removal of Hong Kong's manufacturing industry to the Mainland in the 1980s and 1990s.

Many of those factories that still remain are only involved in a small part of the manufacturing process. Probably the most common example is the partial finishing of China-made garments in Hong Kong to satisfy import quota restrictions in some countries. Small-scale food processing plants which make noodles, fish-balls, soybean sauces and similar items are also quite common; some of these brands are locally famous, and have been in operation in eastern Kowloon for decades.

Wong Tai Sin Road
黃大仙道

Wong Tai Sin Road, right in the middle of northeast Kowloon's 'Housing Estate Heartland', has one of Kowloon's major elements of interest — the massive religious complex-cum-fairground atmosphere of Wong Tai Sin Temple. Like much of eastern Kowloon, the temple complex and its varied throng of worshippers are appealing in its own right — an essential, vital aspect of the 'real Hong Kong'.

Better renowned for its principal deity's skill in granting worshipper's wishes than for any aesthetic appeal, the regionally famous Wong Tai Sin Temple is an endlessly fascinating, all-out assault on the senses that attracts every social type and physical condition of worshipper imaginable.

Devotees range from rich businessmen seeking out a quick horseracing tip to wizened old women beseeching Heaven for better days to come, as they eke out a bare existence on social welfare subsidies. Mainland and overseas Chinese tourists snap photographs of one other, Hong Kong's legions of ever-present *see lai* (housewives) come to ask the deity for answers about whatever it is that they want or need to know, and high school students in uniform earnestly pray for success in forthcoming examinations.

① Wong Tai Sin Temple
② Temple touts
③ Charms and joss-sticks stalls/fortune-telling complex
④ Morse Park

STREETS

Wong Tai Sin Road

Wong Tai Sin Temple must be one of the most un-self-conscious displays of animism to be witnessed in any post-industrialized society today, as fascinating and enlightening to serious students of social anthropology as it remains the casual visitor.

1. Wong Tai Sin Temple

In 1915 a portrait of Wong Tai Sin was brought to Hong Kong from Guangdong Province and initially installed in a small temple in Wan Chai. In 1921 the temple moved to Chuk Yuen — then a small village, now a massive resettlement estate — and was re-established as a private Taoist (Daoist) abbey. In 1956 the abbey opened to the general public and has greatly expanded over the last four decades into today's massive religious complex.

Sometimes described as the 'Refugee God', Wong Tai Sin is, along with Tin Hau, one of the most popular Chinese deities worshipped in Hong Kong. A highly significant, yet sometimes overlooked, reason for Wong Tai Sin's massive popularity with Hong Kong people is that it is one of the most conveniently situated temples in the entire urban area. Wong Tai Sin MTR Station is right next to the gates, so no one needs to walk very far to get there!

Stepping into the temple complex, one is immediately struck by the rampaging colours and statuary, the sandalwood-like smell of smouldering joss-sticks, and the clickety-clack of the bamboo *cheem* (fortune sticks) being cast. Perhaps surprisingly to some, given the temple's 'spiritual' nature, the tentacle-like presence of Mammon makes itself manifest in all its forms. Incense sticks are scooped out from the censers by the temple attendants, doused with water and then thrown away to make way for new ones, long before they have fully burnt down. Simply lighting them is considered devotion enough.

Wong Tai Sin Temple's fame and appeal reach far beyond the shores of Hong Kong itself. Worshippers from the Mainland, Taiwan, Japan, Thailand, Singapore, Malaysia and other parts of Southeast Asia flock here in their thousands every year in the hope that their prayers can be answered, and a stop at the temple is an essential feature on tour itineraries catering to Chinese visitors to Hong Kong.

Wong Tai Sin Road

Adjacent to the temple complex, the Sik Sik Yuen Clinic is really meant to make people well. Established in line with the motto 'Helping the Underprivileged', the clinic's extensive charitable work has greatly expanded over recent few decades to reflect the steadily evolving needs and expectations of Hong Kong society. The Sik Sik Yuen is a Taoist (Daoist) organization devoted to 'Spirituality, Tranquillity, Intuition, and Purification' and has been very closely linked with the Wong Tai Sin Temple since its foundation.

A free herbal and medical consultation clinic for the poor was established in 1924 by the abbey attached to Wong Tai Sin Temple. In 1980 the clinic was expanded to provide Western medical treatment at heavily subsidized rates. More than 140 patients are treated at the clinic every day; there is also a popular physiotherapy section as well.

In 1999 a dental clinic was also established by Sik Sik Yuen; those patients aged over sixty-five enjoy substantial concessionary rates. Five residential care homes for the elderly are currently run by Sik Sik Yuen, as well as three subsidized day care nurseries for the children of working-class parents.

② *Temple touts*

Notorious for their aggressive persistence, the touts that gather outside Wong Tai Sin's temple gates prey on unsuspecting lone tourists and first-time visitors to the complex. One of the more common tactics employed by these pests involves stuffing a folded paper charm into your hands and demanding immediate payment in return for the 'blessing'. The talisman's cost is usually $20 or so, but sometimes *much* more; the price depends on how you are dressed, your race and physical robustness, and the degree of fear, superstition or gullibility the tout detects.

Attempts to return the unwanted, unasked-for charm to the tout are energetically rebuffed by noisy claims that the charm's unique, individual essence has been absorbed by your *hei* ('vital energy'). Thus transformed, the charm is now — funny that — both non-returnable *and* non-refundable.

If this ploy has no apparent effect, the touts will resort to unsubtly expressed threats that 'evil' and 'calamity' will befall you and your nearest and dearest, if

Wong Tai Sin Road

you should *dare* reject a charm so self-evidently *fated* to be yours. While these touts and their heavy-handed antics are completely illegal, and signs put up by the temple authorities warn visitors to beware of them, they nevertheless continue to aggressively force their 'charms' on visitors to the temple.

Pushy temple touts are a problem at a great many other Chinese temples elsewhere in Hong Kong, in particular those frequently visited by overseas Chinese from Taiwan and Southeast Asian countries, and tourists from mainland China. Stories of harassment at local temples are frequently reported in newspapers from time to time, but — this being Hong Kong after all — little effective action is ever taken.

③ *Charms and joss-sticks stalls/fortune-telling complex*

Just to the right of the main temple gateway stands a row of stalls selling all manner of charms, talisman, joss-sticks and religious paraphernalia. Each stall claims its wares to be the one most favoured by brand- and status-conscious gods (this *is* Hong Kong, after all) and thus are, naturally, more potent than those sold by their competitors. Red and gold colours dominate the scene and representations of very large gold ingots seem to lend credence to the view that most worshippers are far more interested in the wherewithal for a good time in the here and the now than with what may take place in the afterlife.

To the right of the temple itself is a newly built complex, which houses a plethora of English-speaking, tourist-friendly fortune-tellers. The temple has a curious arrangement whereby the individual worshipper draws the lot but not the slip of paper explaining what the lot means. This is where the fortune-tellers come in. For about $20, or a lot more depending on your perceived susceptibility, your numbered slip is interpreted in deliberately vague terms.

For a larger fee, however, the soothsayers can offer various forms of life-altering advice. These range from helping punters choose winning Mark Six numbers or determining an astrologically suitable date for moving house, to changing the

Wong Tai Sin Road

shape of your tattooed eyebrows to a more auspicious pattern, or finding out whether a facial mole represents good or bad luck. All possible forms of advice and prognostication are just there for the asking!

4. Morse Park

Morse Park was named after Sir Arthur Morse, the popular chief manager of the Hongkong and Shanghai Banking Corporation who retired in 1953. Morse publicly proclaimed that 'what was good for the colony was good for the Bank' — a rare indication from a businessman that in times of real crisis, the interests of Hong Kong must come first.

Morse's confident foresight in the future of Hong Kong and willingness on the part of the Bank to take considerable financial risks during the war years did much to help rehabilitate Hong Kong's shattered economy in the immediate postwar period.

Like many of Kowloon's large parks, Mor See Gung Yuen (Morse Park) is probably most heavily used in the hour or so before dawn. At this time numerous *tai chi* practitioners go through their motions, as well as ranks of sword and fan dancers and various impromptu exercise and aerobics groups; most have long since gone their way by eight o'clock or so.

How To Get There

By Bus:	No. 106 from Quarry Bay to Wong Tai Sin, No. 2F from Cheung Sha Wan to Tsz Wan Shan North, No. 3C from Hong Kong–China Ferry Terminal, Tsim Sha Tsui to Tsz Wan Shan North, No. 11C from Chuk Yuen to Sau Mau Ping Upper. All alight when you see the Wong Tai Sin Temple.
By MTR:	Wong Tai Sin Station.
By Taxi:	九龍黃大仙道嗇色園 (*'Gau Loong, Wong Dai Seen Doh, Sik Sik Yuen'*).

STREETS

Clear Water Bay Road
清水灣道

Clear Water Bay Road extends through the hillside towards the commuter countryside of the Sai Kung peninsula. This area is perhaps best known, both within Hong Kong and overseas, for its expansive country parks and wild open spaces with magnificent vistas of islands and sea in every direction. The genuinely cosmopolitan town area in Sai Kung is attractive as well, with a thriving, international, reasonably priced restaurant and bar scene, and extensive scenic views.

As in much of Hong Kong if one gets slightly off the beaten track, a wide variety of interest can be found in this bustling corner of Kowloon's sprawling 'Housing Estate Heartland'. Just beyond the MTR Station crowds one can find quiet parks and corners of considerable serenity and enchantment, including what is probably the most strikingly beautiful Buddhist temple in Hong Kong.

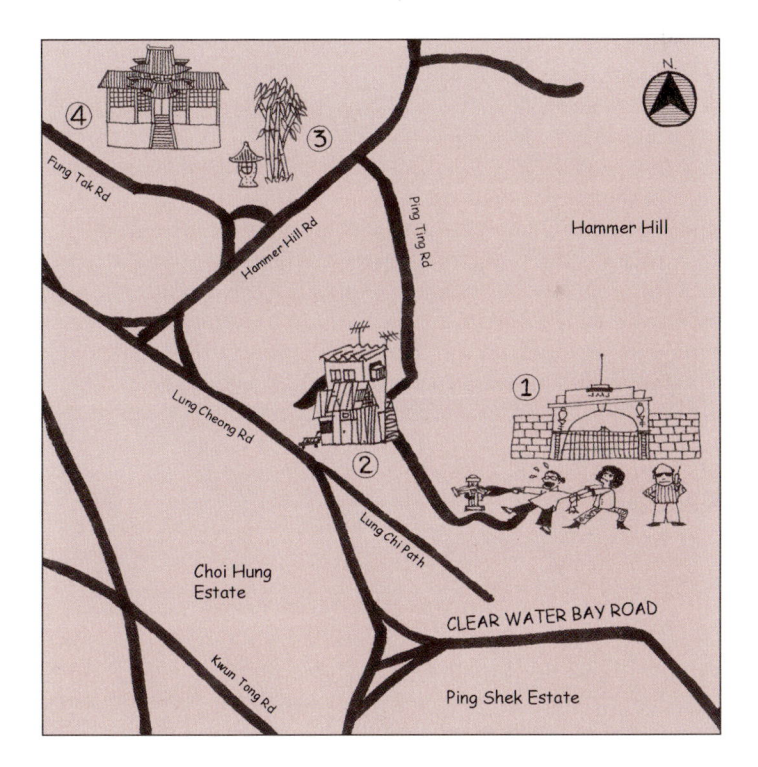

❶ Little Sisters of the Poor
❷ Ngau Chi Wan Village and squatter settlement
❸ Hammer Hill Park
❹ Chi Lin Nunnery

STREETS

Clear Water Bay Road

1 Little Sisters of the Poor

Built in the early 1930s as part of a major expansion of Roman Catholic charitable establishments across Hong Kong, the convent of the Little Sisters of the Poor was designed and built by the Franco-Belgian consortium Credit Foncierre d'Extreme Orient. The red-brick Carmelite Convent at Stanley and the Anglican St Mary's Church in Causeway Bay, which looks like a highly stylized Chinese temple, are other pleasing examples of their work.

The attractive, tree-shaded Little Sisters of the Poor convent offers a serene retirement refuge for the indigent elderly, and has been popular ever since its inception. Another affiliated old age complex has also been built near Sheung Shui in the northern New Territories. Adherence to Roman Catholicism is not a strict requirement for admittance to the home. Some of the pleasant old buildings within the compound have recently been slated for preservation. The convent's garden and grounds are particularly pleasant, and shaded with numerous old trees. Access by the general public is restricted, but passers-by can nevertheless get a good view of the old buildings through the convent's main gates on Clear Water Bay Road.

2 Ngau Chi Wan Village and squatter settlement

The ongoing, more or less thriving contemporary existence of Ngau Chi Wan ('Cattle Pond Bay') Village comes as something of a shock. How does this rundown squatter settlement still exist in modern-day Hong Kong, right in the middle of dozens of high-rise apartment blocks and modern shopping complexes, with the MTR line snaking through the middle? Ngau Chi Wan and others parts of Kowloon offer similar decrepit examples.

The continued survival of Ngau Chi Wan Village into the twenty-first century is probably one of the urban area's best reminders that contemporary Hong Kong, despite its veneer of affluence and modernity, is in reality a series of extended,

Clear Water Bay Road

overgrown villages, with many of the associated values and habits of much smaller localities. Most of the inhabitants in Ngau Chi Wan Village have been living there for decades now; a pleasing continuity in contemporary Hong Kong, which, even for many lifelong residents, remains an extremely transient society.

Once overwhelmingly inhabited by refugees from war and political upheaval in mainland China, general living conditions in the few remaining squatter hut settlements have greatly improved with more widespread general prosperity in recent decades. Even ramshackle huts like these in Ngau Chi Wan have usually installed built-in air-conditioning units — an almost undreamed-of luxury in such places even a generation ago.

③ *Hammer Hill Park*

Occupying an area of 6,800 square metres, the spacious, recently laid-out Hammer Hill Park is far larger than the living room carpet-sized 'parks' and grubby, concreted 'sitting out areas' littered throughout the vast tracts of urban jungle in Hong Kong. When so many of Hong Kong's public gardens are a frank disappointment, it is wonderful to see one like Hammer Hill Park that has so obviously received thoughtful planning and careful attention to detail.

Hammer Hill Park has a very attractive, well-tended Japanese-style garden featuring granite lanterns, Zen-like rock gardens (the rocks used in the garden's

Clear Water Bay Road

construction were obtained from nearby Diamond Hill), spectacular autumn-tinted Japanese maples, slowly spreading elms and numerous gnarled pines. The gardens also incorporates various species of luxuriant tropical flora to tremendous visual effect, such as scarlet bougainvillea (*Bouganvillea spectabilis*), multicoloured crotons (*Codiaeum varigatum pictum*), feathery leafed varieties of palm such as Dwarf Date (*Phoenix roebelini*), Alexandra palm (*Archontophoenix alexandrae*) and Golden Cane (*Chysalidocarpus lutescens*), as well as interesting indigenous species such as wild banana (*Musaceae*) and colourful varieties of flowering 'native ginger' (*Alpinia*).

With the serenely austere Chi Lin Nunnery forming an atmospheric backdrop, Hammer Hill Park makes a very pleasant, tranquil respite from the nearby crowds and somehow seems a whole world removed from the teeming streets only a short distance away. Or that is what it is like on an average weekday afternoon; like many similar locations elsewhere in Hong Kong, the crowds found here on weekends are *quite* another story.

4. Chi Lin Nunnery

First established in 1934 and substantially renovated and rebuilt since then, the Chi Lin Nunnery has even been featured on Hong Kong's postage stamps. The nunnery's patrons and directors have included, among many others drawn from the great and the good of Hong Kong society, the Aw family of *Sing Tao* and *Hong Kong Standard* newspapers and Tiger Balm Gardens fame. Reopened in 2001 after a major refurbishment, the beautiful, serene Chi Lin Nunnery completely refutes the often-held notion that a newly built Chinese temple is hardly worth looking at until it has had some time to age and mature.

Closely derived from Tang dynasty temple architecture, Chi Lin's austere grey roofline and unadorned cedar pillars wonderfully complement the brilliantly gilded images of the Buddhist pantheon housed in various halls within the complex. The temple courtyard, interspersed with gnarled potted pines and a water lily pond, has a haunting,

Clear Water Bay Road

almost Japanese starkness completely at variance with the red-and-gold, incense-and-gongs, fairground atmosphere so generally prevalent in temples in southern China.

But Chi Lin *is*, after all, a temple in Hong Kong. After ambling about the courtyards and meditating for a while on the varied meanings of life and the universe, the visitor can adjourn to the nunnery's well-stocked gift shop. Catering more to the requirements of the local Buddhist faithful than the more upmarket 'Boutique Buddhist', a 'dharma' shoulder bag will set you back a couple of hundred dollars while bracelets of prayer beads made from various types of semi-precious stones, an increasingly popular item in Hong Kong, can be found in varying colours and prices.

How To Get There

By Bus:	No. 10 Choi Hung–Tai Kok Tsui (circular route), No. 21 Choi Hung–Hung Hom (KCR Kowloon Station), No. 606 Choi Hung–Siu Sai Wan.
By MTR:	Choi Hung Station.
By Taxi:	彩虹清水灣道 (*'Choi Hung, Ching Shui Wan Doh'*).

Cha Kwo Ling Road
茶果嶺道

Along with neighbouring Lei Yue Mun, this tiny, settlement is one of the last remaining original, pre-urban villages in eastern Kowloon. Cha Kwo Ling somehow manages to survive, for the most part left behind and forgotten by the overwhelming urbanization found only a few hundred metres away. Cha Kwo Ling was originally located on the shores of Kowloon Bay, and despite reclamation work in recent years the village remains very close to the present-day waterfront.

Cha Kwo Ling provides a rare contemporary glimpse of the days when this eastern area of Kowloon was a remote place of quarries and rough hamlets. Seldom frequented by outsiders, the few inhabitants scratched a bare living by quarrying, coastal fishing and small-scale market gardening.

Cha Kwo Ling derives its name from the *cha kwo* ('tea fruit'), a local shrub (*Paederia scandens*) whose leaves were used to line the steaming baskets in which a particular variety of Hakka cake was cooked. *Cha kwo* bushes were extensively found on the low range of hills situated behind the village, and the early Hakka stonecutter's settlement derived its name, Cha Kwo Ling ('Tea Fruit Range') from these plants.

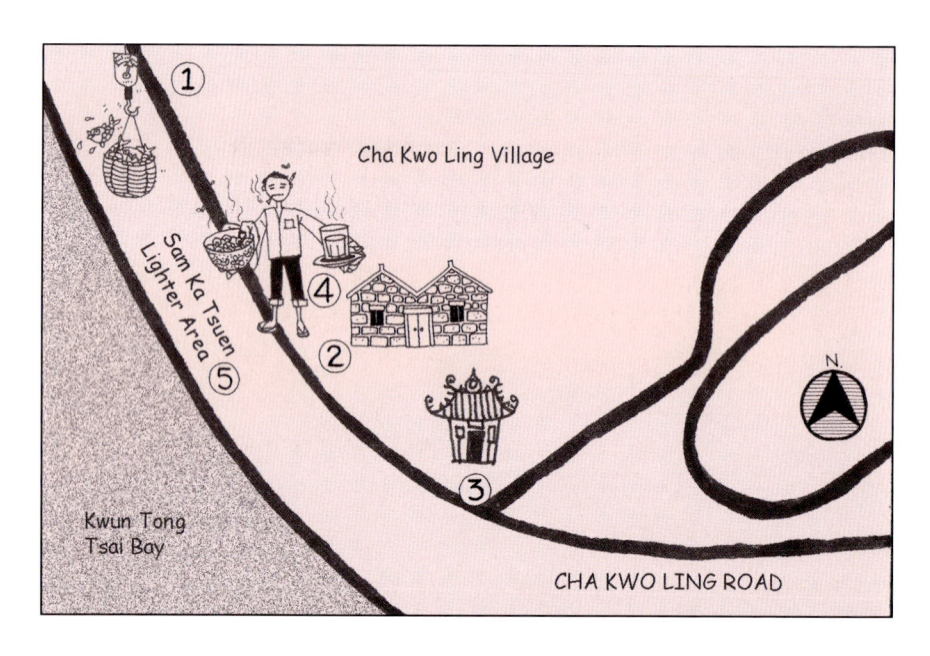

❶ Seafood wholesalers
❷ Stone houses
❸ Tin Hau Temple
❹ Local café (Hoi Tin Jau Gar)
❺ Sam Ka Tsuen Lighter Area

Cha Kwo Ling Road

The village is perceived by many urban residents — if they have heard of it at all — as a somewhat down-at-heel corner of eastern Kowloon. The name of the village (but nothing else about it) was nevertheless featured in a well-known song by Cantonese pop singer Sam Hui Koon-kit. First released in 1977, the lyrics remain popular and well-remembered.

At first glance, closely built, straggling Cha Kwo Ling Village, situated between the former waterfront — now Cha Kwo Ling Road — and the worked-out stone quarries behind, seems to offer little of interest. But walk a few paces behind the main street and an entirely different aspect of Kowloon life reveals itself.

Cha Kwo Ling is widely known elsewhere in Hong Kong and Kowloon for its acclaimed *kee lun* (unicorn) dance troupe. Utilizing *kung fu* movements, dance routines partially derived from martial arts techniques and marvellously coloured costumes, Cha Kwo Ling's *kee lung* troupe is often asked to perform elsewhere in Hong Kong during temple festivals, *ta chiu* (protective rituals) and official opening ceremonies. Numerous prominent Hong Kong citizens, including local magnate the late Henry Fok Ying-tung, have been major sponsors for the *kee lung* troupe over the years.

① Seafood wholesalers

Every day of the year, Hong Kong consumes a tremendous quantity of fresh fish and seafood. Until the 1960s, most *fruits de mer* sold in Hong Kong's markets and restaurants were caught locally. But since the early 1960s, a combination of steadily worsening marine pollution and massive overfishing in the Hong Kong region has greatly diminished the once important local fishing industry.

These days much of Hong Kong's better quality fresh seafood is imported from the Philippines, Indonesia, the Maldives and the central Pacific. Live reef fish much in demand by the restaurant trade, such as speckled garoupa, various types of wrasse, rock lobsters, clams and other sought-after species are air-freighted live to Hong Kong, and then resold by seafood wholesalers such as these located along Cha Kwo Ling Road.

Cha Kwo Ling Road

A note of caution: live seafood is *not* necessarily as fresh, and therefore healthy to eat, as it would apparently seem. Numerous species of reef fish taken from tropical waters are highly prone to ciguatera, an algae-borne contamination complicated by prolonged live storage in marine-water tanks. Ciguatera can badly poison those who eat seafood affected by it and outbreaks in Hong Kong are common.

The last two decades have seen an annually increasing, seemingly insatiable demand for imported seafood among the *nouveau riches* in Hong Kong and southern China, whose desire for exotic varieties of *yau shui yue* (swimming fish) is mostly based on reasons of ostentatious public display at banquets, rather than valid concerns about freshness and quality.

This annually increasing pressure continues to put marine breeding grounds in countries such as Indonesia and the Philippines under increasingly severe threat. The problem is, of course, complicated by what is — at the very best — scanty official protection for natural resources in these and other places.

② Stone houses

Appropriately enough for an area that got its start in life from small-scale quarrying, many of the older houses in Cha Kwo Ling are built of roughly dressed, locally quarried granite blocks. As late as 1960, many of the local villagers were described in official reports as 'skilled stonemasons'. Quarrying had largely died out here, however, by the end of that decade.

Cha Kwo Ling Road

According to villagers, Cha Kwo Ling's numerous *shek lau* (stone buildings) are warm in winter, pleasantly cool in summer and are easily able to withstand annual typhoons and weeks of monsoon rains in Hong Kong. Despite steadily increasing affluence, many remaining village houses have had little structural alteration in generations, although air-conditioners and television aerials — as well as piped water and more modern sanitation — are now standard additions.

③ Tin Hau Temple

Situated at the southern end of Cha Kwo Ling village is that most unusual of Hong Kong sights, a sympathetically restored, fully functioning, genuinely old temple. Village temples in many parts of Hong Kong, especially in the newly affluent parts of the New Territories, are often subjected to insensitive 'restoration' efforts that usually involve far too much paint and re-roofing in vivid buff-yellow or bottle-green tiles.

In the process, any sense of connection between the building's past and present is lost. Here at Cha Kwo Ling, however, the roughly dressed local stone is clearly visible, and villagers take an obvious pride and enjoyment in the building. On the hillside just behind the temple, disused, overgrown quarries can still be seen.

Cha Kwo Ling's Tin Hau Temple is mostly still used by descendants of the Hakka people who first built it in the mid-nineteenth century. Inside on the wall, among the black and white portraits of village elders taken when the temple was restored, is a photograph of R. R. Todd, secretary for Chinese affairs when the temple was previously renovated in 1950.

Cha Kwo Ling Road

④ Local café (Hoi Tin Jau Gar)

Cha Kwo Ling still possesses many facets of local life that have vanished from a lot of places in the urban area. One such feature is the Hoi Tin Jau Gar traditional eating place, which is simple and largely unchanged in recent years. Locally patronized cafés like this one were once a very common sight all over Hong Kong, but with rising local affluence and changing expectations they are now a slowly dying species.

Thirty years ago, a small local café like Hoi Tin Jau Gar would have been the favoured venue for village wedding banquets and other Cha Kwo Ling celebrations. These days, however, the café's clientele are mostly workers from the cargo handling basin across the road, truck and goods van drivers, or village people having a light lunch.

While the menu is fairly basic, the staff are generally friendly and welcoming; very few non-Cha Kwo Ling locals ever come here, or have reason to do so, and visitors, especially non-Chinese ones, are something of a novelty.

Cha Kwo Ling Road

⑤ Sam Ka Tsuen Lighter Area

The combined cargo-working basin and typhoon anchorage at Sam Ka Tsuen ('Three Families' Village') is a smaller version of the much larger feature at Yau Ma Tei. Most large-scale shipping to Hong Kong these days relies on containerization, which offloads at the port of Kwai Chung. A considerable amount of coastal and riverine shipping still passes through Victoria Harbour, however, and much of this is processed at small cargo lighter areas such as this one at Cha Kwo Ling.

The labour force employed at Sam Ka Tsuen is, for the most part, drawn from the local village, and sampans can be seen bustling about here at all hours of the day and night. Lighter areas such as this one see above average amounts of smuggling taking place, as the vessels that pass through here are small and fast, and the origins and destinations of their crews somewhat obscure. Few questions are ever asked — or answered — around here.

How To Get There	
By MTR:	Yau Tong Station, A2 or B2 Exits.
By Taxi:	油塘茶果嶺道 ('*Yau Tong, Cha Gwo Leng Doh*').

Lei Yue Mun Road
鯉魚門道

Lei Yue Mun Village remains perhaps one of the most pleasant and, at least on the surface, most unlikely corners in this part of Kowloon. One of the four original villages in the eastern side of the Kowloon hills, Lei Yue Mun, along with Cha Kwo Ling, Ngau Tau Kok and Sai Cho Wan, only came into existence in the 1850s as a result of Hakka migration into the Hong Kong region, after British settlement on Hong Kong Island.

The present-day village straggles along narrow Lei Yue Mun Praya Road and gradually extends around the coastline past the Sam Ka Tsuen Typhoon Shelter. Beyond there the village peters out on a small sandy beach just beyond the Tin Hau Temple — permanently strewn, unfortunately, with broken Styrofoam boxes, discarded fishing nets, abandoned glass buoys and all the other marine detritus sadly so commonplace on beaches all over Hong Kong.

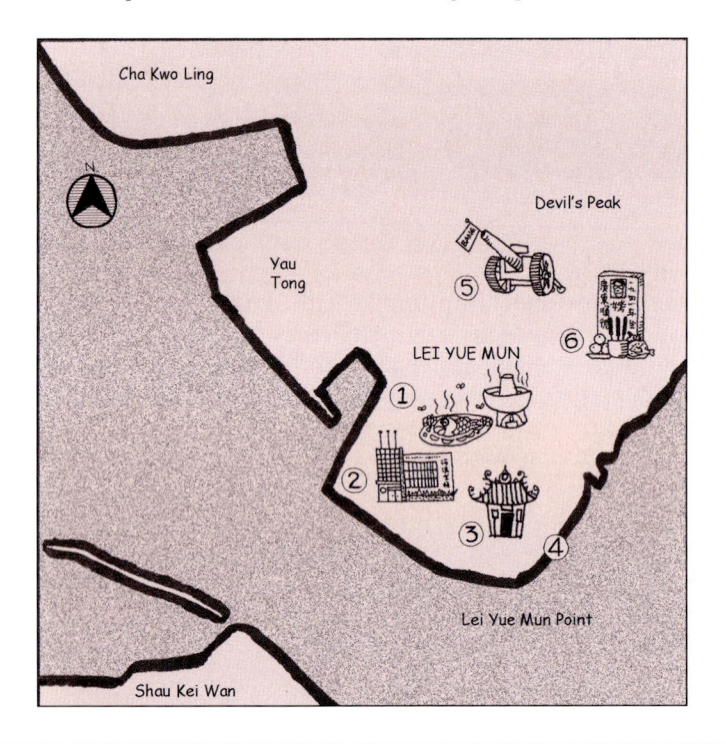

❶ Seafood retailers and restaurants, Lei Yue Mun Village
❷ Aw Boon Haw School
❸ Tin Hau Temple, Lei Yue Mun Village
❹ Stone loading ramps
❺ Abandoned gun batteries on Devil's Peak
❻ Junk Bay Chinese Permanent Cemetery

STREETS   278

Lei Yue Mun Road

① *Seafood retailers and restaurants, Lei Yue Mun Village*

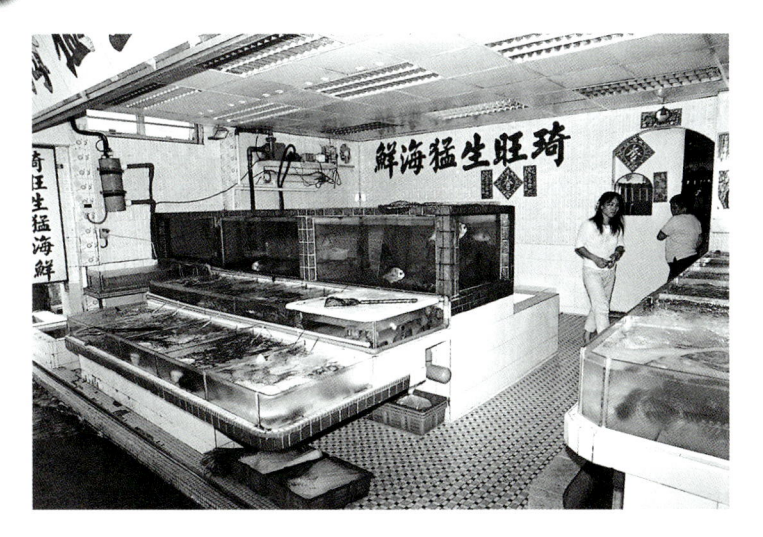

Lei Yue Mun's numerous live seafood shops and attached restaurants have been a popular attraction for visitors to the village for many years. Although not on the standard tourist route, these restaurants are well-known among local seafood aficionados and are always well patronized, especially at weekends.

While some of the seafood on offer here is still caught locally, most sea creatures sold in Lei Yue Mun these days are imported into Hong Kong. Whilst the greater proportion from Indonesia, the Philippines and elsewhere in Southeast Asia, increasing quantities of live fish are, however, imported from as far away as Sri Lanka, Fiji and the Maldives.

Some stock even originates from France and the Maritimes of eastern Canada. Live turbot from these places are accommodated — for what brief span remains of their earthly lives — in specially refrigerated tanks, designed to replicate the chilly waters off the Normandy and Newfoundland coasts. More budget-conscious diners need not even bother asking how much these well-travelled fish cost!

A popularly held belief in this part of the world, especially prevalent among the Hong Kong Chinese, is that if a fish is still swimming then by definition it *must* be fresher than one that is frozen or refrigerated. Contaminated storage water obtained from typhoon shelters and other heavily polluted sources can quickly taint live fish, and completely preventable cholera outbreaks are, alas, an annually recurring summer feature in 'Asia's World City'.

Lei Yue Mun Road

② *Aw Boon Haw School*

An unexpected Kowloon-side glimpse of the now sadly demolished Tiger Balm Gardens, which stood for many years on the hillside above Causeway Bay on Hong Kong Island, can be found in the playground of this village school in Lei Yue Mun. Animal-shaped statuary and concrete mouldings somehow evoke a reminder of the fantastic carvings and grotesque imagery formerly found in the Aw brothers' extensive pleasure grounds on Hong Kong Island, in a similarly themed garden complex in Singapore, and in the Kek Lok Si Temple in Penang.

Burma-born Hakka entrepreneurs Aw Boon Haw and Aw Boon Par were the inventors of Maan Kam Yau (Tiger Balm), the menthol-based cure-all renowned and sold wherever in the world that Chinese settled. Claimed to alleviate everything from headaches, insect bites, and menstrual pain, to giddiness and nausea, Maan Kam Yau created the basis of one of the largest ever Overseas Chinese family fortunes.

During their lifetimes the Aw brothers endowed numerous charities in Singapore, Malaya, Hong Kong and China, as well as in their native Burma. As well as the universally popular Tiger Balm, the Aw brothers established a significant Chinese-language publishing empire in Hong Kong and elsewhere among the Overseas Chinese diaspora. Titles included the *Sing Tao*, *Singapore Standard* and *Hong Kong Standard* newspapers.

The family eventually lost control of the Tiger Balm side of the business in the early 1970s, and during the late 1990s the Tiger Balm Gardens above Causeway Bay were sold for redevelopment. As a result of the usual Hong Kong combination of private greed and public and official apathy, the gardens and the magnificent Tiger Pagoda were all demolished. The ornate private residence was retained, but now stands unoccupied, and its future use is still uncertain.

Lei Yue Mun Road

③ Tin Hau Temple, Lei Yue Mun Village

Still an atmospheric boat people's temple right by the seashore and not — like numerous Tin Hau Temples in Hong Kong — marooned hundreds of metres inland by successive waves of reclamation, Lei Yue Mun's Tin Hau Temple is very quiet most of the time. This distinctive and small temple really comes alive during the annual Tin Hau Festival when dozens of vessels converge on the waterfront in front of the building, a smaller version of the much larger Tin Hau Festival around the coast at Joss House Bay.

One of the more noted features of Lei Yue Mun's temple — at least to some people — is a rarely seen link with many centuries ago. Behind the main altar is a cave-like, vulva-shaped crevice, which ethnologists speculate was a pre-Chinese fertility shrine that existed long before a formalized temple was even built here.

This shrine is assumed to be the female equivalent of the phallic-shaped, so-called 'Amah's Rocks' found at Bowen Road on Hong Kong Island, Lamma, Sha Tin and elsewhere. If you are a male and ask to see the rocky crevasse in an appropriately 'nudge-wink' manner, the temple's (also male) keepers will turn the lights on and give you a discreet peep. Do not bother if you are a woman — it is not even worth asking them — as the attendants will disclaim all knowledge of the rock's existence!

Lei Yue Mun Road

④ *Stone loading ramps*

Lingering reminders of one of the major early industries in Hong Kong can be found spread out along the water's edge at Lei Yue Mun. Stone quarrying was a major early industry in the Kowloon hills. Much of Kowloon's stone ended up being used to build the solid Victorian city across the harbour.

Dressed building stone from the 'Four Hills' was transported as far away as Canton, where Kowloon's premium quality granite was used in the construction of the Roman Catholic Cathedral in that city, built in the 1860s and still standing today. So much Kowloon stone was incorporated into the new structure that it became known as the Shek Lau ('Stone Building') — a name which still persists today.

These ramps were used to load stone blocks onto barges for transport across the Victoria Harbour and beyond. The overgrown disused quarries scattered around the hillsides are among the few local reminders of this once important industry.

⑤ *Abandoned gun batteries on Devil's Peak*

Rugged and almost wild, Devil's Peak rises directly above the narrow Lyemun Strait and directly overlooks the eastern approaches to Victoria Harbour. Once remote, Devil's Peak now looks down and out on extensive urbanization in every direction, in particular the massive New Town conurbation built on reclaimed land at Junk Bay — perhaps better known in contemporary Hong Kong as Tseung Kwan O.

Lei Yue Mun Road

The hill has been known locally for almost a century as Pau Toi Shan, literally 'Gun Battery Hill'. Construction of landward defences started on this stretch of the eastern Kowloon hills soon after the New Territories was leased to Great Britain in 1898, followed by two substantial gun batteries. These emplacements were named the Pottinger Battery, after Sir Henry Pottinger, the first governor of Hong Kong and the Gough Battery, for General Sir Hugh Gough, the new colony's first general officer commanding. The batteries were complemented in 1914 by a stone-built redoubt that commanded the very top of the ridge.

The guns from both batteries were removed from Devil's Peak in 1936 and subsequently used to further reinforce Mount Davis, on the western end of Hong Kong Island. When the Japanese passed through Devil's Peak in 1941, the battery housings were completely disused.

Devil Peak's empty, mostly overgrown gun emplacements are still there today, and are a popular venue for Hong Kong's growing legions of weekend war gamers, as well as kite flyers and bird watchers. The Wilson Trail, a popular hiking path, starts near Stanley and winds across Hong Kong Island, past the gun batteries and into the Kowloon hills and the mountains of the eastern New Territories.

6 Junk Bay Chinese Permanent Cemetery

Stretching around the hillside from Devil's Peak towards the massive new town of Tseung Kwan O (Junk Bay) is a sprawling Chinese cemetery. Attractively and — this being Hong Kong — correctly geomantically situated on a steep mountainside with the sea and islands in front, Junk Bay contains thousands of graves. Cemeteries in Hong Kong contain either permanent burials, in the sense that the word usually

Lei Yue Mun Road

conveys elsewhere in the world, or temporary occupancy. In the latter case graves are exhumed after several years, the remains cremated or pulverized and then stored in an urn or columbarium space, and the plot recycled for another burial.

From time to time visitors may encounter lost-looking cockerels wandering about the cemetery. These roosters, known as *jiu wan gai*, have been brought here as part of a Chinese ritual to 'call back' the souls of the dead. As they are believed to subsequently contain the ghost of the departed, the fowls are left abandoned after the ceremony. It is considered *very* inauspicious to either touch them or eat them — but not, apparently, to simply abandon them to their fate. Most *jiu wan gai*, it seems, are subsequently killed and eaten by hawks or the numerous wild dogs that prowl around the cemetery.

At the bi-annual grave-sweeping festivals of Ching Ming and Chung Yeung, the approach road up from Yau Tong to Junk Bay Chinese Permanent Cemetery is usually blocked by dozens of buses and private cars, all headed towards the cemetery for ritual grave-sweeping and the laying of offerings for the souls of the deceased.

How To Get There

By Bus:	KMB Bus No. 14C to Lei Yuen Mun Sam Ka Tsuen, and then walk along to Lei Yue Mun Praya Road.
By MTR:	Yau Tong Station.
By Taxi:	鯉魚門海旁道 (*'Lei Yue Mun Hoi Pong Doh'*).

Bibliography

Allister, William. *Where Life and Death Hold Hands.* Toronto, Stoddart Publishing Ltd., 1989.
Andrew, Kenneth. *Hong Kong Detective.* London, The Adventurer's Club, 1962.
Andrew, Kenneth. *Chop Suey.* Devon, Arthur H. Stockwell Ltd., 1975.
Angus, Marjorie Bird. *Bamboo Connection.* Hong Kong, Heinemann Publishers Asia Ltd., 1985.
Anslow, Barbara. *The Young Colonials.* United Kingdom (privately published), 1997.
Bard, Solomon. *Traders of Hong Kong: Some Foreign Merchant Houses, 1841–1899.* Hong Kong, Urban Council, 1993.
Bartlett, Frances. *The Peninsula: Portrait of a Grand Old Lady.* Hong Kong, Roundhouse Publications (Asia) Ltd., 1997.
Booth, Martin. *Gweilo: Memories of a Hong Kong Childhood.* London, Doubleday, 2004.
Braga, José Pedro. *The Portuguese in Hong Kong and China.* Macao, Fundação Macau, 1998.
Bray, Denis. *Hong Kong Metamorphosis.* Hong Kong, Hong Kong University Press, 2001.
Cameron, Nigel. *The Hong Kong Land Company Ltd: A Brief History.* Hong Kong, The Hong Kong Land Company Ltd., 1979.
Cameron, Nigel. *Power: The Story of China Light.* Hong Kong, Oxford University Press, 1982.
Chan, Mary Mai-lai. *Egg Woman's Daughter: A Tanka Memoir.* Hong Kong, Asia 2000 Ltd., 2001.
Cheng, Po-hung. *A Century of Kowloon Streets and Roads.* Hong Kong, Joint Publishing Co. (H.K.) Ltd., 2000.
Chu, Chindy Yik-yi. *The Maryknoll Sisters in Hong Kong 1921–1969: In Love with The Chinese.* New York, Palgrave Macmillan, 2004.
Clinton, David. *The Lion in the East: The Story of King George V School, 1900–2002.* Hong Kong, PTA, KGV and FPA of King George V School, 2002.
Coates, Austin. *Myself a Mandarin.* London, Frederick Muller Ltd., 1968.
Coates, Austin. *Whampoa: Ships on the Shore.* Hong Kong, South China Morning Post Ltd., 1980.

Bibliography

Coates, Austin. *Quick Tidings of Hong Kong*. Hong Kong, Oxford University Press, 1990.

Collis, Maurice. *Foreign Mud: An Account of the Opium War*. London, Faber and Faber Ltd., 1946.

Collis, Maurice *Wayfoong*. London, Faber and Faber, 1965.

Drage, Charles. *Taikoo*. London, Constable and Co. Ltd., 1970.

Dunnaway, Cliff (ed.). *Wings over Hong Kong – A Tribute to Kai Tak: An Aviation History 1891–1998*. Hong Kong, Odyssey Books, no date.

Eitel, E. J. *Europe in China*. Hong Kong, Oxford University Press, 1983.

Elliott, Elsie. *Crusade for Justice: An Autobiography*. Hong Kong, Heinemann Educational Books (Asia) Ltd., 1981.

Endacott, G. B. *A History of Hong Kong*. Hong Kong, Oxford University Press, 1993.

Endacott, G. B. and Birch, Alan. *Hong Kong Eclipse*. Hong Kong, Oxford University Press, 1978.

Endacott, G. B. and She, Dorothy. *The Diocese of Victoria, Hong Kong: A Hundred Years of Church History, 1849–1949*. Hong Kong, Kelly and Walsh Ltd., 1949.

Endacott, G. B. *A Biographical Sketchbook of Early Hong Kong*. Hong Kong, Hong Kong University Press, 2005.

Faure, David. 'Notes on the History of Tsuen Wan', *Journal, HKBRAS*, 1984, pp. 46–104.

Field, Ellen. *Twilight in Hong Kong*. London, Frederick Muller Limited, 1960.

Fonoroff, Paul. *Silver Light: A Pictorial History of Hong Kong Cinema 1920–1970*. Hong Kong, Joint Publishing Co. (H.K.) Ltd., 1997.

Gleason, Gene. *Hong Kong*. London, Robert Hale Ltd., 1964.

Gleason, Gene. *Tales of Hong Kong*. London, Robert Hale Ltd., 1967.

Gittins, Jean. *Eastern Windows – Western Skies*. Hong Kong, South China Morning Post Ltd., 1969.

Hase, P. H. (ed.). *In The Heart of The Metropolis: Yaumatei and Its People*. Hong Kong, Joint Publishing (H.K.) Co. Ltd., 1999.

Hase, P. H. 'Beside the Yamen: Nga Tsin Wai Village', *Journal, HKBRAS*, 1999, pp. 1–82.

Bibliography

Hase, P. H., Hayes, J. W., and Iu, K. C. 'Traditional Tea Growing in the New Territories', *Journal, HKBRAS,* 1984, pp. 264–281.

Hayes, J. W. 'Old British Kowloon', *Journal, HKBRAS,* 1966, pp. 120–137.

Hayes, James. *The Rural Communities of Hong Kong: Studies and Themes.* Hong Kong, Oxford University Press, 1983.

Hayes, James. *Tsuen Wan: The Growth of a New Town and Its People.* Hong Kong, Oxford University Press, 1993.

Herklots, G. A. C. *The Hong Kong Countryside.* Hong Kong, South China Morning Post Ltd., 1965.

Hoe, Susanna. *The Private Life of Old Hong Kong: Western Women in the British Colony, 1841–1941.* Hong Kong, Oxford University Press, 1992.

Holdsworth, May. *Foreign Devils: Expatriates in Hong Kong.* Hong Kong, Oxford University Press, 2002.

Hutcheon, Robin. *Wharf: The First Hundred Years.* Hong Kong, The Wharf (Holdings) Ltd., 1986.

Hutcheon, Robin. *The Blue Flame: 125 Years of Towngas in Hong Kong.* Hong Kong, The Hong Kong and China Gas Co. Ltd., 1987.

Ingrams, Harold. *Hong Kong.* London, Her Majesty's Stationery Office, 1952.

Jarvie, I. C. (ed.). *Hong Kong: A Society in Transition.* London, Routledge and Kegan Paul, 1969.

Jenner, W. F. C. *A Gazetteer of Place Names in Hong Kong, Kowloon and the New Territories.* Hong Kong, Government Printer, 1960.

Johnson, David. *Star Ferry: The Story of a Hong Kong Icon.* Auckland, Remarkable View Ltd., 1998.

Kirkup, James. *Cities of the World: Hong Kong and Macao.* London. J. M. Dent and Sons Ltd., 1970.

Knight, Margaret C. *Hong Kong Journal 1949.* United Kingdom (privately published), 1950.

Ko Tim Keung and Wordie, Jason. *Ruins of War: A Guide to Hong Kong's Battlefields and Wartime Sites.* Hong Kong, Joint Publishing (H.K.) Co. Ltd., 1996.

Lang, Graeme and Ragvald, Lars (eds.). *The Rise of a Refugee God: Hong Kong's Wong Tai Sin.* Hong Kong, Oxford University Press, 1993.

Bibliography

Lindsay, Oliver. *The Lasting Honour: The Fall of Hong Kong 1941.* London, Hamish Hamilton, 1978.

Lindsay, Oliver. *At the Going Down of the Sun: Hong Kong and South-East Asia 1941–45.* London, Hamish Hamilton, 1981.

Maryknoll Convent School. *Maryknoll Convent School 1925–2000.* Hong Kong, Maryknoll Convent School, 2000.

Miners, Norman. *Hong Kong under Imperial Rule 1912–1941.* Hong Kong, Oxford University Press, 1987.

Morgan, W. P. *Triad Societies in Hong Kong.* Hong Kong, The Government Printer, 1960.

Munn, Christopher. *Anglo-China: Chinese People and British Rule in Hong Kong 1841–1880.* Surrey, Curzon Press, 2001.

Neale, Dorothy. *Green Jade.* Australia (privately published), 1995.

Ng, Peter Y. L. *New Peace County: A Chinese Gazetteer of the Hong Kong Region.* Hong Kong, Hong Kong University Press, 1983.

Ommanney, F. D. *Eastern Windows.* London, Longman, and Green and Co. Ltd., 1960.

Ommanney, F. D. *Fragrant Harbour: A Private View of Hong Kong.* London, The Travel Book Club Ltd., 1962.

Oxford University Press, *The Hong Kong Guide 1893,* with an introduction by H. J. Lethbridge. Hong Kong, Oxford University Press, 1986.

Pryor, E. G. *Housing in Hong Kong.* Hong Kong, Oxford University Press, 1983.

Ride, Edwin. *British Army Aid Group: Hong Kong Resistance 1942–45.* Hong Kong, Oxford University Press, 1981.

Sayer, Geoffrey Robley. *Hong Kong 1862–1919.* Hong Kong, Hong Kong University Press, 1975.

Sayer, Geoffrey Robley. *Hong Kong 1841–1862. Birth, Adolescence and Coming of Age.* Hong Kong, Hong Kong University Press, 1980.

Schofield, W. 'Further Notes on the Sung Wong Toi', *Journal, HKBRAS,* 1968, pp. 67–73.

Selwyn-Clarke, Selwyn. *Footprints: The Memoirs of Sir Selwyn Selwyn-Clarke.* Hong Kong, Sino-American Publishing Ltd., 1975.

Sinn, Elizabeth. 'Kowloon Walled City: Its Origin and Early History', *Journal, HKBRAS,* 1987, pp. 30–45.

Bibliography

Siu, Anthony K. K. 'The Kowloon Walled City', *Journal, HKBRAS,* 1980, pp. 139–140.

Siu, Anthony K. K. 'More About the Kowloon Walled City', *Journal, HKBRAS,* 1986, pp. 265–266.

Smith, Carl T. *A Sense of History: Studies in the Social and Urban History of Hong Kong.* Hong Kong, Hong Kong Educational Publishing Co., 1995.

Smith, C. T. and Hayes, J. W. 'Hung Hom: An Early Industrial Village in Old British Kowloon', *Journal, HKBRAS,* 1975, pp. 318–323.

Stephenson, Ralph. *Colonial Sunset: A Worm's Eye View.* London, Pen Press Publishers Ltd., 2004.

Symons, Catherine Joyce. *Looking at the Stars: Memoirs of Catherine Joyce Symons.* Hong Kong, Pegasus Books, 1996.

Theroux, Paul. *Kowloon Tong.* London: Penguin Ltd., 1998.

Tong Cheuk Man, Toong, David P. M., Cheung, Alan S. K. and Mo Yu Kai (compilers). *A Selective Collection of Hong Kong Historic Postcards.* Hong Kong, Joint Publishing (H.K.) Co. Ltd., 1995.

Tsai, Jung-fang. *Hong Kong in Chinese History: Community and Social Unrest in the British Colony, 1842–1913.* New York, Columbia University Press, 1993.

Tsang, Steve. *A Modern History of Hong Kong.* Hong Kong, Hong Kong University Press, 2004.

Waley, Arthur. *The Opium War through Chinese Eyes.* London, George, Allen and Unwin, 1958.

Wesley-Smith, Peter. *Unequal Treaty 1898–1997: China, Great Britain and Hong Kong's New Territories.* Hong Kong, Oxford University Press, 1980.

Wilson, Brian. *Hong Kong Then.* Durham, The Pentland Press, 2000.

Wilson, Dick. *Hong Kong! Hong Kong!* London, Unwin Hyman, 1990.

Wordie, Jason. *Streets: Exploring Hong Kong Island.* Hong Kong: Hong Kong University Press, 2002.

Wright, Arnold (ed.). *Twentieth Century Impressions of Hong Kong: History, People, Commerce, Industries and Resources.* Singapore, Graham Brash (Pte) Ltd., 1990.

Photograph Credits

The page numbers are shown. Where more than one photograph appears on a page, 'a' denotes the upper and 'b' the lower one.

Anthony Hedley

18, 24, 25a, 32, 37a, 38, 39, 44, 48, 50, 52, 54, 55, 61, 62, 63, 72, 74, 77, 88, 97, 109, 112a, 112b, 114, 115, 119, 120, 126a, 127, 130, 131, 132, 133, 139, 140, 147, 153, 155b, 159, 161a, 161b, 164, 165, 171, 173, 174, 175, 177, 178, 179, 192, 193a, 193b, 197, 198, 202b, 203, 207, 208, 212, 213, 214, 215, 218, 219a, 219b, 232, 240, 242, 244, 247b, 253, 257, 258, 263, 264, 265, 266, 268, 269a, 269b, 273, 275, 277, 279, 281, 283, 284

John Lambon

19, 23, 25b, 27, 29, 33, 36, 40, 42, 43, 53, 64, 71, 73, 76, 78a, 78b, 82, 83, 87, 93, 98b, 99, 105, 106, 117, 118, 123, 125, 154, 155a, 181, 234, 235, 236, 246, 248, 252a, 256

Colin Day

21, 30, 31, 37b, 45, 47, 49, 57, 59, 67a, 67b, 68, 69, 81, 84, 89a, 89b, 92, 95, 98a, 107, 108, 111, 113, 124, 126b, 141, 143, 144a, 144b, 145, 148, 149, 150, 152, 156, 158, 160, 166, 169, 170, 180a, 180b, 184, 185, 186, 187, 188, 189, 191, 196, 202a, 209, 210, 217, 222, 223, 224, 225, 229, 230, 231, 237, 241, 247a, 251, 252b, 259, 270, 274, 276, 280, 282